IMAGES
of America

EARLY LIVERMORE

ON THE COVER: The Dutcher brothers' first hardware store and tin shop was located on Livermore Avenue north of First Street, behind what is now *The Independent* newspaper office. A cast-iron stove is on the roof to the left and a hand pump to the right.

IMAGES
of America

EARLY LIVERMORE

Livermore Heritage Guild

ARCADIA
PUBLISHING

ISBN 978-0-7385-3099-4

Published by Arcadia Publishing
Charleston, South Carolina

Printed in the United States of America

Library of Congress Catalog Card Number: 2005936023

For all general information contact Arcadia Publishing at:
Telephone 843-853-2070
Fax 843-853-0044
E-mail sales@arcadiapublishing.com
For customer service and orders:
Toll-Free 1-888-313-2665

Visit us on the Internet at www.arcadiapublishing.com

CONTENTS

ACKNOWLEDGMENTS

The Livermore Heritage Guild wishes to acknowledge the efforts of Don Meeker, Gary Drummond, Loretta Kaskey, and Larry Mauch in putting this book together. Without the many hours of scanning photographs by Bill Nale, this publication would not have happened. Most of these images come from the archives of the Livermore Heritage Guild History Center. Many thanks to those associated with the Livermore Rodeo for permission to use their photographs. Apologies for photographs not included. They are all very good; we just ran out of pages. And finally, thanks to our editor, Hannah Clayborn, for keeping us focused.

INTRODUCTION

The Livermore Valley has played an important part in the Bay Area's history for thousands of years. Situated between the San Francisco Bay, Sacramento Valley, and the San Joaquin Valley, it first served as a passageway for Native American traders.

Archeological evidence suggests that the first Native Americans settled in the valley 4,500 years ago. Baptism records kept at Mission San Jose indicate that in the late 1700s there were four tribes in the valley: the Pelnen near Pleasanton, the Causen near Sunol, the Ssaoam near Brushy Peak in Livermore, and the Seunen near Dublin. The average size of each tribe was 50 to 200 individuals, with no more than 500 in total population. Water was much more plentiful, as was wildlife. Each year, a winter lake known as Willow Marsh formed between Pleasanton and Dublin. In Livermore, the Springtown area was mostly marsh.

Mission San Jose, founded in 1797, had a profound impact on the valley's Native Americans. By 1800, Mission San Jose cattle were disrupting the native flora and fauna and driving away native food sources. Between 1801 and 1805, most of the Native Americans left the valley to become neophytes at Mission San Jose or retreated into the hills, joining other tribes. By 1836, when the mission was secularized and closed, nearly all the Native Americans originally from the valley had died from disease or old age.

In 1836, upon their release from the mission, a large group of Native Americans from various tribes did return to the area south of Pleasanton, known as Alisal at the time. By then, Robert Livermore, Jose Amador, and Augustine and Juan Bernal had established their ranchos. With indigenous food resources depleted, the Native Americans tried to support themselves by working as laborers. After the gold rush, as the population in the valley started to grow, the Native American population moved away, searching for open land or seeking work on other ranches. The influx of Chinese laborers in 1869 to work on the railroad made it even harder for the few remaining Native Americans to find work. The population continued to decline until 1906, when Charles Kelsey reported finding only 28 individuals. By 1914, most of the remaining Native American population was gone.

The valley's importance continued throughout the gold rush period as travelers passed through on their way to and from the gold fields. The valley became known as Livermore's Valley because Robert Livermore, who settled here in the 1830s, would offer food and shelter to those showing up at his doorstep. In 1847, Edwin Bryant devoted one full page in his book, *What I Saw in California,* to his visit with the Livermore family.

Robert Livermore Sr. never saw the town of Livermore, as he died in 1858. He is buried in the Mission San Jose church floor. In 1869, William Mendenhall would establish the town of Livermore, naming it after his good friend, on 680 acres he had purchased the previous year. But Livermore was not the first town here. Alphonso Ladd established a small community in 1865 (near present-day Old First Street) that was known as Laddsville. There were two hotels and several businesses, including a bakery, a jewelry store, a blacksmith, a drugstore, and undoubtedly several saloons. Joseph Le Conte mentions his visit to Laddsville in 1878 in his book *A Journal of Ramblings through the High Sierra of California.* Laddsville was ultimately absorbed into Livermore because of several fires and businesses locating closer to the railroad depot in downtown Livermore.

Originally the town's income came primarily from wheat. The wine industry began to grow in the 1880s. Coal and oil, found in the surrounding hills, also contributed to the town's prosperity. In the early 1900s, the town was known for its healthful climate, and five hospitals thrived in Livermore in the late 1920s—the Livermore Sanitarium, located on College Avenue; the Arroyo Sanatorium, Del Valle Farm children's hospital, and the Veterans Hospital, all located on Arroyo Road; and the smaller St. Paul's Hospital located on J Street. By the mid-1960s, all but the Veterans Hospital had shut down due to high costs and obsolescence. Today most people know Livermore for its rodeo, its two national laboratories, and the area's wine heritage.

This work covers Livermore before World War II. If you have comments or would like to see a second volume covering the later years in Livermore, send an e-mail to Docent@lhg.org or contact the Livermore Heritage Guild, P.O. Box 961, Livermore, California, 94551. If you would like more information about the Livermore Heritage Guild and our history center in the old Carnegie library, visit our web page at www.lhg.org.

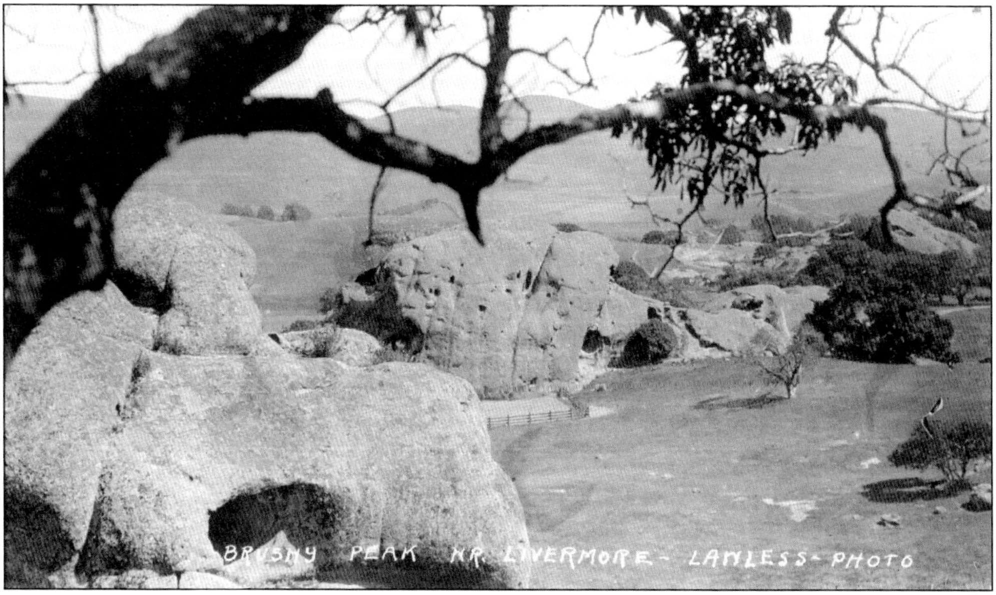

Because of its proximity to Mount Diablo, Brushy Peak was a sacred place for the valley's Native Americans. By the 1920s, it had become a place for social gatherings and dances. Visible for miles around, it is also a local landmark. Today it is part of Livermore Area Recreation and Park District's holdings and is accessible to walkers and hikers.

One

BEGINNINGS

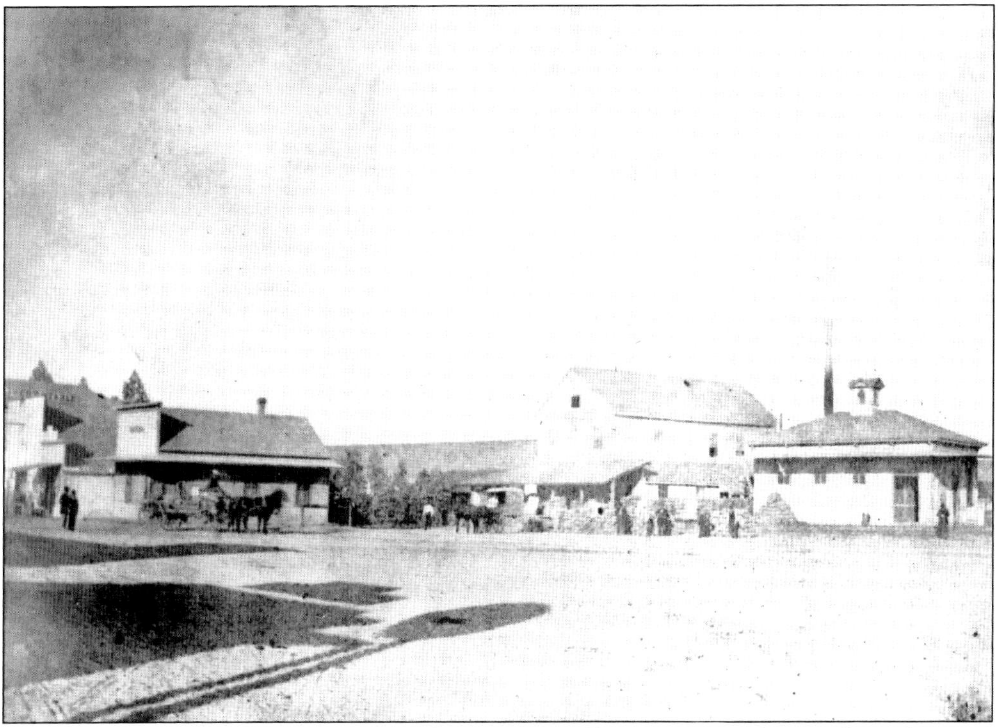

One of the earliest known photographs of Livermore, Mill Square is seen here in the early 1880s. The Magnolia Saloon, to the left, is on the corner, with a livery stable next door. The IOOF building is located left of the livery stable, just out of view in this photograph. Stevens's mill is in the center. The photographer appears to be standing about where the flagpole is today.

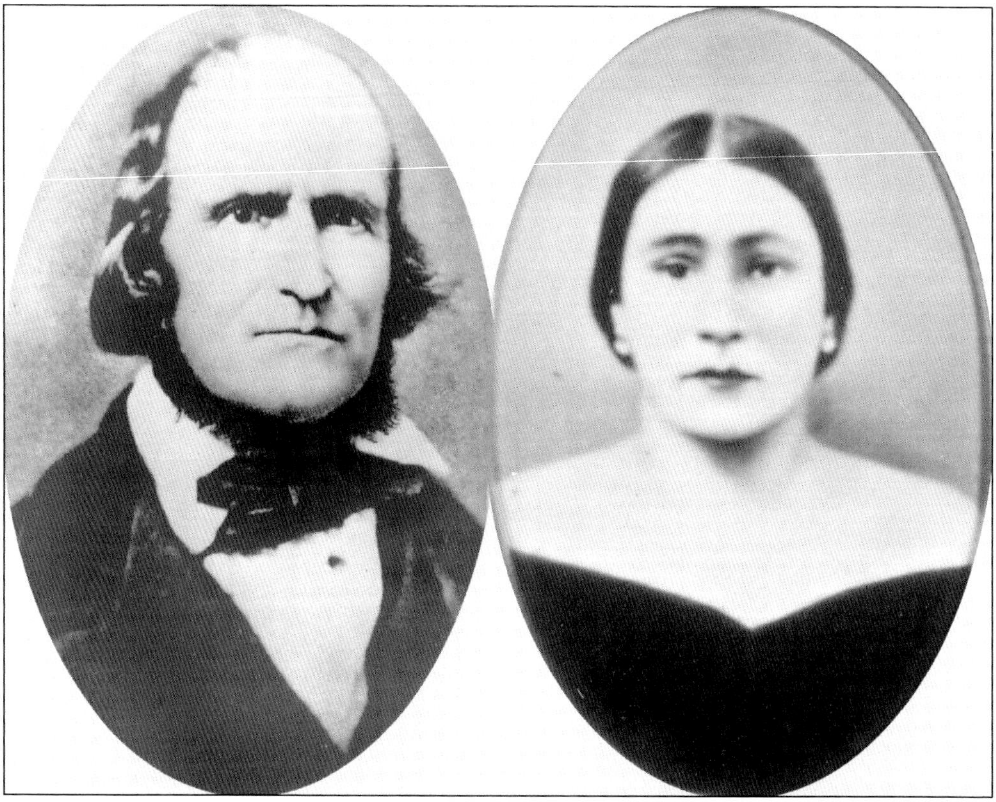

Robert Livermore, born in England in 1799, came to the West Coast around 1821 and worked his way up to the Bay Area. He petitioned the Mexican government for a land grant of 40,000 acres around 1835. He called his holding Rancho Las Positas for the many small streams near his home. Josefa Higuera Molina was a young widow with a daughter when Robert Livermore married her in 1838. Livermore died on February 14, 1858.

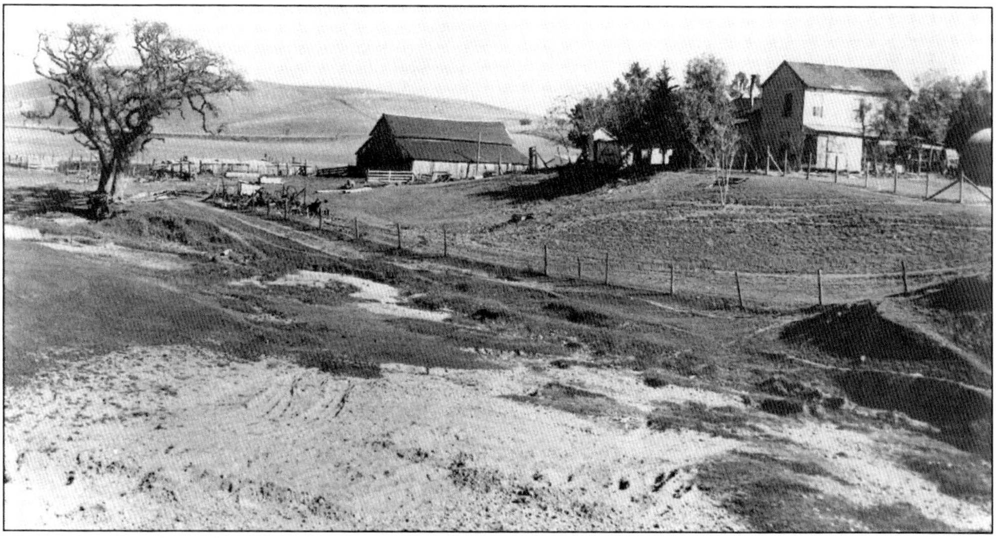

Livermore purchased an "around the horn" house and had it assembled on his ranch in 1851. It was placed so that the original two adobe buildings could be used as wings.

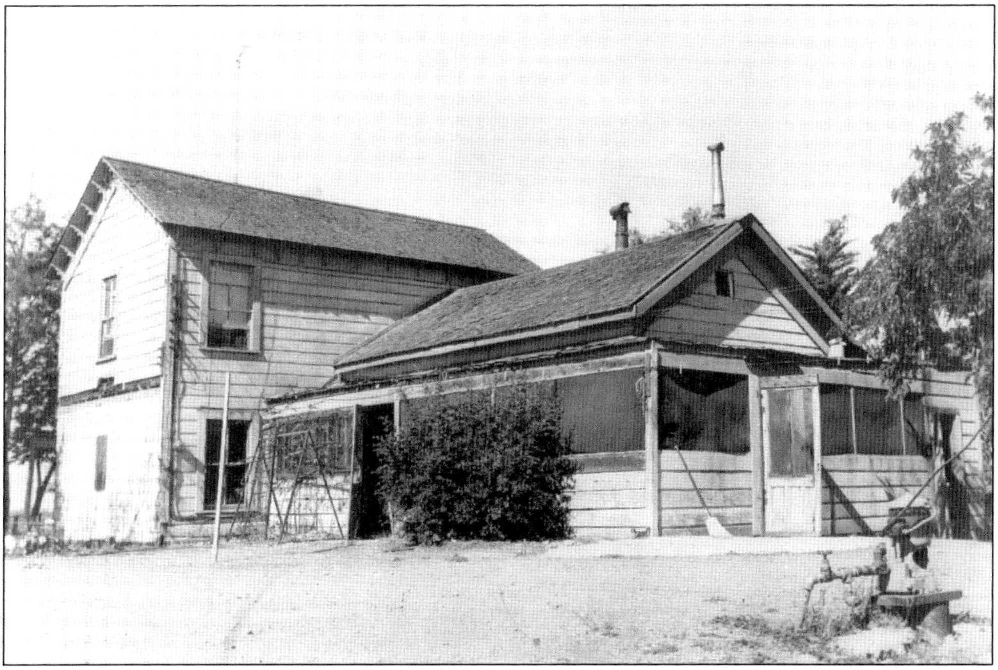

Livermore's house served his family for many years. By the time it was demolished around 1953, it had seen better days.

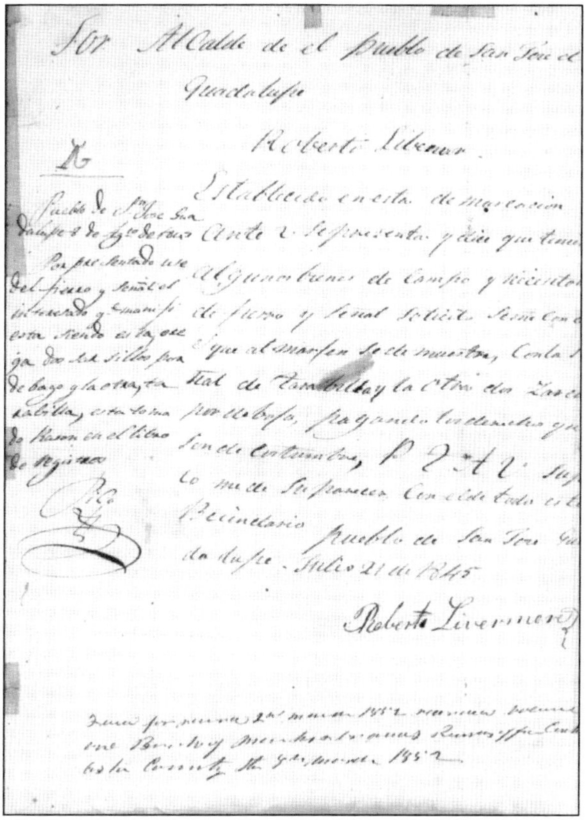

Sor Alcalde de el Pueblo de San José de Guadalupe

Roberto Livermore

Pueblo de San José Guadalupe. Julio 21 de 1845

Roberto Livermore

Robert Livermore was using a cattle brand as early as 1827. Livermore's stock in trade was cattle. In the 1840s and 1850s, he would slaughter large numbers of cows, save the hides, and render the tallow for sale to Yankee traders. When he next saw his hides, they had probably been turned into shoes and boots. The original official application, signed in 1845 by Robert Livermore and California's last Mexican governor, Pio Pico, is in the archives of the Livermore Heritage Guild.

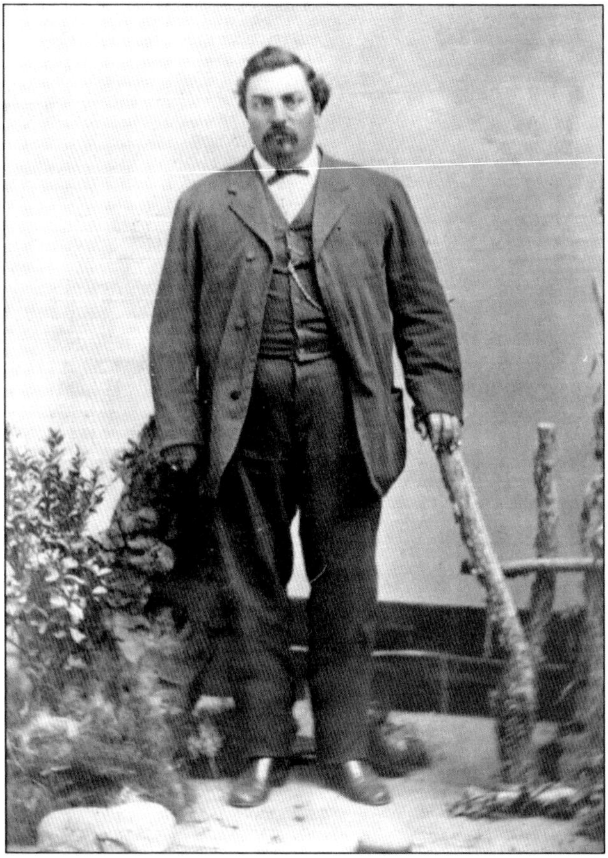

Robert Livermore Jr., like his father, was engaged in stock-raising until 1868. Seeing the advantages of the rich farmland, he turned to raising cereal crops. Although his father's estate was comprised of over 20,000 acres of land, after dividing it among his heirs (and selling off pieces of it to pay the inheritance taxes) Robert Livermore Jr.'s share was only 400 acres. He died in 1886.

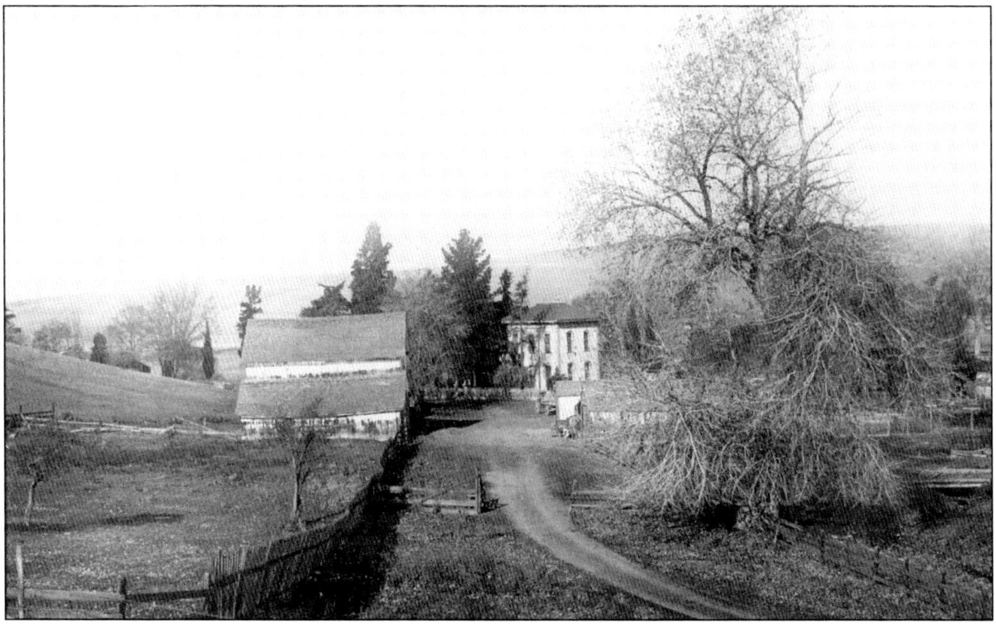

Robert Livermore Jr.'s home and barn were built around 1890, a mile east of his father's ranch house. The house burned in 1915.

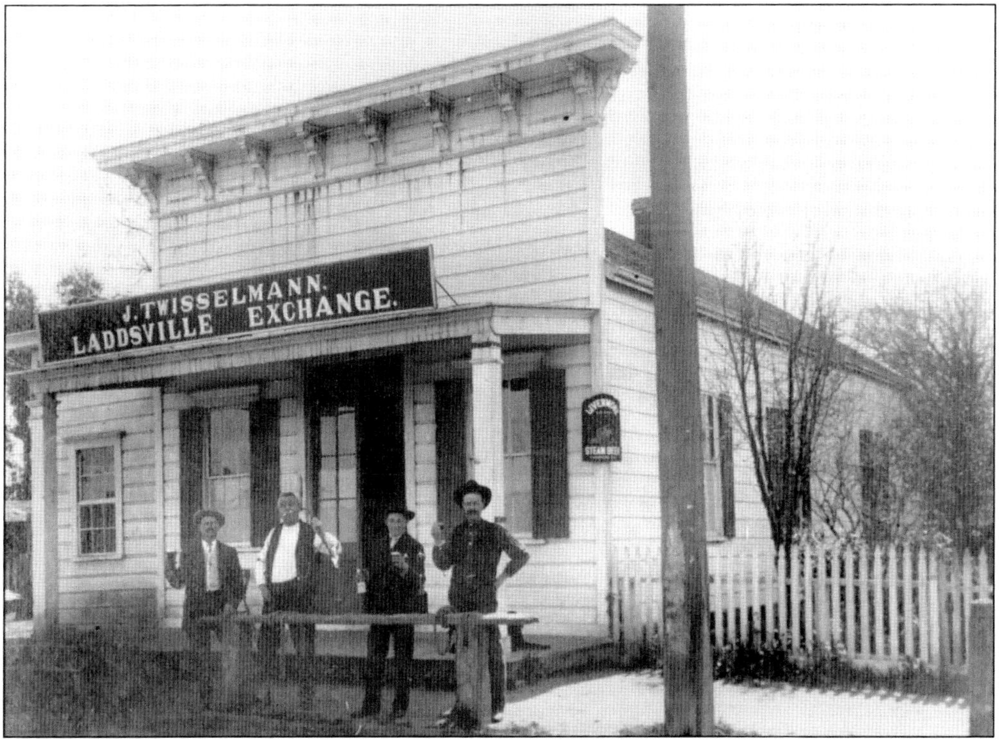

Laddsville was the first community in the eastern end of the valley. It was established by Alonzo Ladd in 1864 on preempted land. It was described as a village that had "50 citizens and 150 dogs, none of whom could vote." Two major fires had decimated the town by 1874.

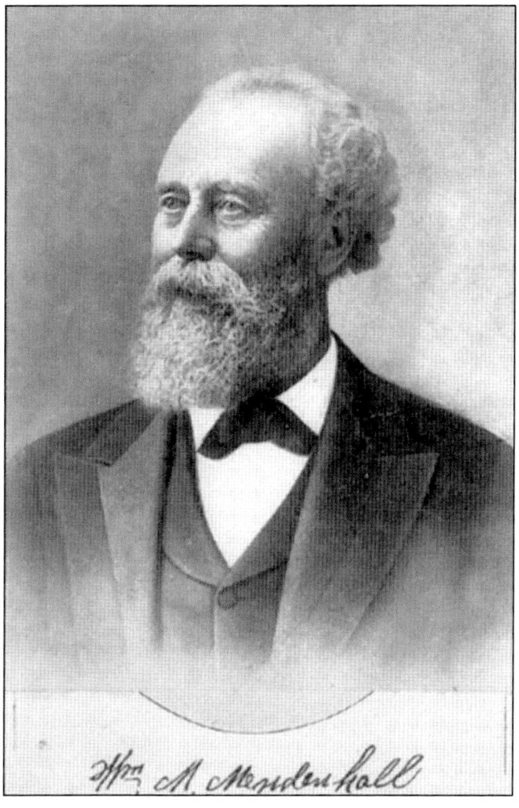

William Mendenhall, farmer, town builder, and stock raiser, arrived in California on Christmas Day in 1845, with a party of 11 young men. Several of his companions, Robert Semple, Henry Clay Smith, and Napoleon Bonaparte Smith, became prominent citizens in the new state.

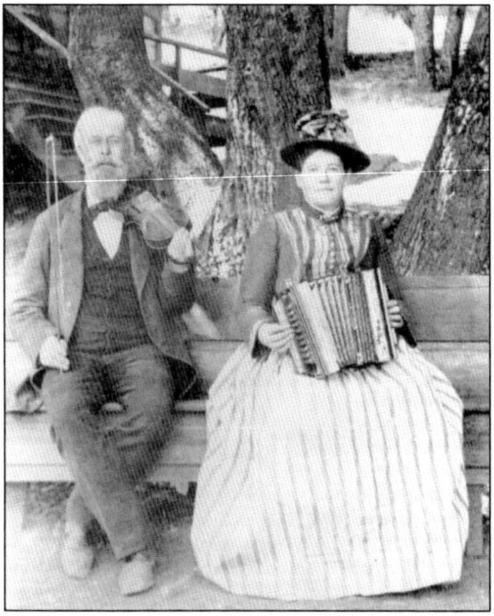

Mendenhall's wife, Mary Allen, arrived the following year. It is said that when they were married on April 18, 1847, theirs was the first marriage of Americans in Contra Costa and Santa Clara Counties. (Alameda County was not established until 1853.)

William Mendenhall hired a railroad surveyor to lay out his new community of Livermore. He named it for his friend, whom he had met during the Bear Flag Rebellion in 1846. The town plat was registered with Alameda County in November 1869.

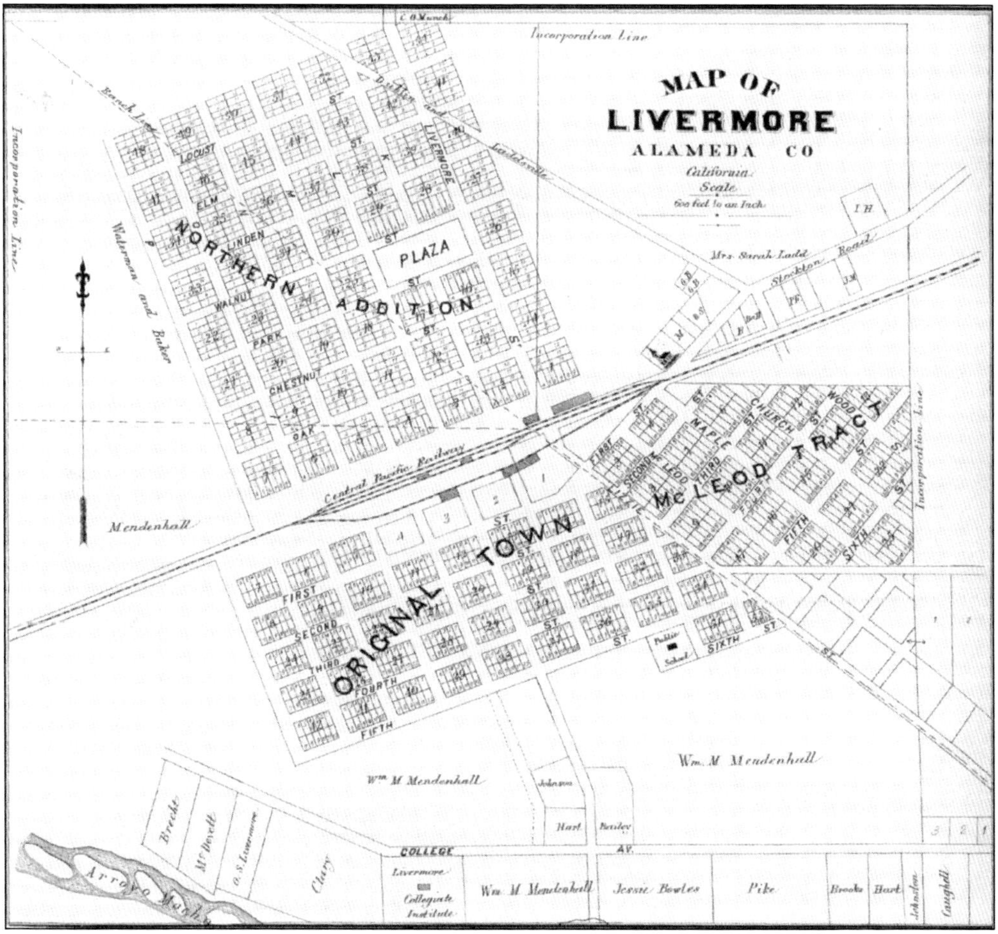

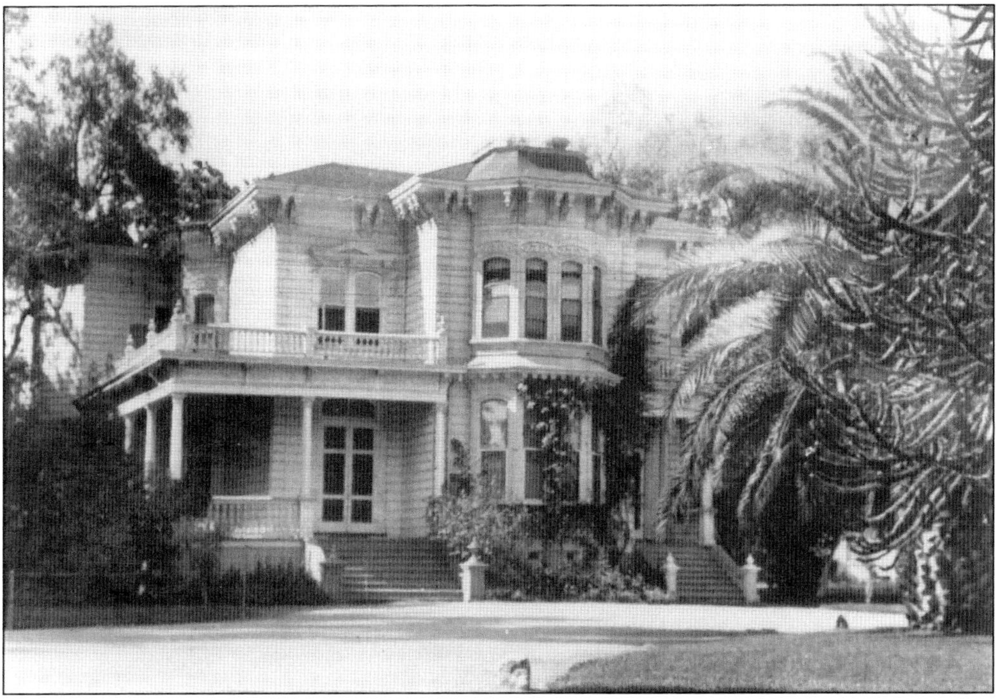

Although William Mendenhall laid out the town of Livermore in 1869 (it was incorporated in 1876), he lived in Santa Clara until his home on College Avenue was finished in 1877.

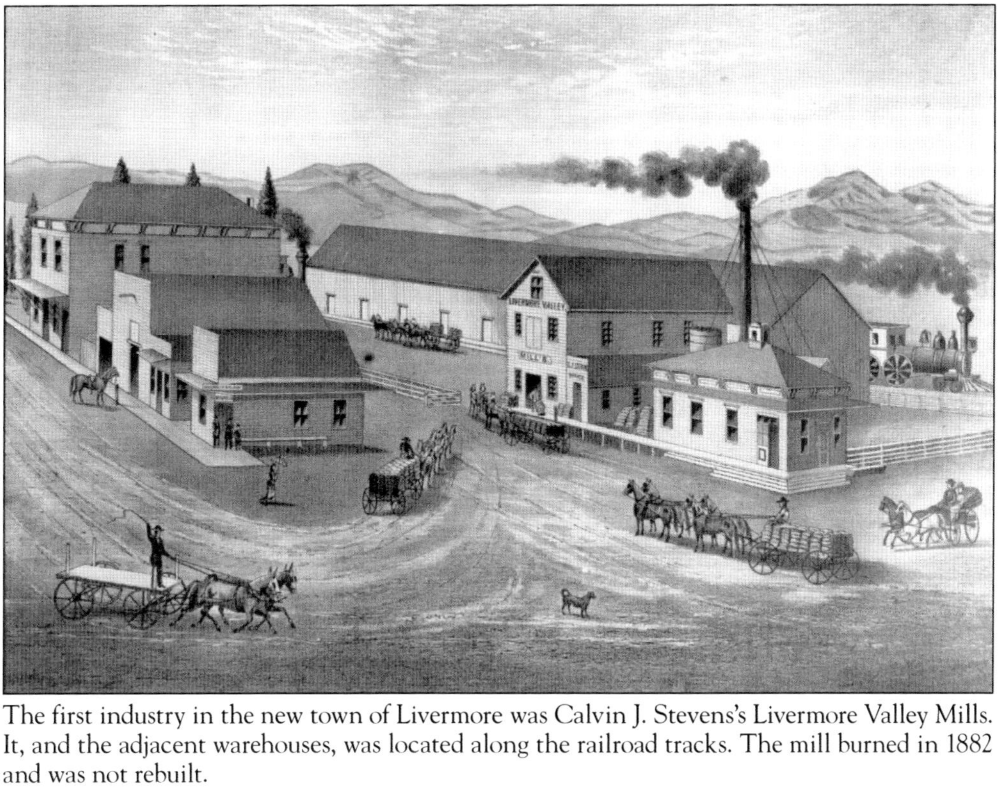

The first industry in the new town of Livermore was Calvin J. Stevens's Livermore Valley Mills. It, and the adjacent warehouses, was located along the railroad tracks. The mill burned in 1882 and was not rebuilt.

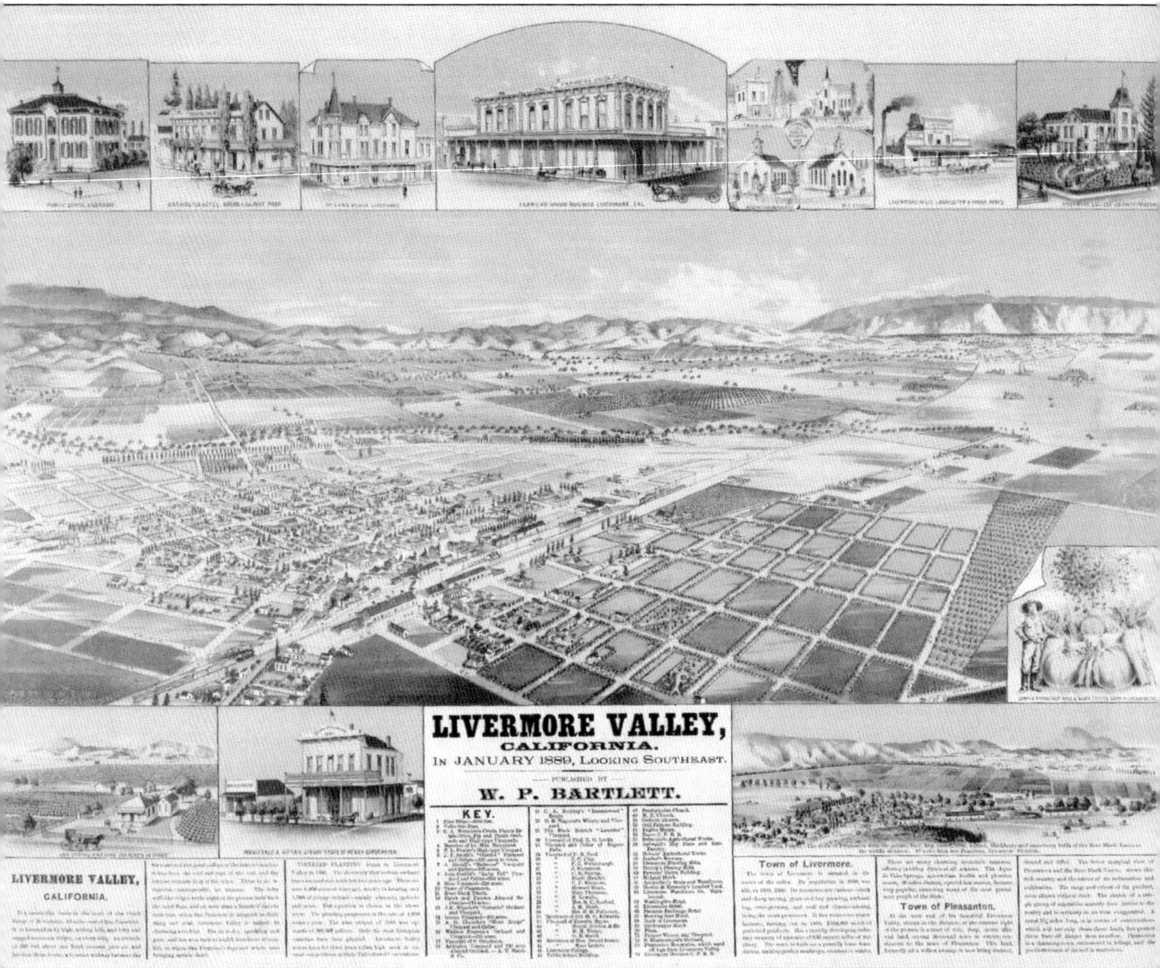

Twenty years after the establishment of the community, William Pitt Bartlett, publisher and editor of the *Livermore Herald*, published this bird's-eye view that emphasized the growth of the town. Regrettably, the artist made an error in the orientation. The view looks to the southwest toward the village of Pleasanton, rather than to the southeast. Prominent buildings in 1889 are illustrated above and below, and of those shown, only the Presbyterian church (third panel from the right, lower left) still remains. The long road shown in the left side led to the vineyard country south of the town. A magnifying glass can be used on the key, which identifies numbered features on the map.

Two

AGRICULTURE/ VITICULTURE

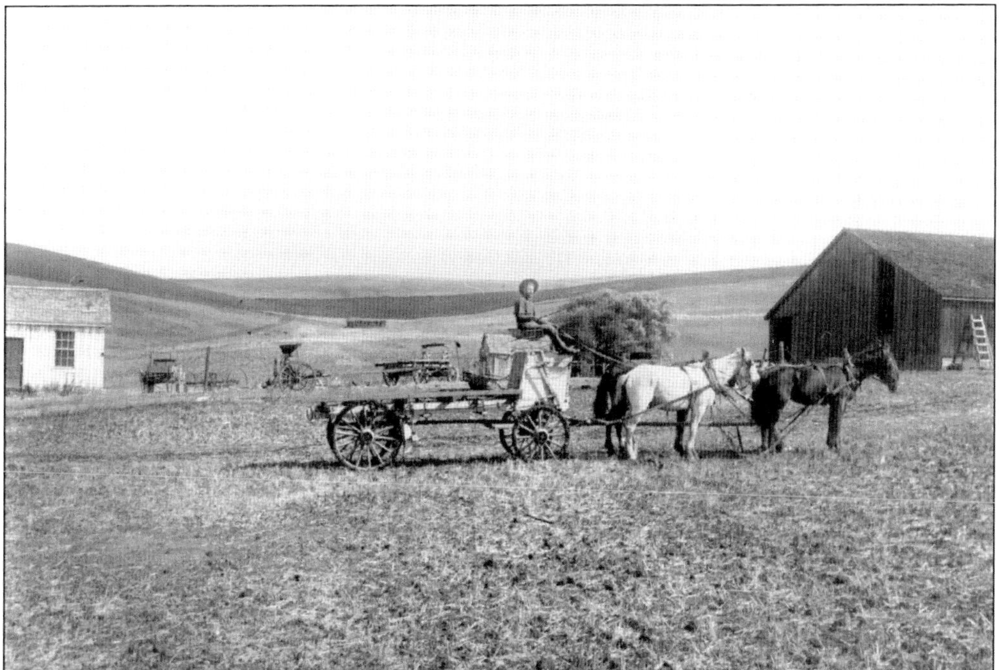

The valley's excellent climate and soil has always been a mainstay in supporting the many families dependent on the land for their income. In the beginning, wheat, and later grapes, were major crops that contributed significantly to the town's growth.

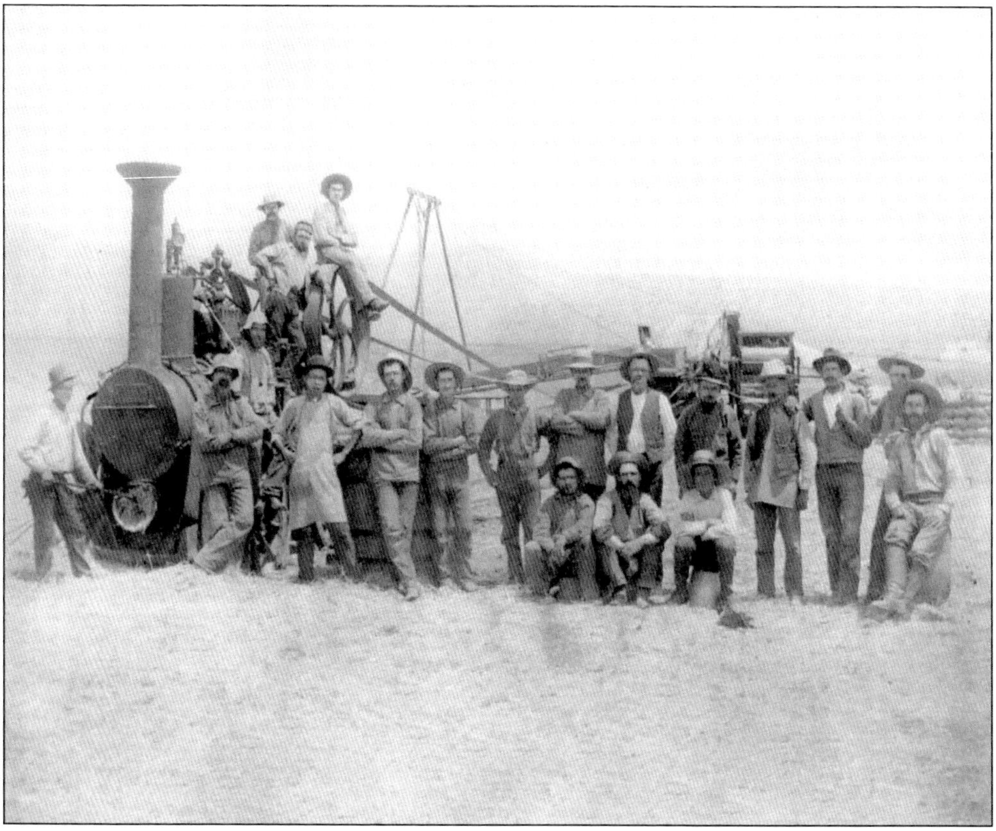

A harvest team on the George May farm in 1896 includes the only known picture of a Livermore Valley Chinese person. The man in the apron was Lee Loo, May's cook, also called Joe May.

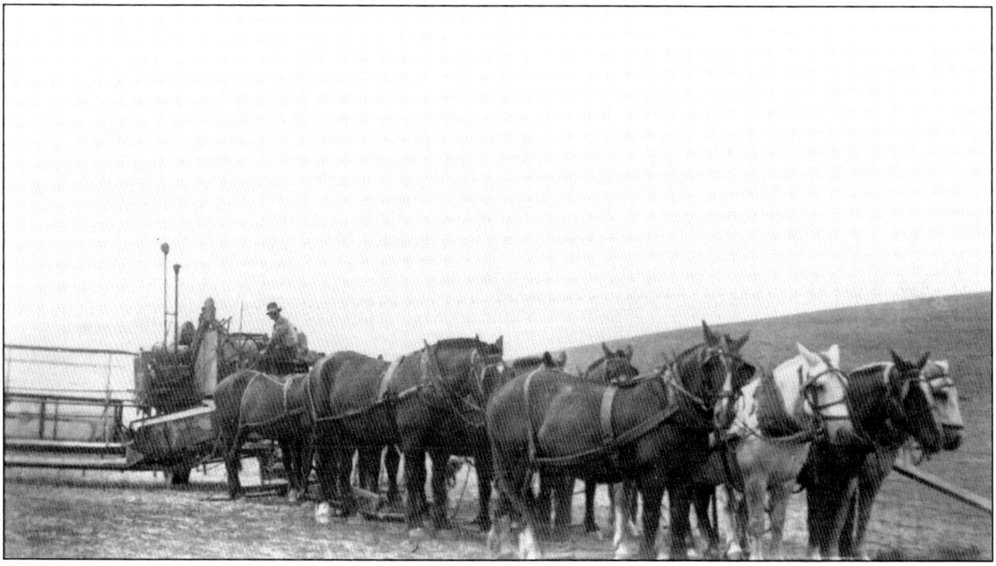

Bill Ralph needed a 16-horse team to pull his harvester in 1924. The horses are four abreast. They may be still placing members in the team, as it is difficult to tell how many are present.

Harvest time utilized as much labor as was available. Pictured in 1924, Bill Ralph (right) is helped by Ernie Gohler and his sister, Marie Ralph Gohler. Wheat and barley cultivation had been the primary economy in Livermore Valley since the 1850s. It was a labor intensive industry that utilized large numbers of both men and horses.

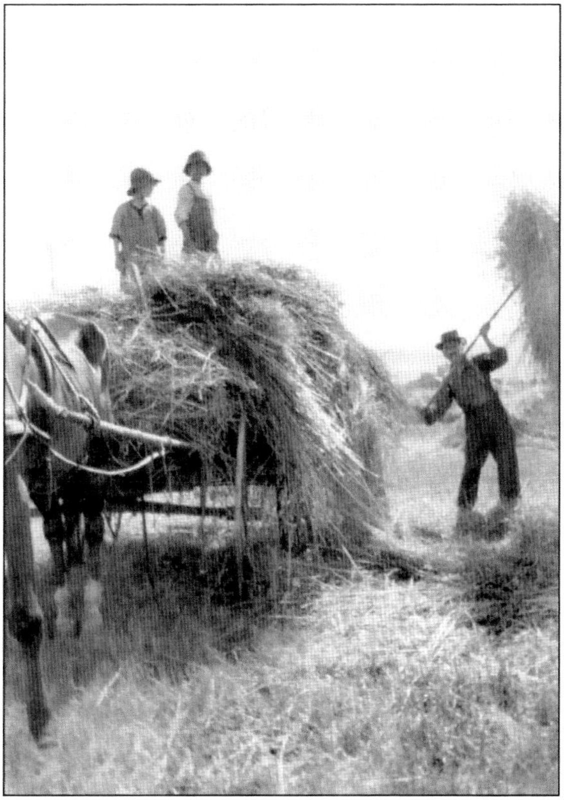

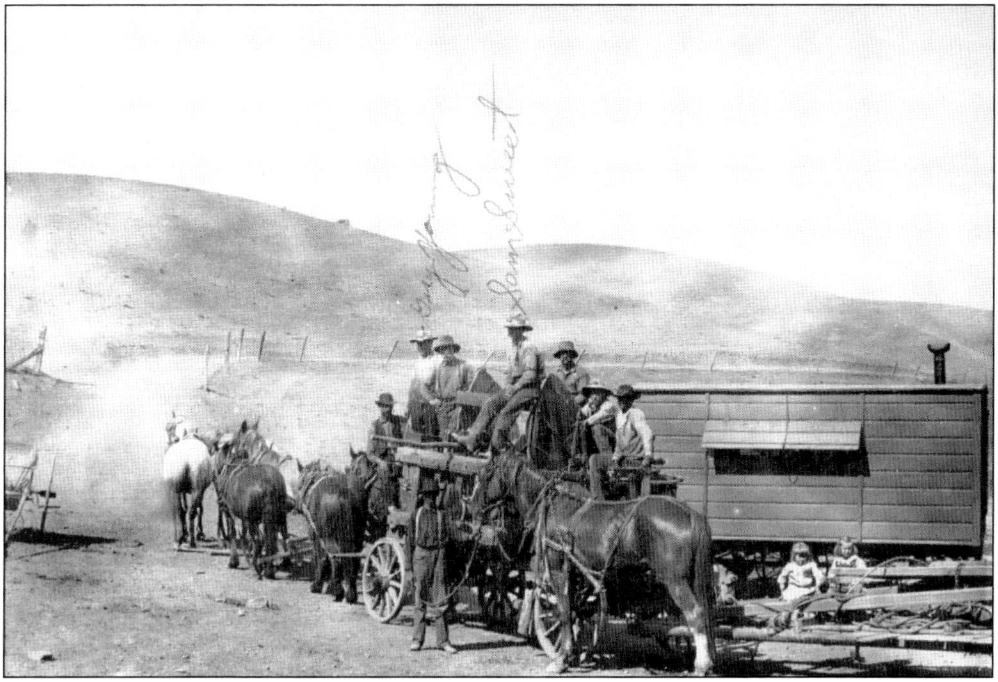

A hay press crew needed a good support team on the Greeley ranch. This team included Tom Greeley, Gerry Young, Sam Sweet, and George Garter.

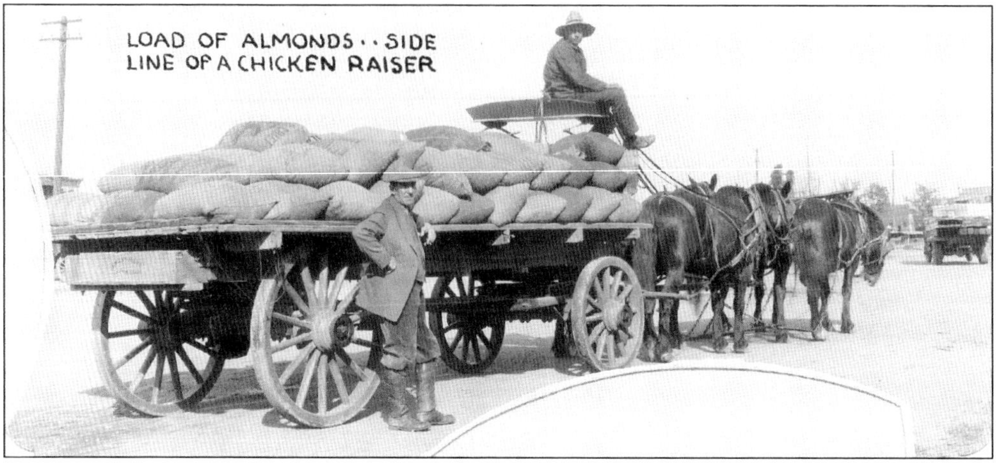

A small farmer's income came from diversified sources. A load of almonds helped supplement what the farmer could get for eggs and chickens. At the beginning of the 20th century, Livermore had a substantial chicken and egg business, so much so that the town of livermore was able to furnish 30,000 hard-boiled eggs for San Francisco earthquake refugees.

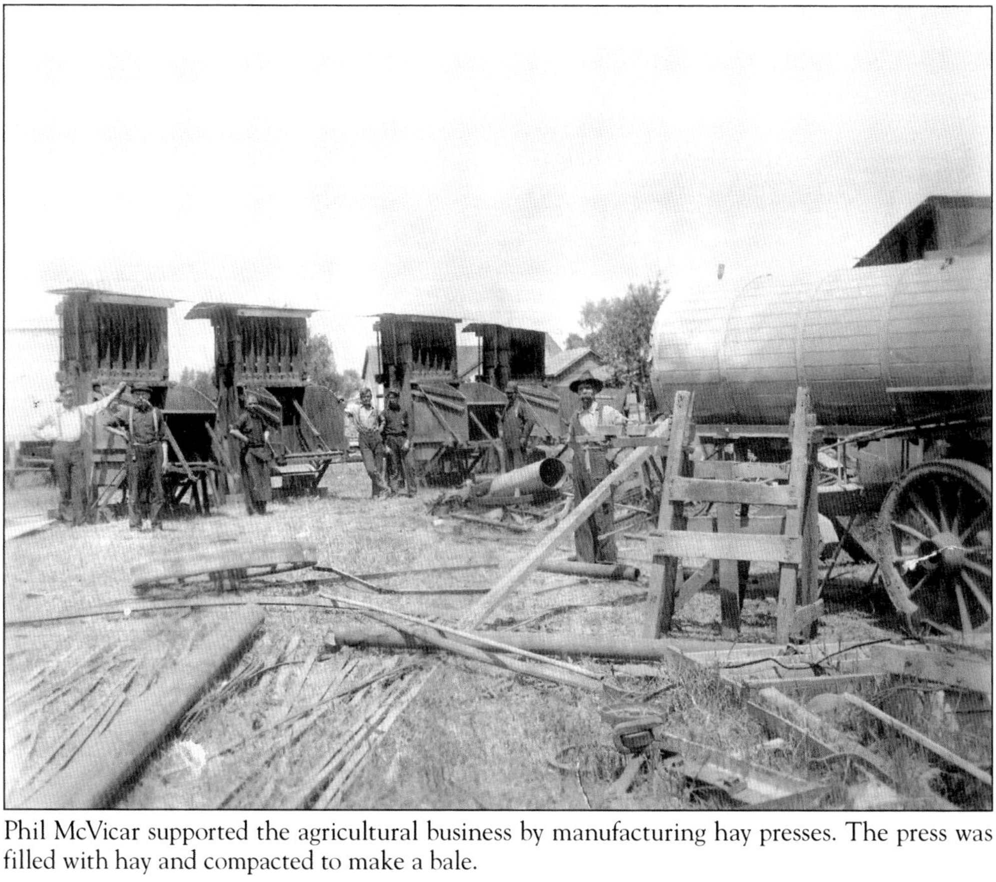

Phil McVicar supported the agricultural business by manufacturing hay presses. The press was filled with hay and compacted to make a bale.

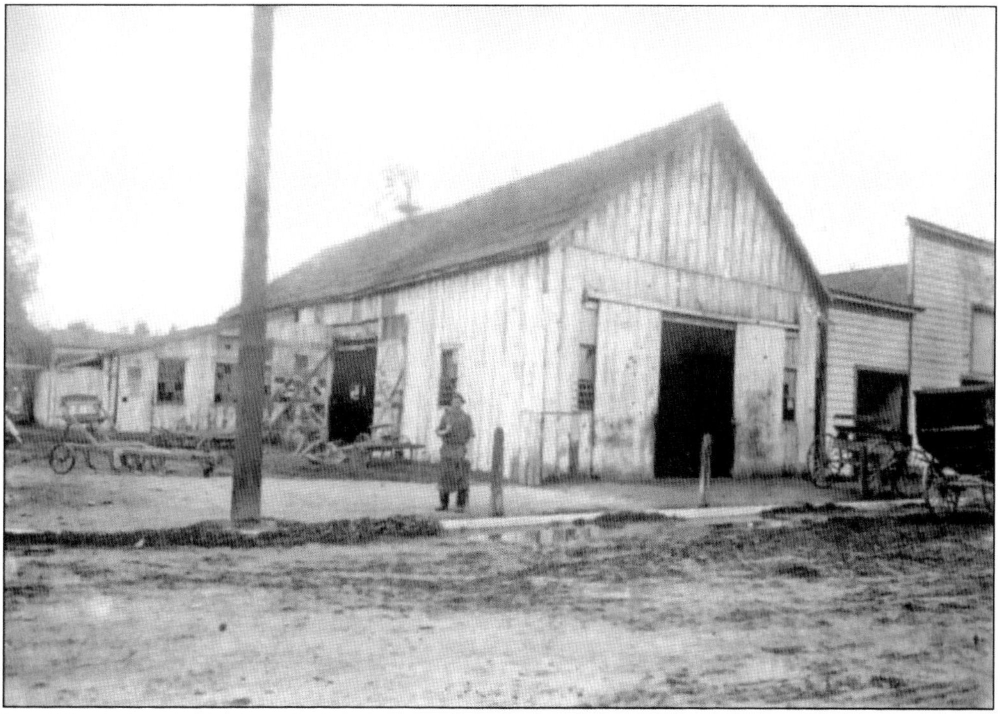

Lars Hendriksen's blacksmith shop was at the corner of Second and M Streets.

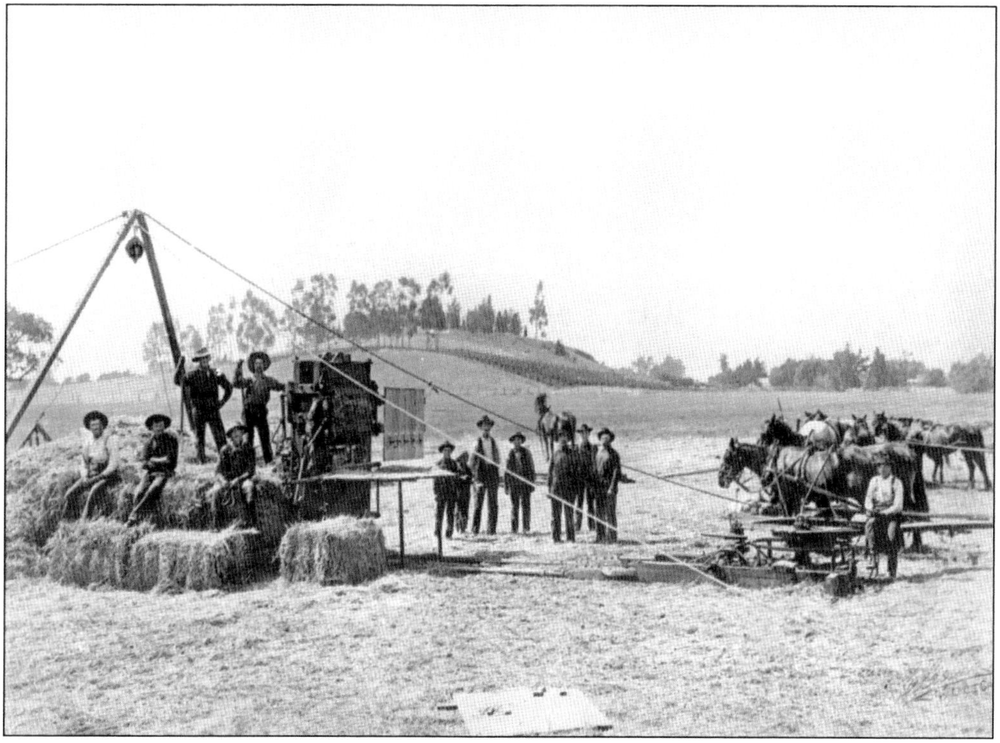

This harvest team is haying west of Livermore, near the site of what is now Granada High School. Oak Knoll Cemetery forms the backdrop.

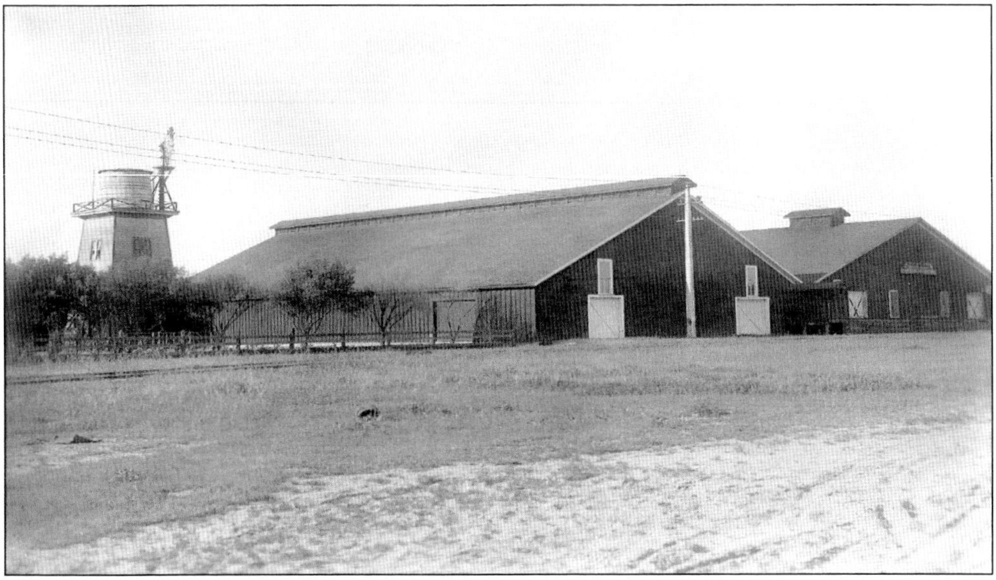

A very early winery in Livermore was owned in 1881 by two Swiss-Italians, Camille Aguillon and Gottardo Bustelli. It was located on the north side of the railroad tracks where Bank of America is currently located. By 1900, the winery, which was acquired by the California Wine Association in 1894, was shipping out 1.6 million gallons of wine annually from Livermore. One of their wine tanks had a 30,000-gallon capacity. It was 20 feet in diameter and rose to a height of 18 feet. The *Height* noted that "two sets of quadrilles could be formed on the bottom of the tank."

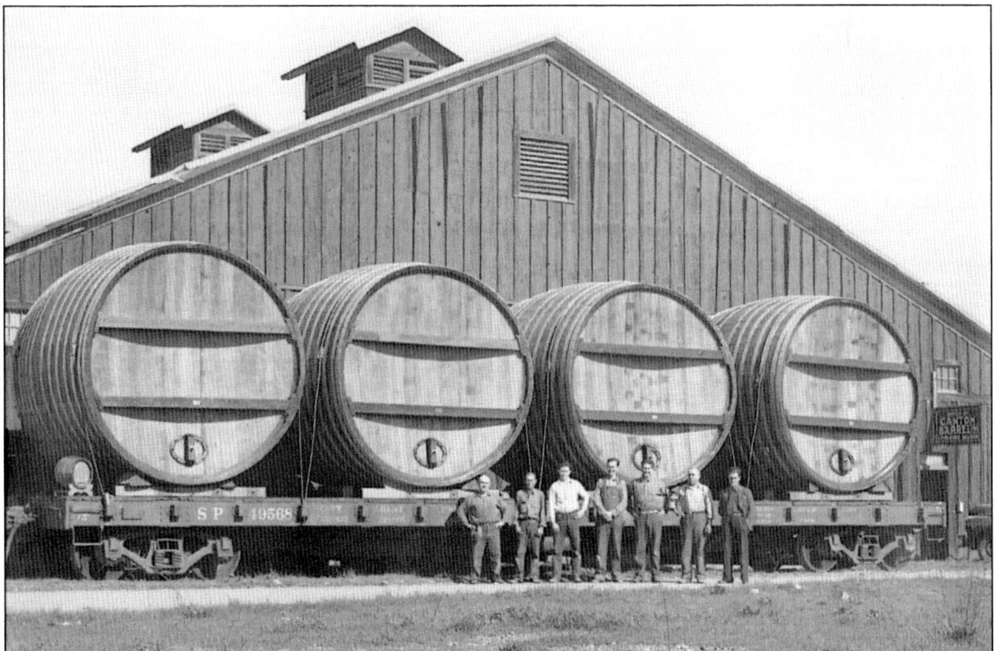

In 1939–1940, the Canton Barrel Company used the old Pioneer Winery building as a factory site for the manufacturing of large, redwood wine tanks. The man second from the right is Ernest Cigliuti. This plant was on the site now occupied by the Bank of America on Railroad Avenue.

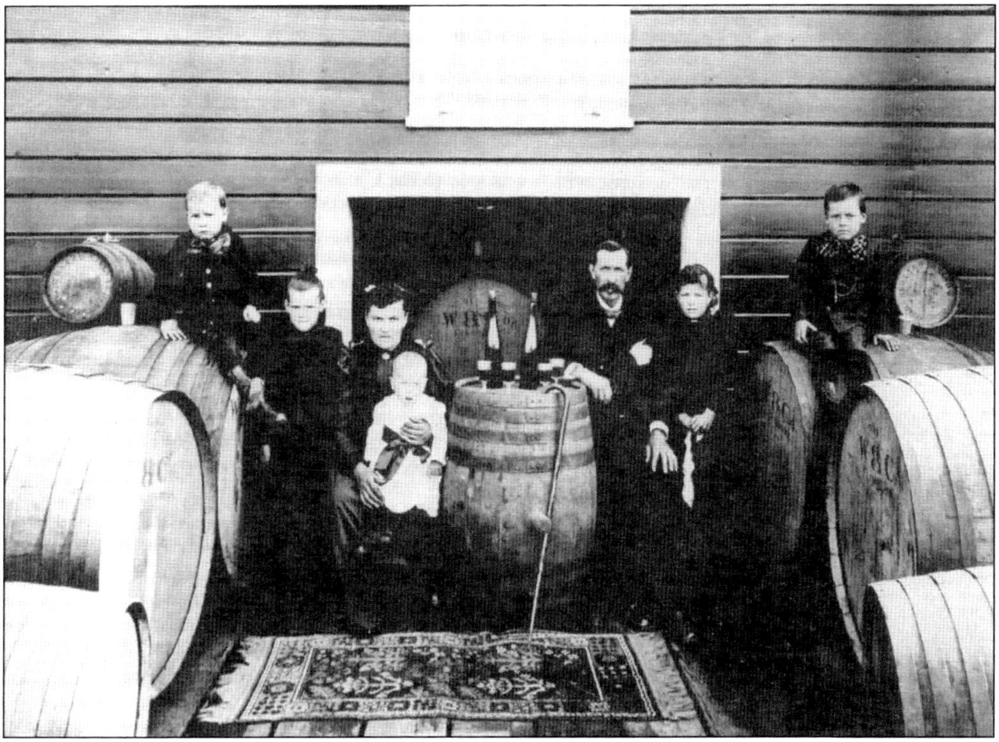

Carl Heinrich Wente came to Livermore Valley in 1883 and the next year acquired half interest in a bearing vineyard. He sold his wine to factors who, in turn, bottled it and applied their own label. At the 1915 Panama-Pacific International Exposition, five of Wente's wines won gold medals, but with another's label. Pictured here in 1898, the Wente family included, from left to right, Ernest, Carolyn, Barbara (holding Frieda), Carl Heinrich, May, and Herman.

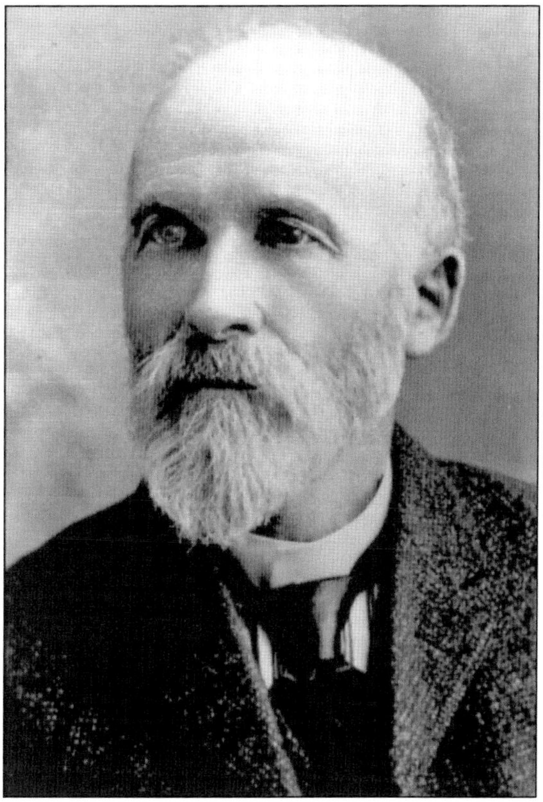

In 1865, James Concannon came to America from the Aran Isles, Ireland. He came to the West Coast about 1875. In San Francisco, he was a bookseller for Anton Roman and a rubber stamp salesman for the S. H. Shepler Company. Concannon was best known as a prominent vintner in the valley.

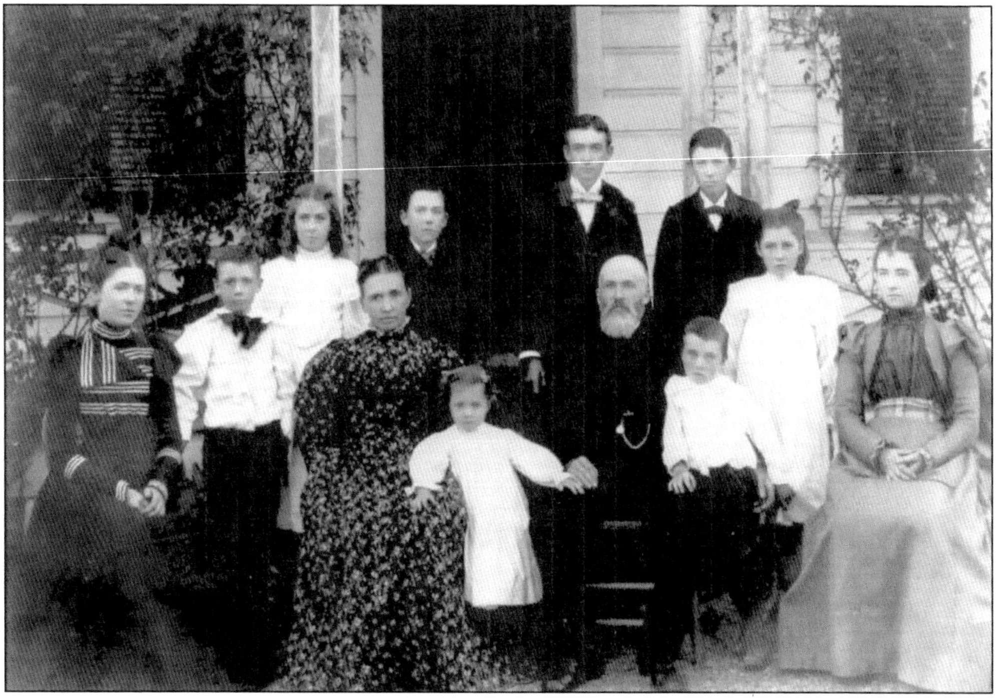

The James Concannon family gathered in 1897 for this portrait. Pictured, from left to right, are May, Robert, Ella, Ellen (mother), Joseph, Veronica, James, James (father), Thomas, John, Sarah, and Sadie.

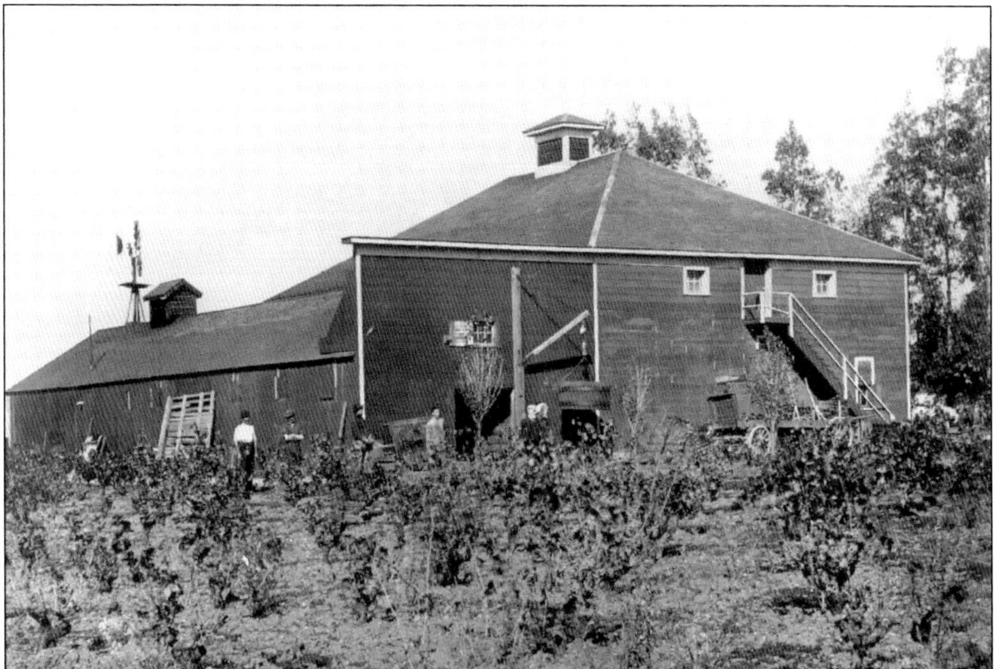

James Concannon made his first wine in the basement of his house in 1886. His winery building was constructed in 1895 and is still in use.

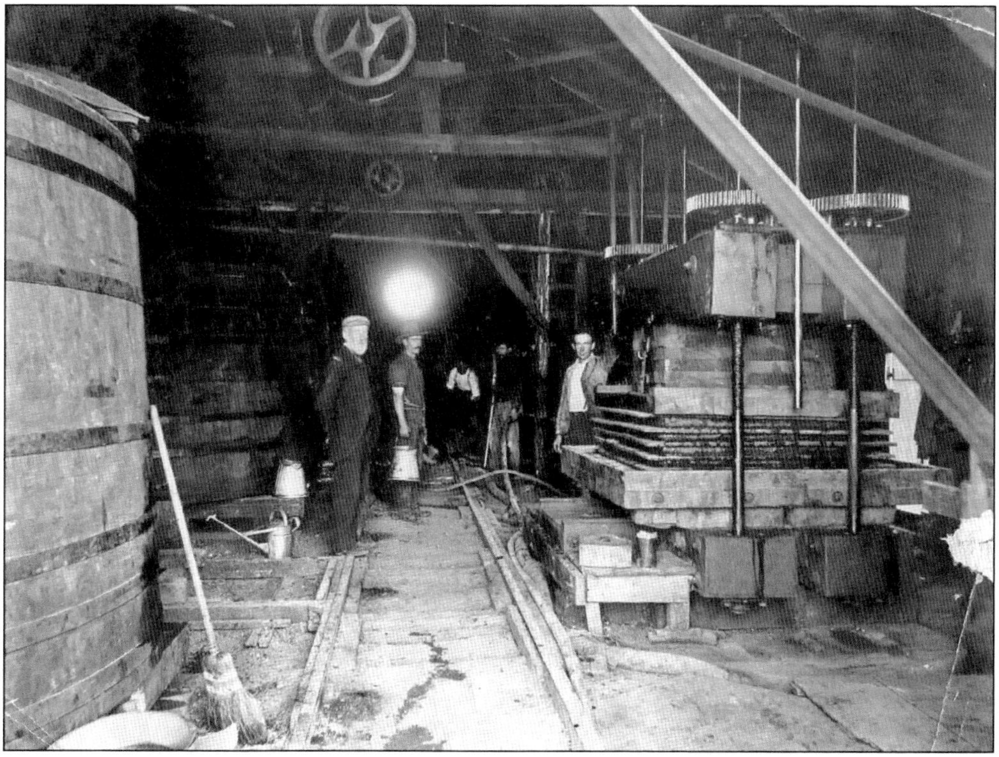

James Concannon used a wine press imported from Germany to crush his grapes. The can with the long nose was used to transfer small amounts of wine from barrel to barrel. To help finance his wine business, Concannon shipped a million grape cuttings a year from 1888 to 1891 to Mexico, to help that country establish its own wine industry.

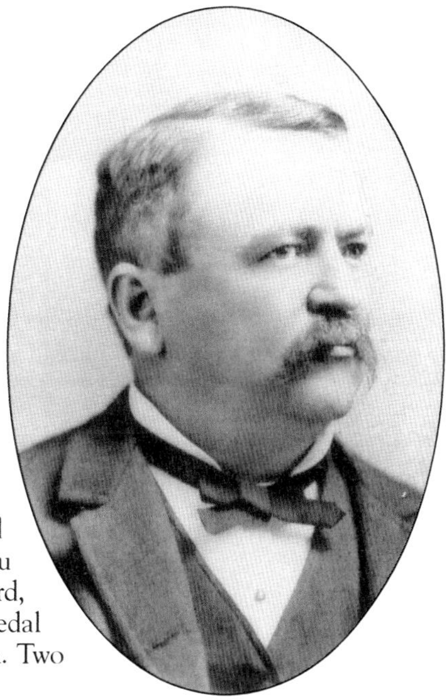

Charles Wetmore learned the concepts of making good wine while visiting the famed French vineyard Chateau d'Quem. He employed those lessons at his own vineyard, Cresta Blanca. His reward was a Grand Prix and a gold medal for his wine at the 1889 Paris International Exposition. Two other Livermore wines also received gold medals.

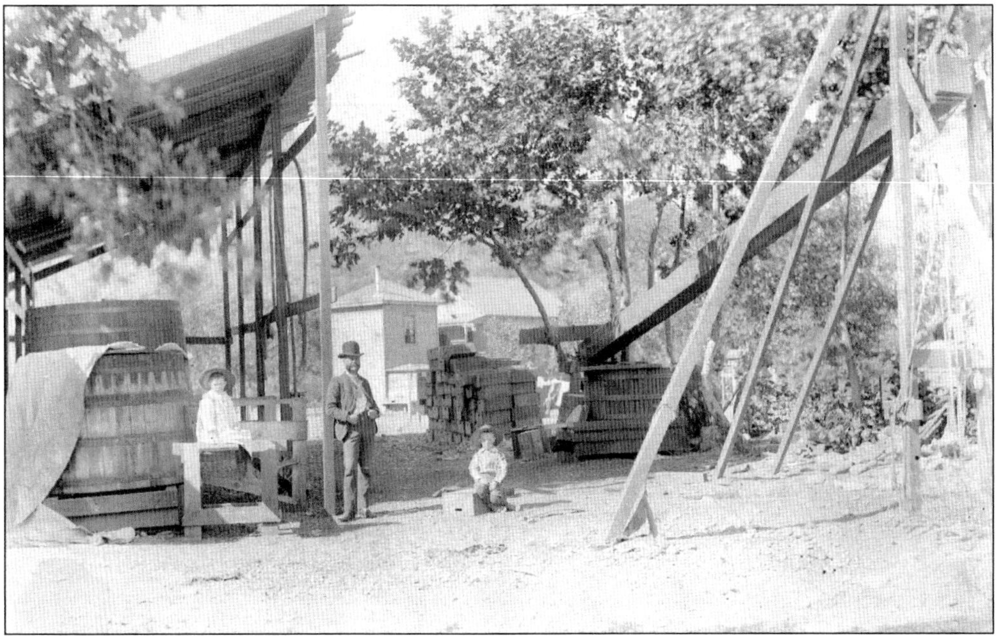

Clarence Wetmore stands near the press that made the wine that won a Grand Prix and a gold medal at the 1889 International Exposition in Paris, France.

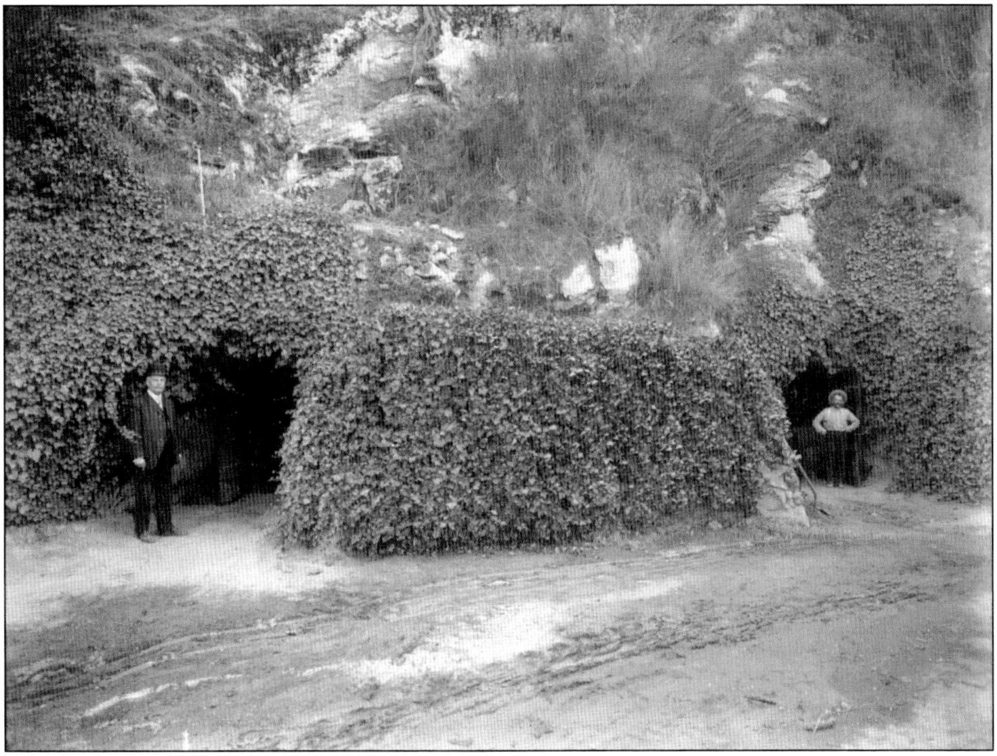

In 1884, Charles Wetmore had two tunnels cut into the hillside for wine storage. Local lore states that Chinese laborers dug them out. At the entrance to the tunnels, Clarence Wetmore (Charles's brother) stands to the left and Frank Minoggio stands on the right.

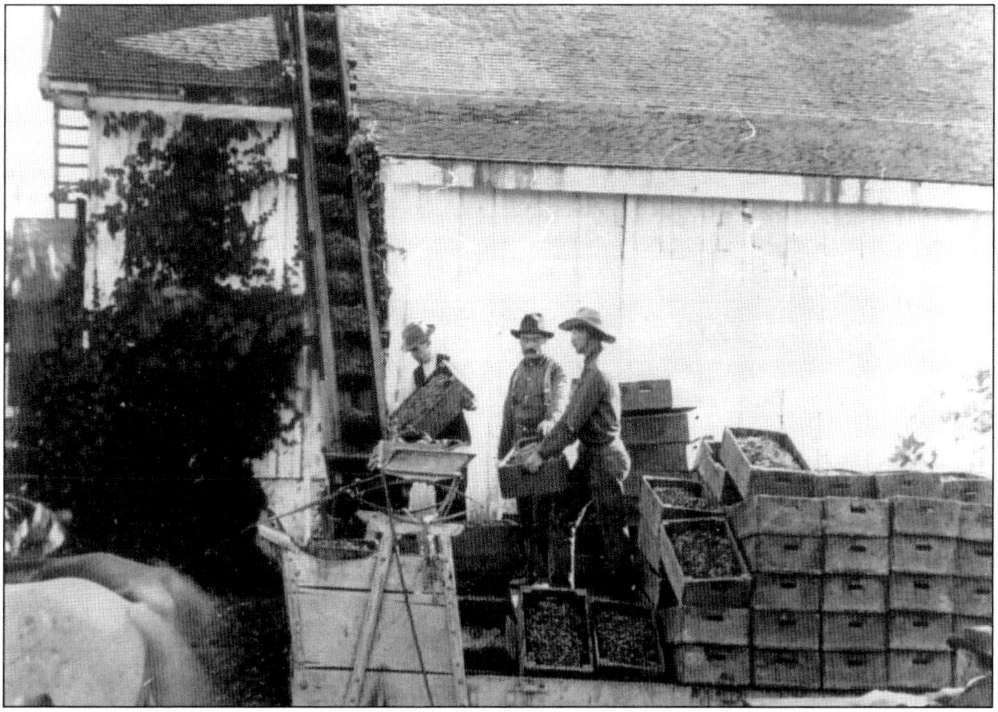

As grapes were brought in from the vineyard, a conveyer lifted the grapes up to the crusher.

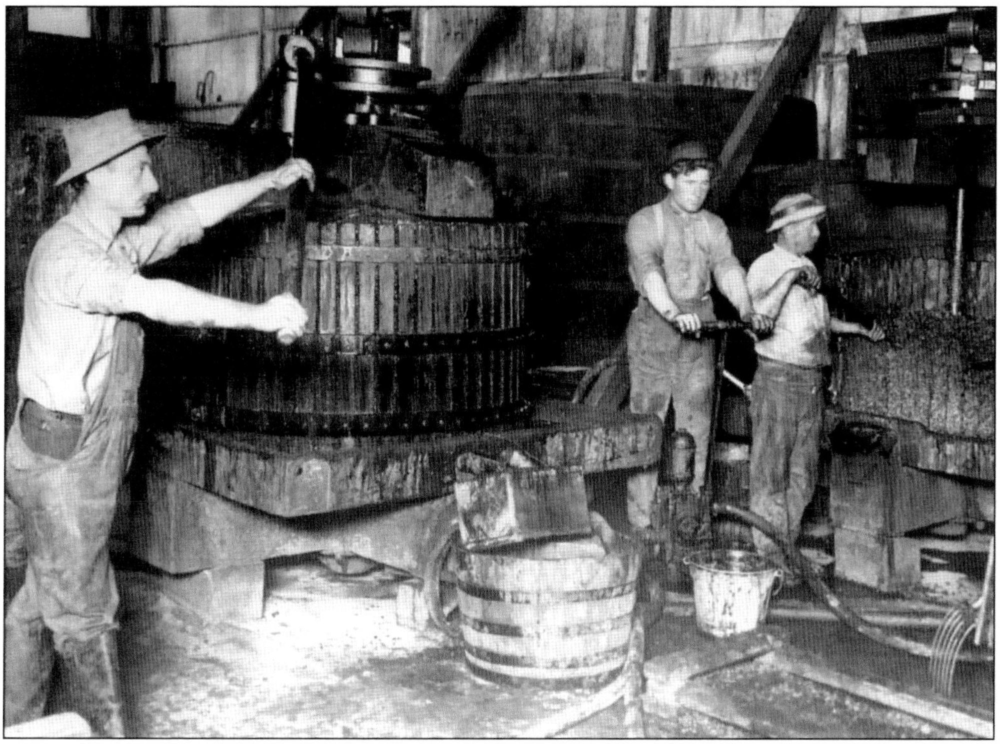

The first process in making wine is the crush. After the juice is extracted from the grape, it is transferred by hand pump into a fermenting tank.

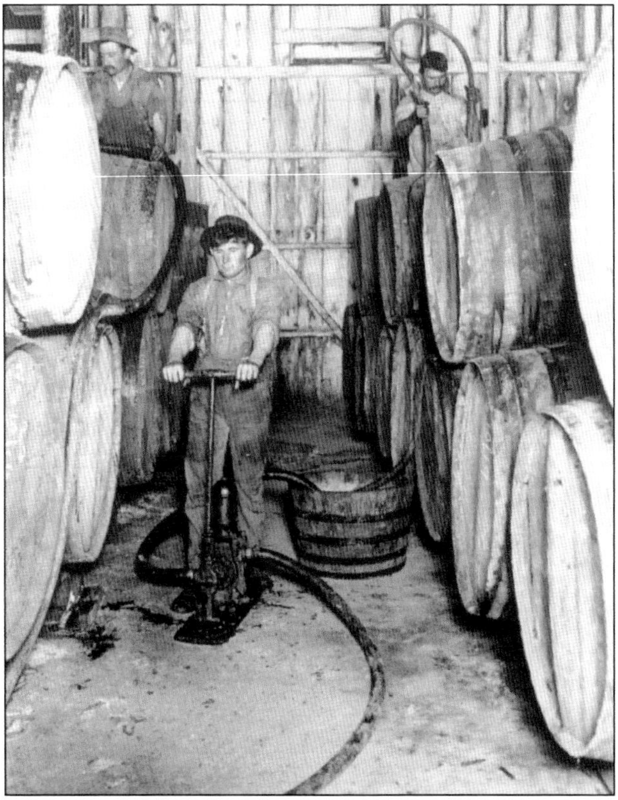

Pumping wine from one tank to another was a strenuous job. The pump used to make the transfer is called an Armstrong pump, and it took strong arms to do this job.

After the bottle was filled with wine, it was labeled and wrapped for shipment.

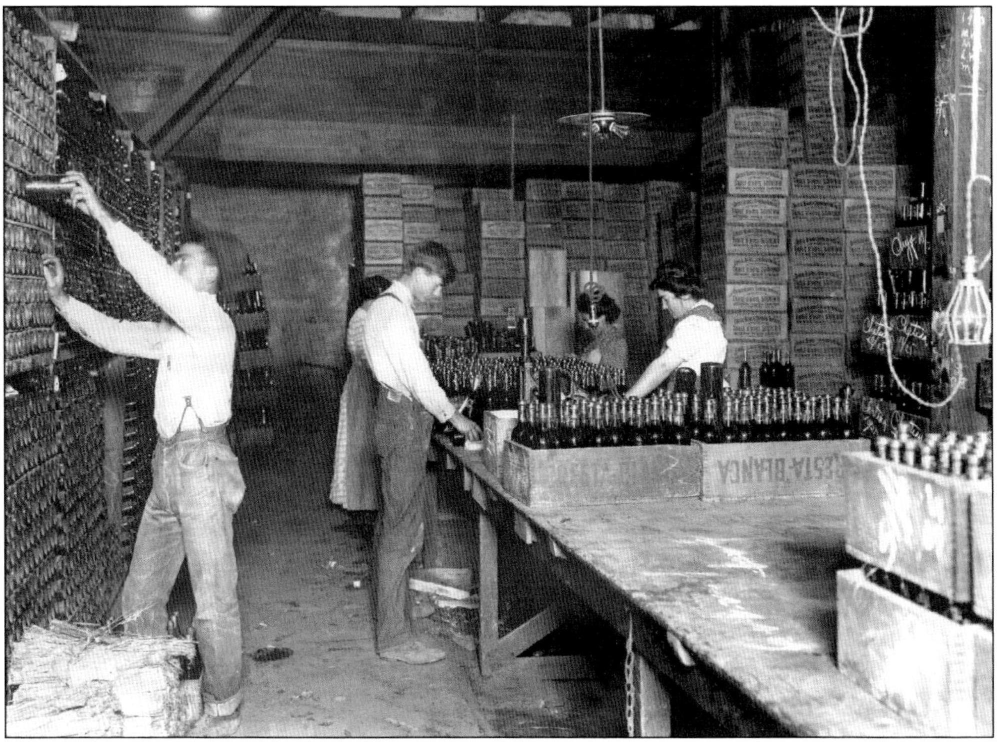

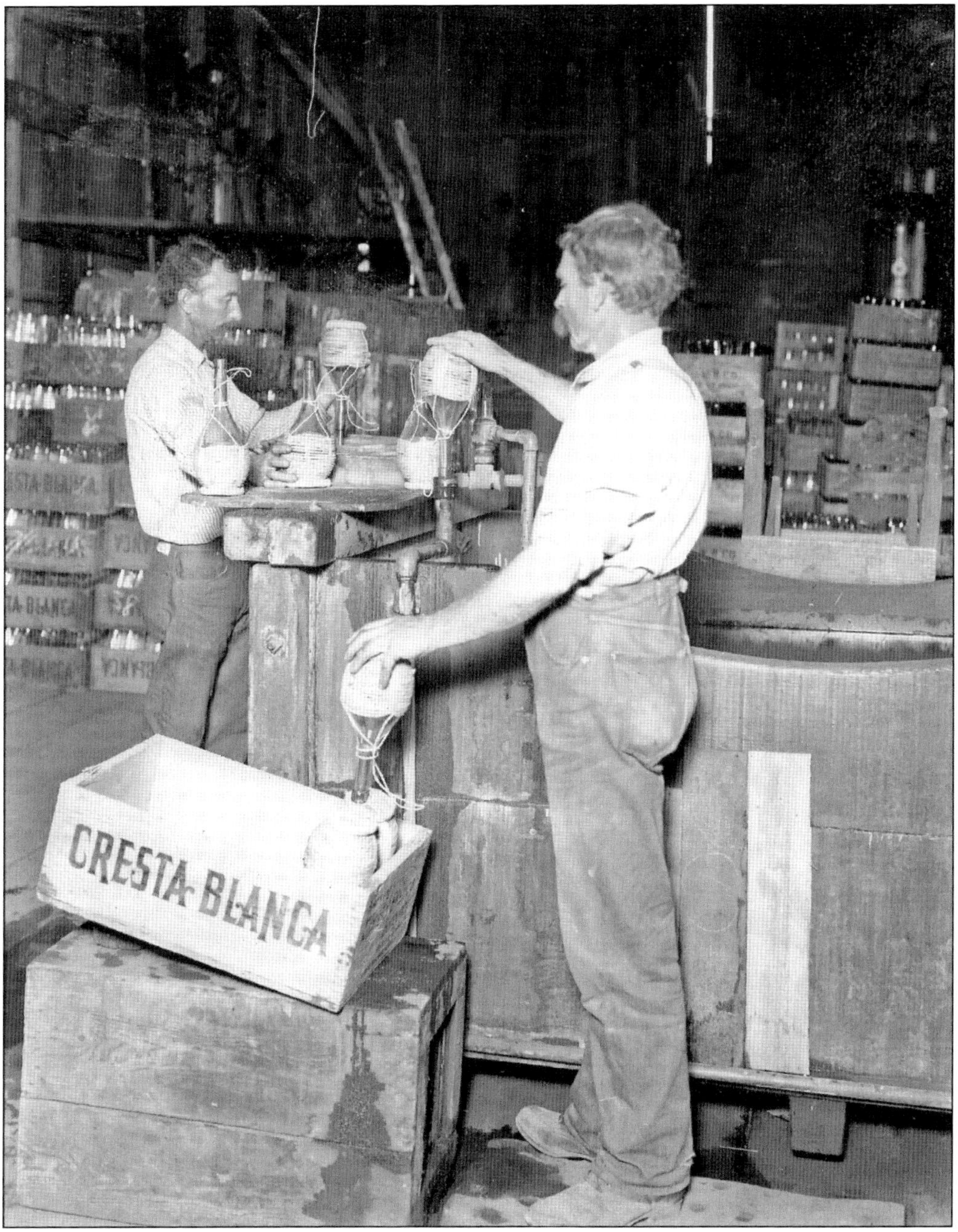

In the late 19th century, it was necessary to wash the residue from glass bottles before filling them with wine and crating them for shipment.

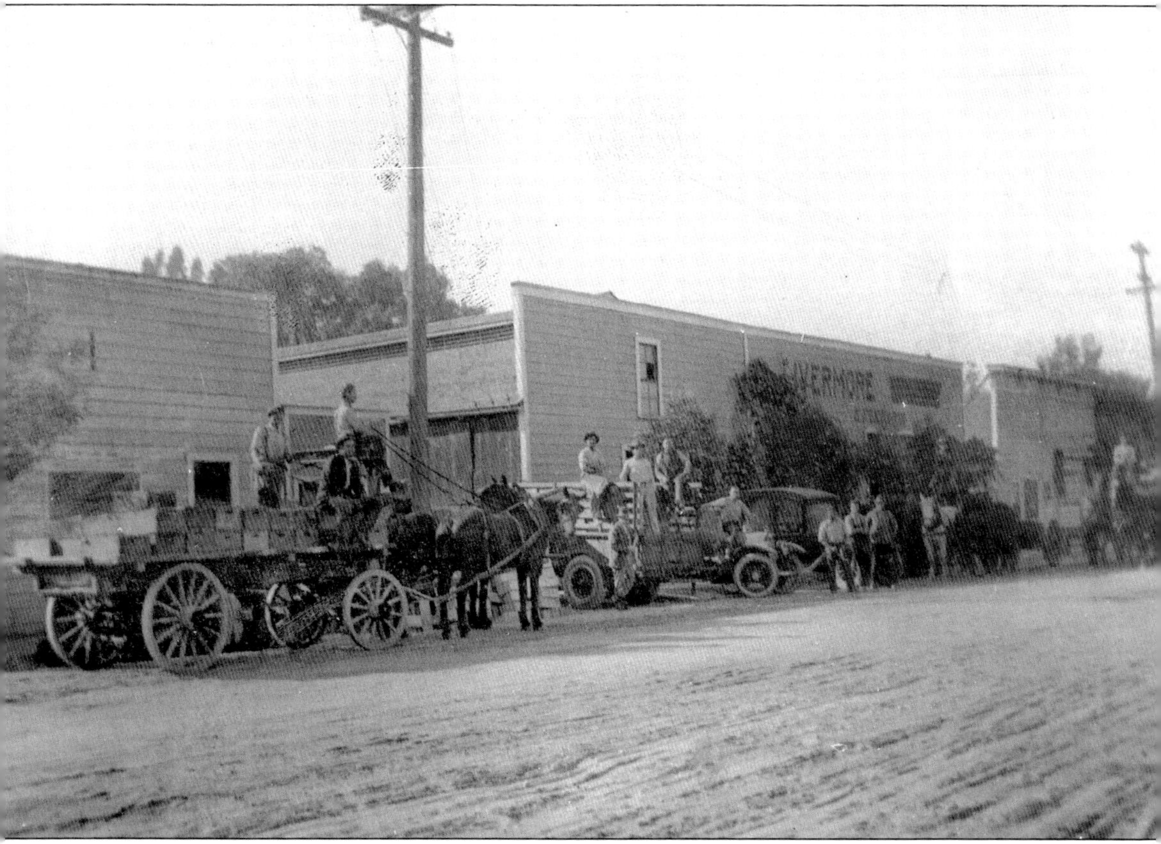

The Livermore Wine Company started business in Livermore in 1904 on the south side of Second Street between K and L Streets (now the site of the Wells Fargo Bank parking lot). Carlo Ferrario, the proprietor, carried on his business during Prohibition by making sacramental and medicinal wine. He moved his plant to South Livermore Avenue in 1936; the building has since been incorporated into the Lutheran church.

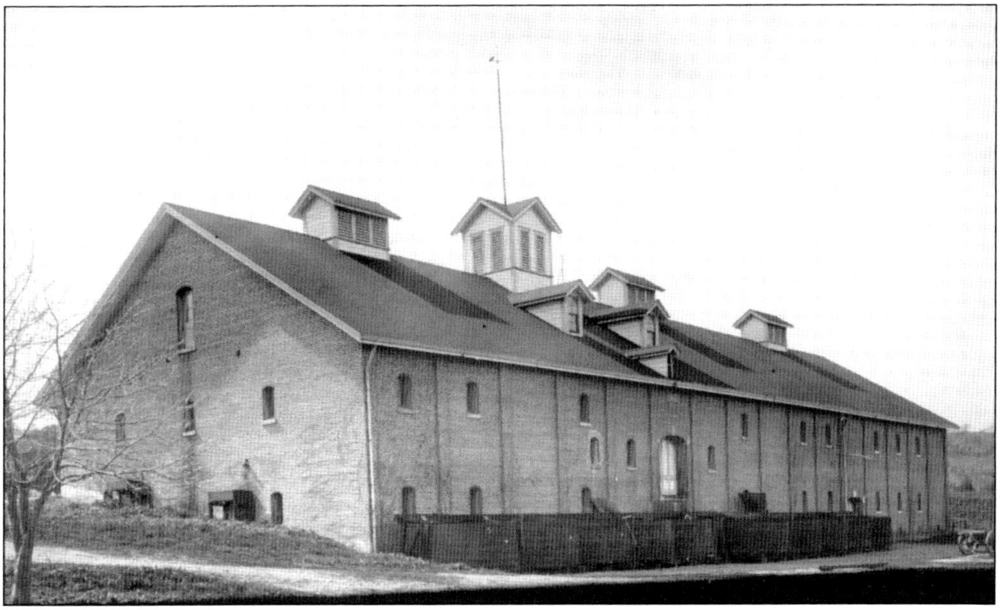

John Crellin started the Ruby Hill vineyard in 1883, naming it for the red earth knoll on his property. The winery building was designed by Hamden W. McIntyre, who had also designed winery buildings for several other vineyards. When it was built in 1887, it was initially to hold 125,000 gallons of wine. Five years later, it was enlarged to accommodate 220,000 gallons.

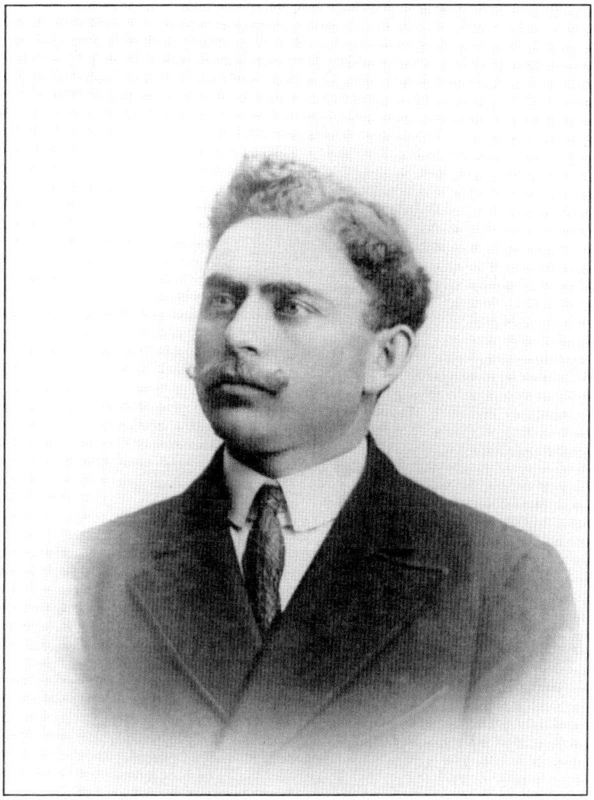

Ernesto Ferrario came to the valley in 1913 and acquired the Ruby Hill vineyard and winery from the Crellin family in 1920. During Prohibition, Ferrario made sacramental wine. It has been said that he maintained some of the old Crellin vines planted between 1896 and 1913 until the 1960s. Ferrario was still active around the winery until it was sold in 1973.

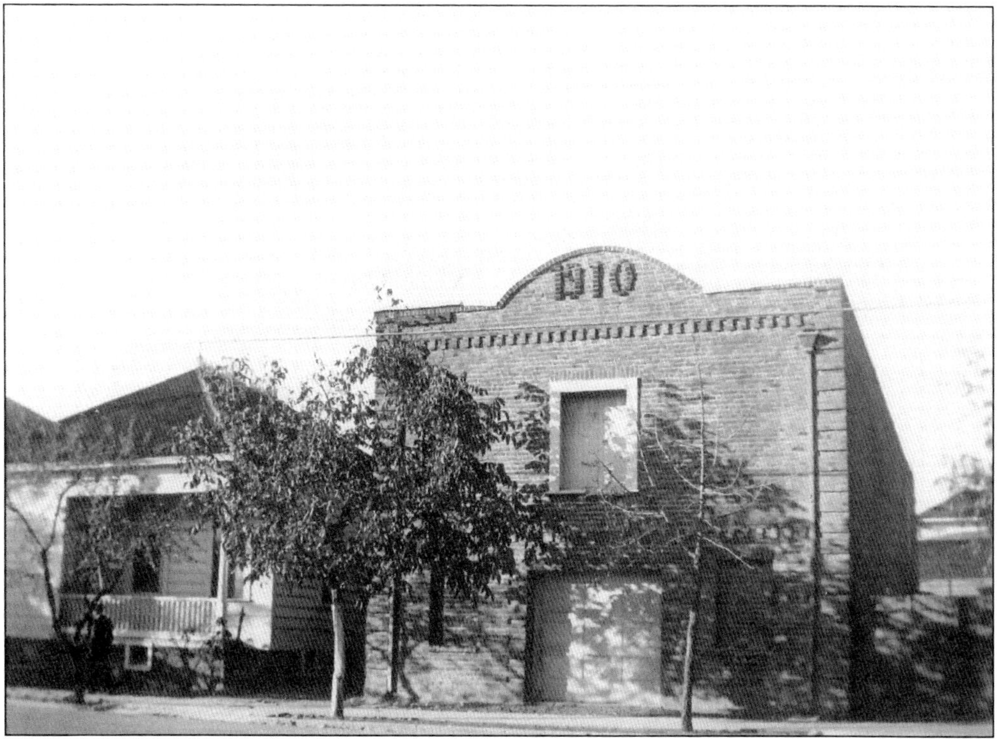

In 1910, the Raboli brothers, Charles and Peter, constructed this winery building at the corner of Second and K Streets. The white house to the left was the residence of one of the brothers.

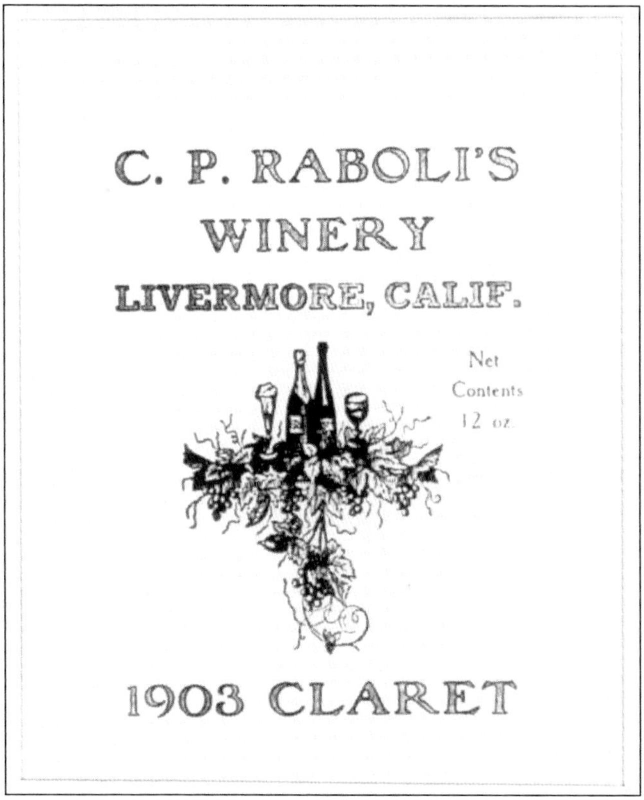

Much of the Raboli wine was sent in bottles rather than barrels to the Tesla coal mining district, located about 15 miles southeast of Livermore in Corral Hollow. Their market substantially decreased when the coal mines closed about 1910.

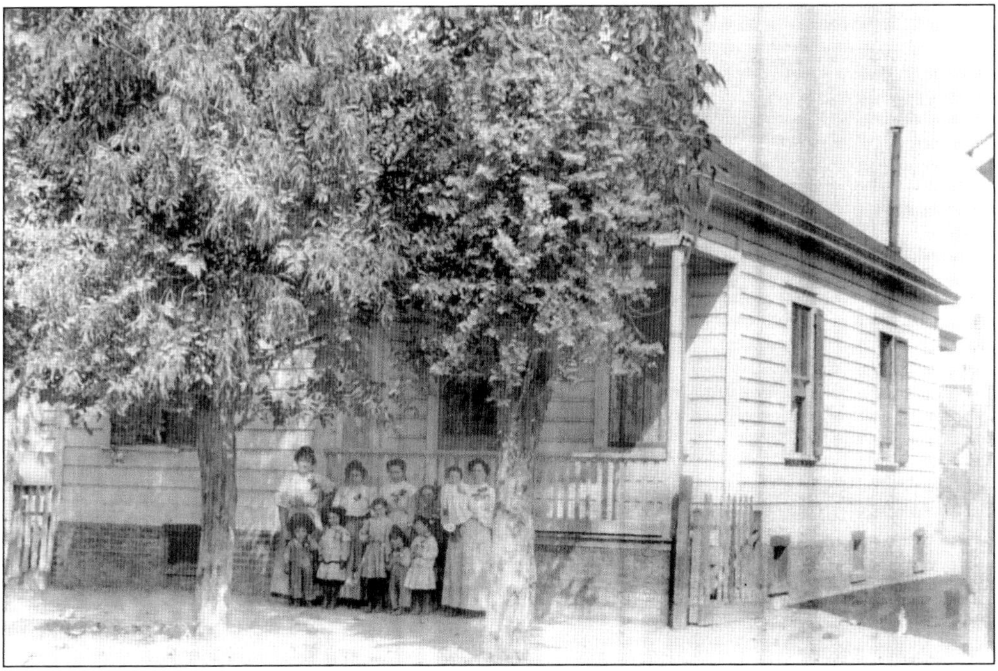

The Raboli wives, sisters-in-law, and children gathered for this photograph near the winery building. The small child in the peaked cap was Lionel Raboli, the last surviving child of that generation.

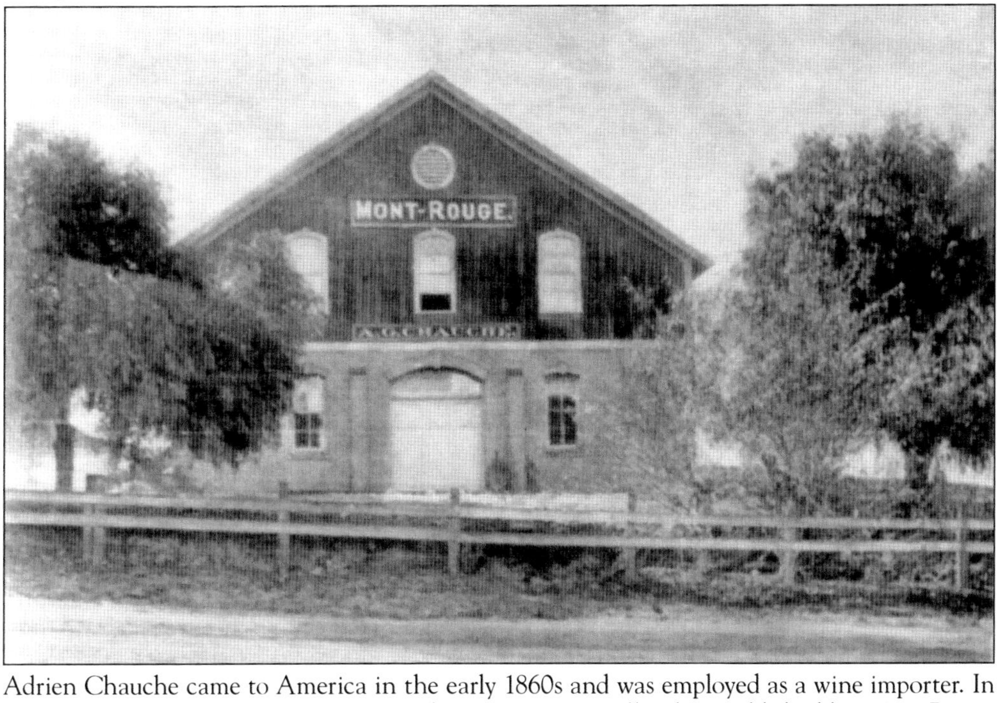

Adrien Chauche came to America in the early 1860s and was employed as a wine importer. In 1884, after seeing the successful vineyards in Livermore Valley, he established his Mont-Rouge vineyard and winery on Stanley Boulevard, near the west slope of Oak Knoll Cemetery. His wine also garnered a gold medal at the 1889 Paris International Exposition.

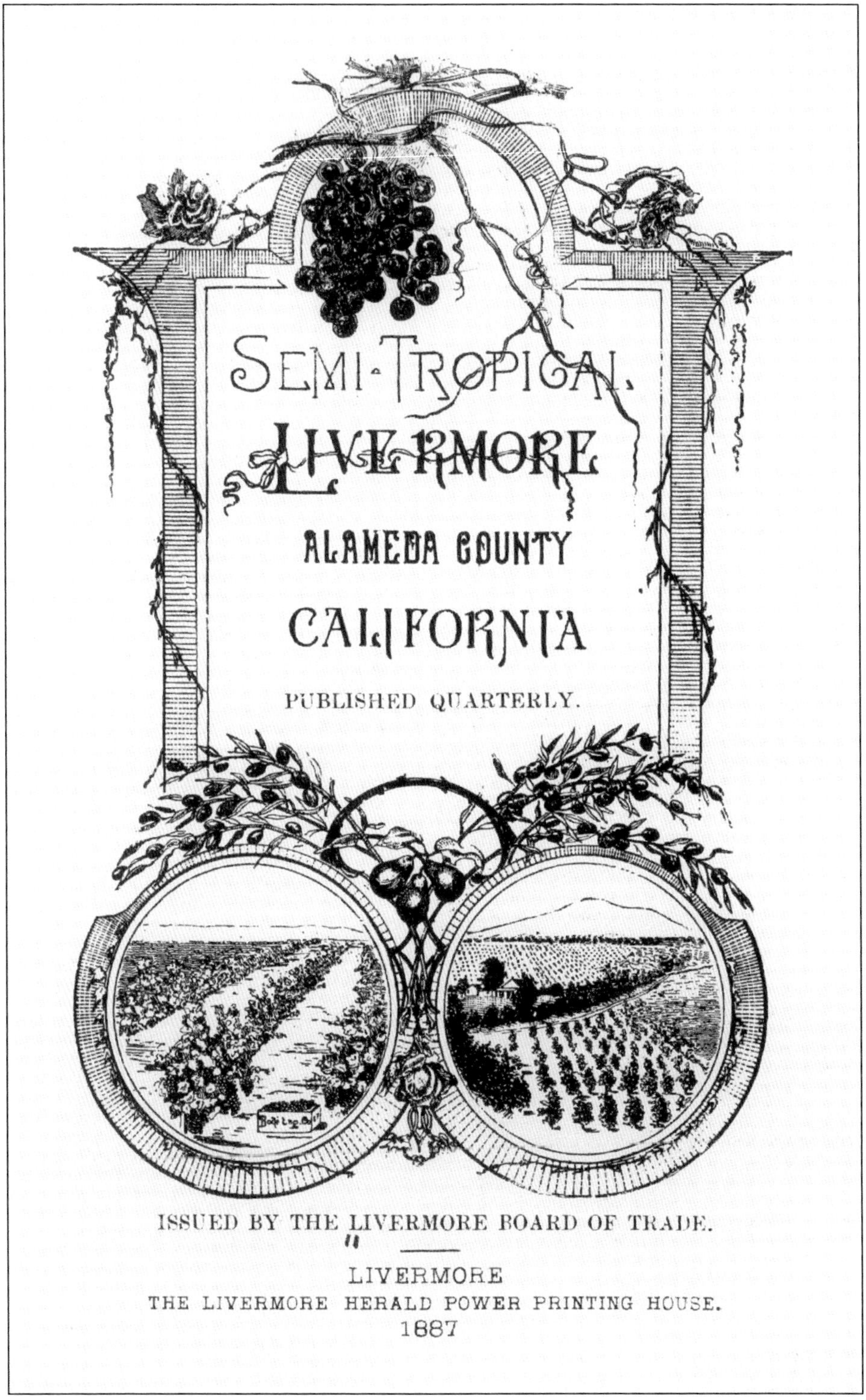

William P. Bartlett, editor of the *Livermore Herald*, boosted Livermore Valley and the advantages of living here at every opportunity. This is the cover of one of his publications.

Three

Transportation

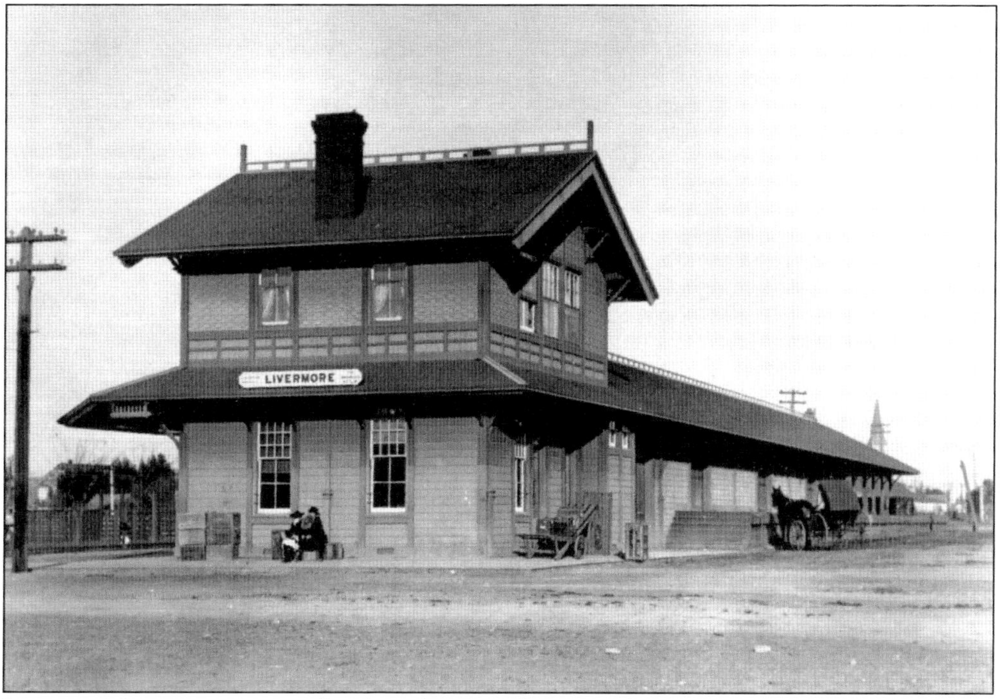

Livermore's beginnings were tied to the railroad. William Mendenhall donated land for a train depot when he founded the town. The railroad helped the town grow quickly, spelling the demise of the neighboring community of Laddsville, which was eventually swallowed up by the new town.

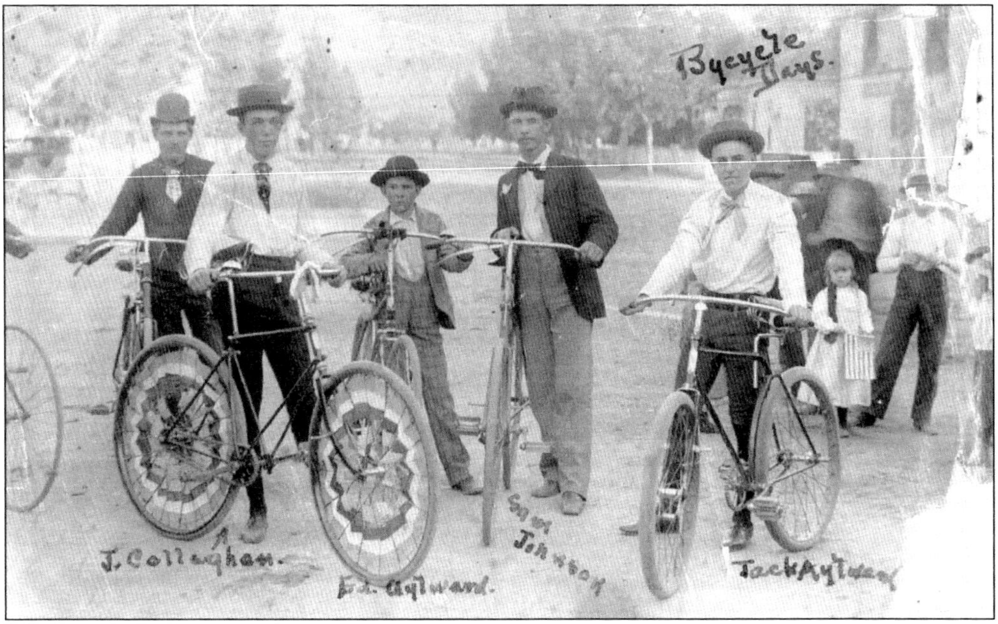

Certainly an alternative to the horse and buggy for the younger set was the bicycle. Here are John Callaghan, Frank Aylward, Sam Johnson, and Jack Aylward, ready to take a spin on Bicycle Day. This affair was a race whose route was First Street to L, down to College and back via Livermore Avenue to First Street. The event was held on July 4, 1895.

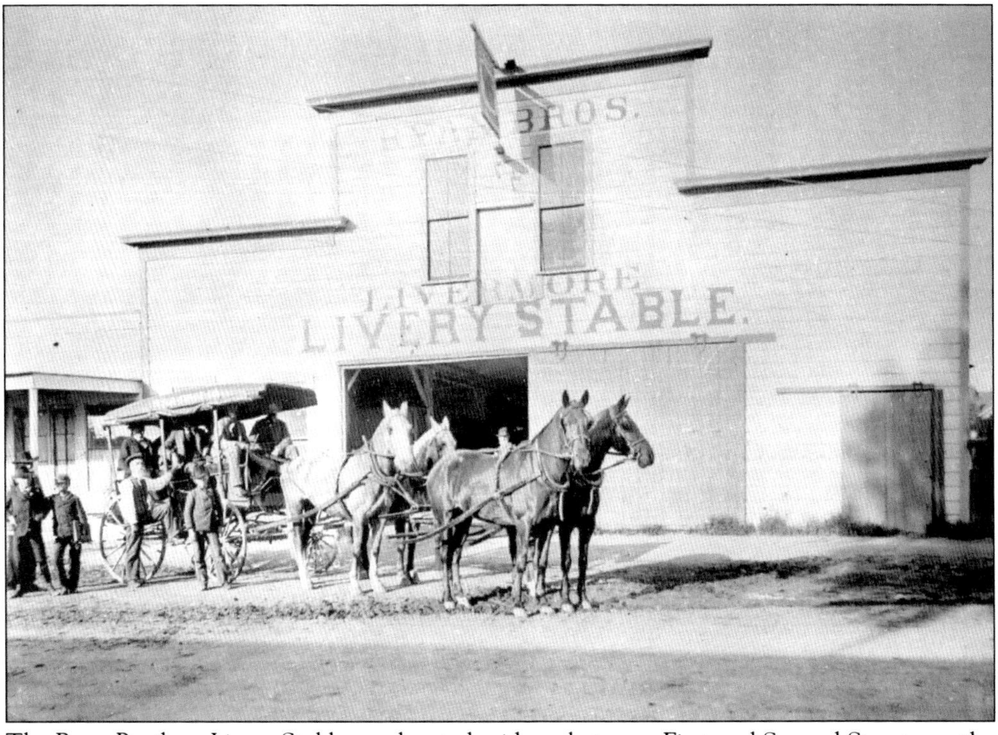

The Ryan Brothers Livery Stable was located midway between First and Second Streets on the east side of Livermore Avenue. It opened in 1885.

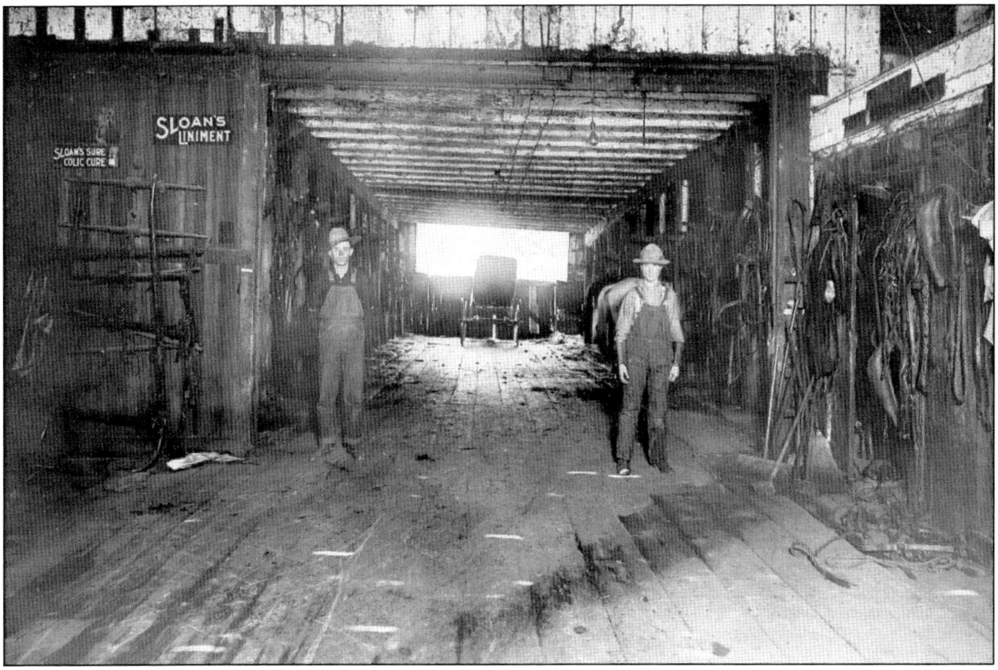

The interior of the Ryan Brothers stable had plenty of space to accommodate their drayage business. The three Ryan brothers had heavy loads of timbers and other materials hauled regularly to Corral Hollow coal mines.

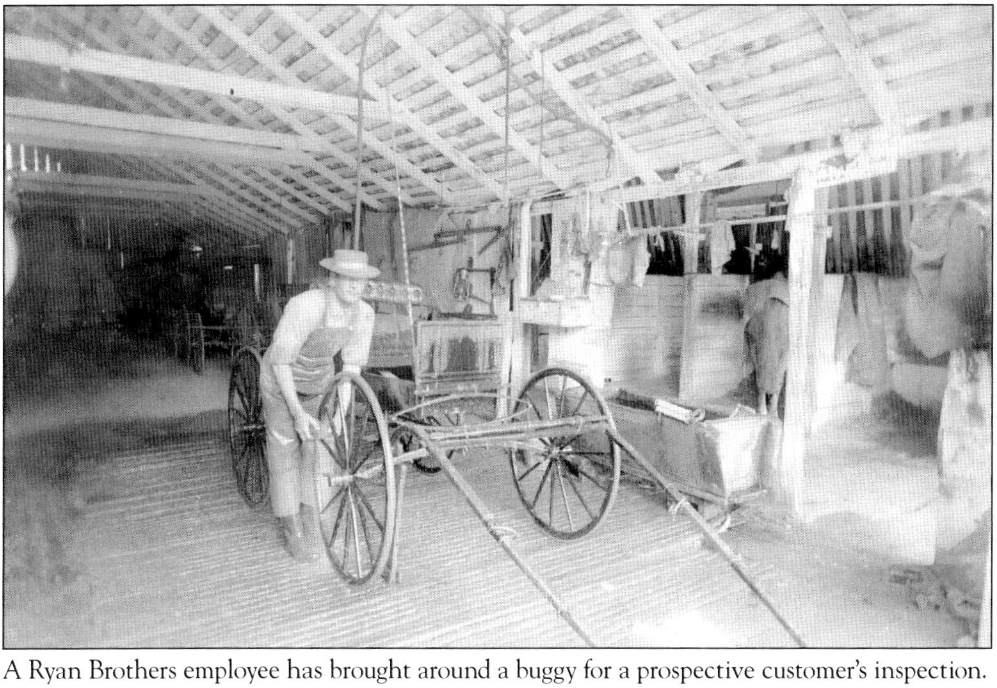

A Ryan Brothers employee has brought around a buggy for a prospective customer's inspection.

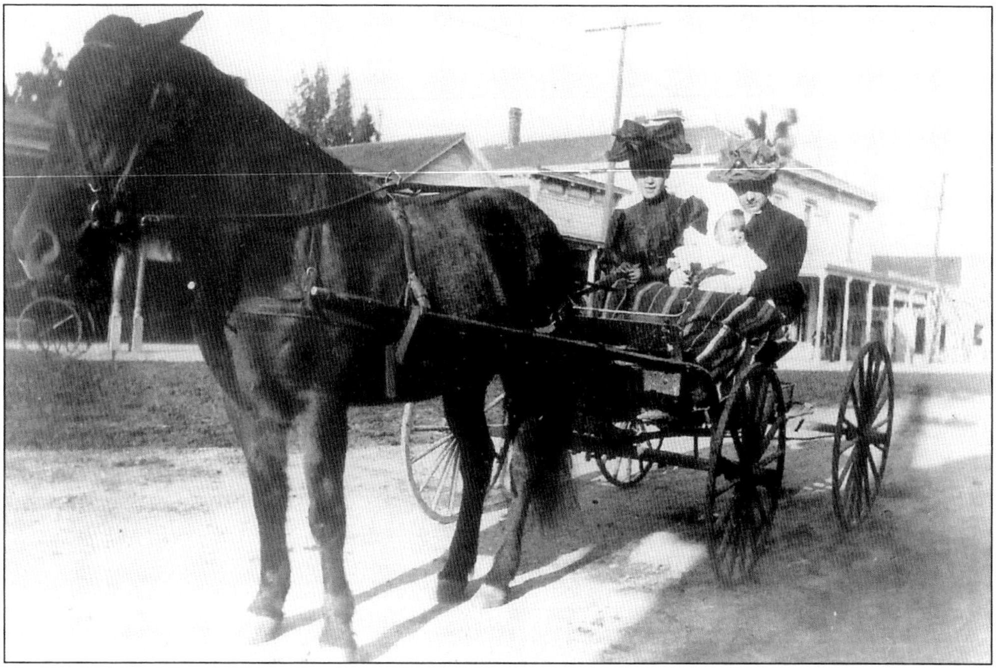

Mrs. George Beck, her son, and the child's godmother run an errand on First Street around 1902.

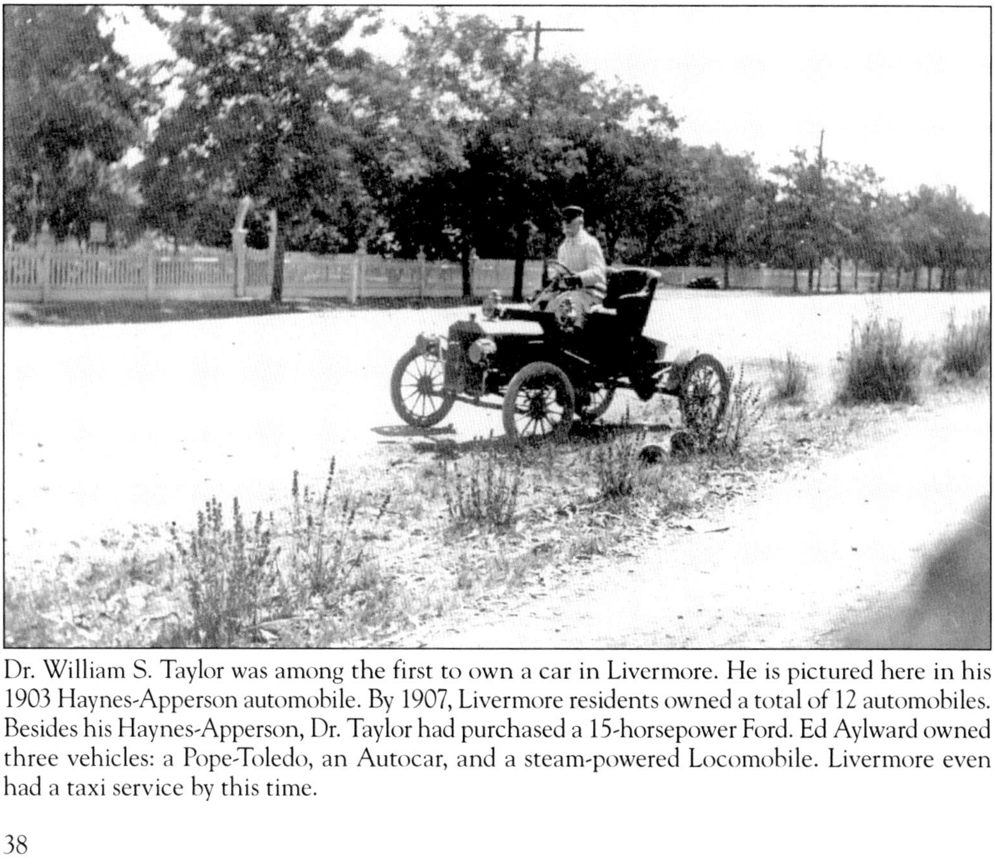

Dr. William S. Taylor was among the first to own a car in Livermore. He is pictured here in his 1903 Haynes-Apperson automobile. By 1907, Livermore residents owned a total of 12 automobiles. Besides his Haynes-Apperson, Dr. Taylor had purchased a 15-horsepower Ford. Ed Aylward owned three vehicles: a Pope-Toledo, an Autocar, and a steam-powered Locomobile. Livermore even had a taxi service by this time.

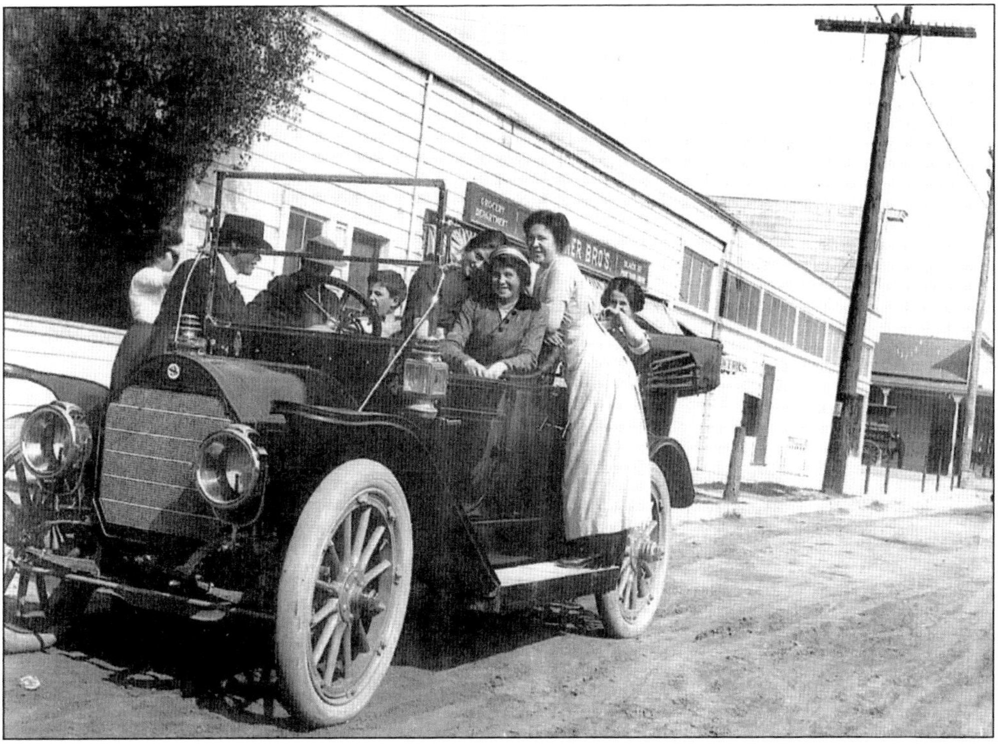

William Regan shows off his new 1913 Stoddard touring car for the benefit of the ladies. In a photograph taken on the north side of First Street between L and M Streets, young John Regan sits at the wheel. Anspacher's Mercantile is in the background. The ladies are Genevieve O'Donnell, far right in the front seat; Kitty McGlinchy, leaning on Genevieve's shoulder; Anna O'Donnell, standing on the runner board; and Gertrude O'Donnell, seated in the back.

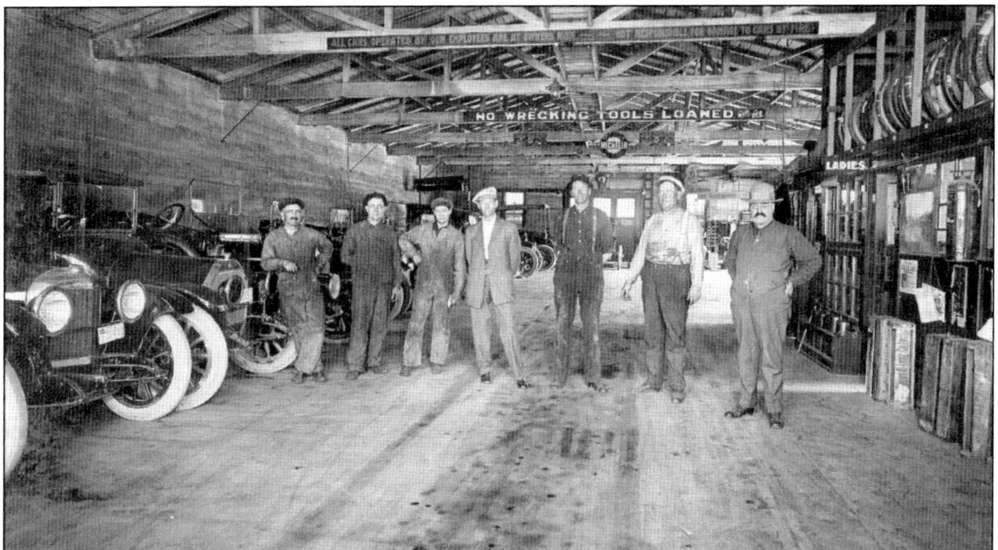

The Livermore Garage Company was organized by Patrick M. O'Donnell in 1911. His was one of the first "car rental" establishments in the community. Later Henry P. Varney took control of the business. Varney stands on the right.

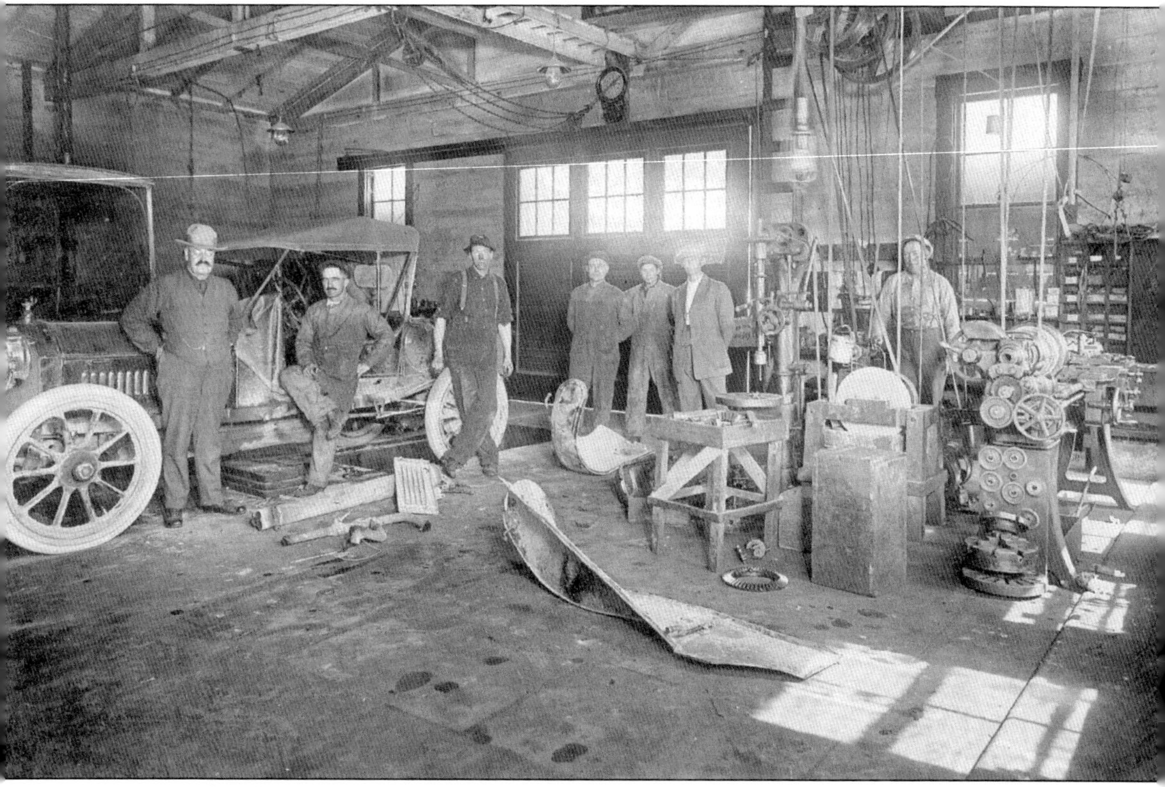

Engine rebuilding and automobile parts replacement were quite common in early-20th-century garages. With the increase in the number of automobiles, the number of horse-drawn vehicles decreased. A parallel change was that as the number of automobile repair facilities went up, the number of blacksmith shops went down. The last livery stable in Livermore closed in 1920.

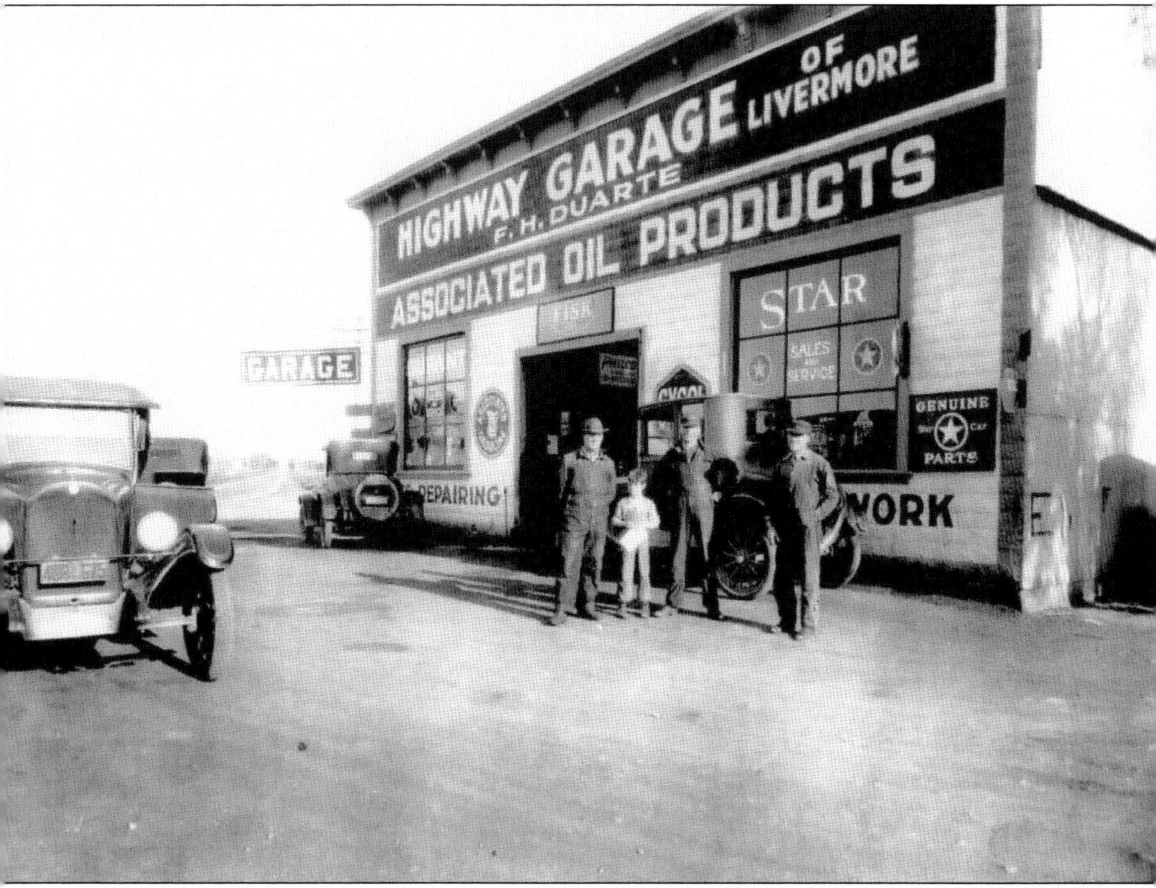

The first transcontinental highway was the Lincoln Highway, extending from Asbury Park, New Jersey, to Lincoln Park in San Francisco. Livermore was on the route as the highway came down through the Altamont Pass in the eastern hills and continued west to the East Bay. By 1922, the highway had been rerouted from Sacramento to San Francisco via the newly completed Carquinez Bridge. F. H. Duarte opened his Highway Garage at the intersection of Junction Avenue, L Street, and the Dublin Road in 1915. His location on the Lincoln Highway made an ideal stop for repairs and refueling.

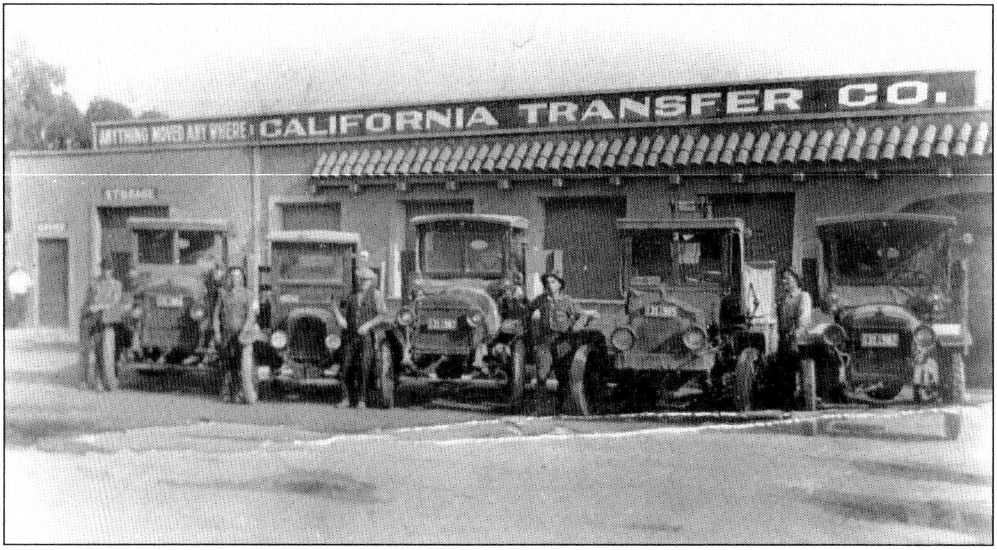

Billy Wilson owned a local trucking company beginning about 1915. His company, California Transfer, specialized in heavy hauling.

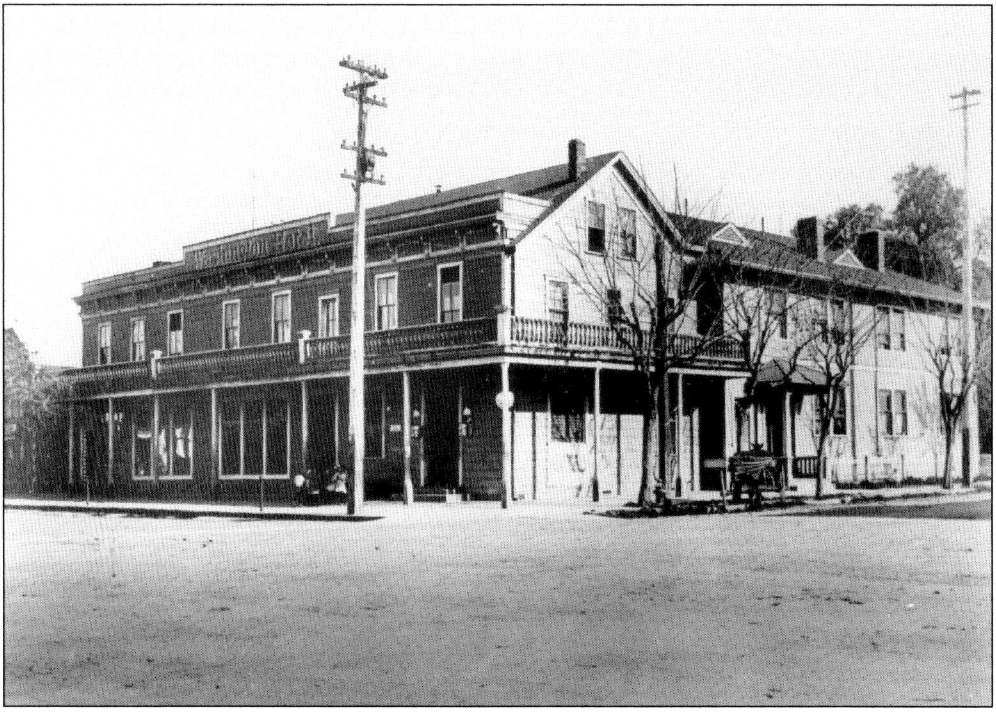

In 1873, the Washington Hotel was built in Livermore by Anton Bardellini after he was burned out in the Laddsville fire of 1871. Located at the intersection of First and L Streets, it was well placed to accommodate guests arriving by train.

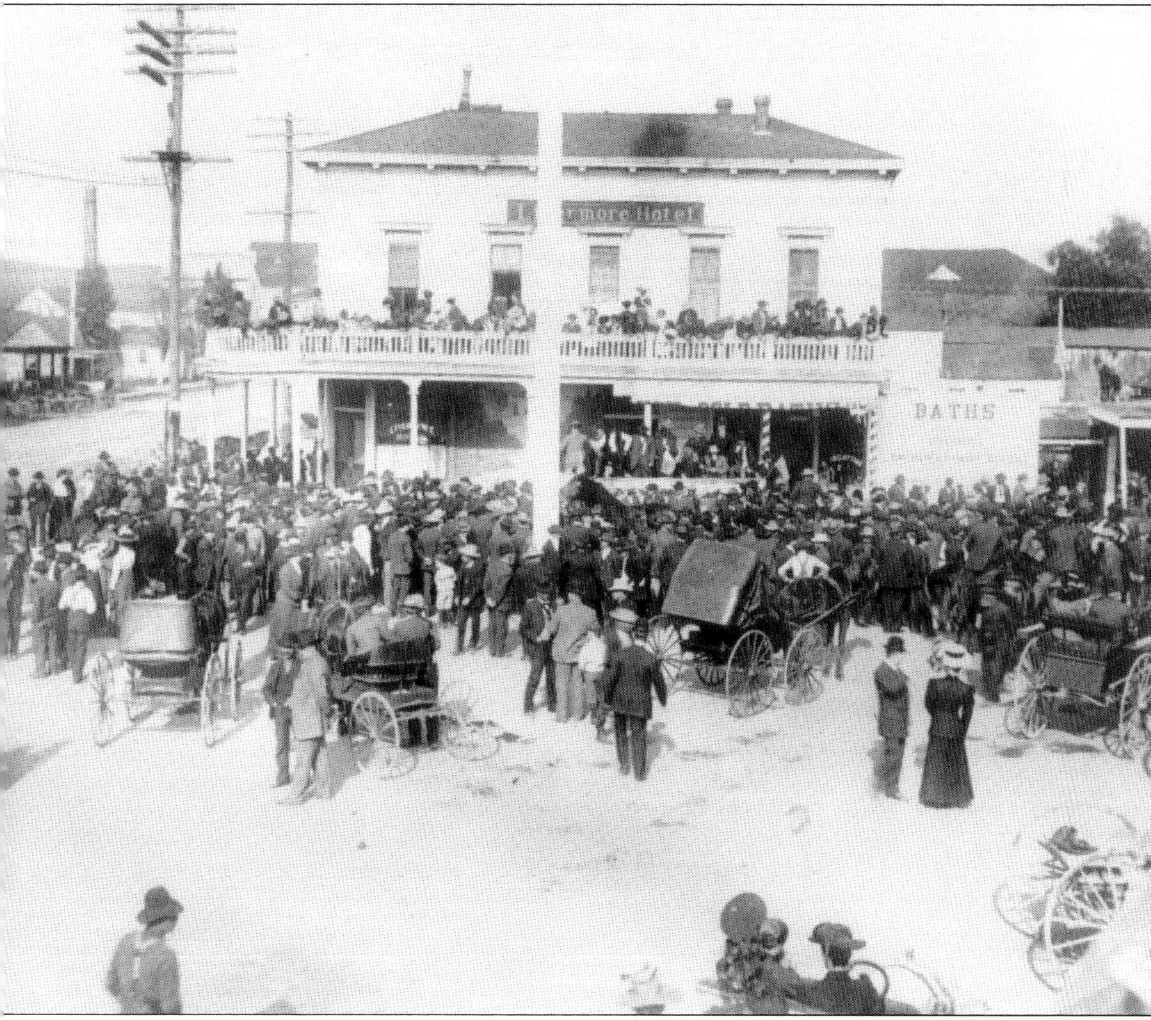

The Livermore Hotel was located at the crossroads of First Street and Livermore Avenue. Being on the east side of the street gave it the advantage of a fine view down First Street, and its position near the town flagpole made it the perfect backdrop for community Fourth of July celebrations, horse shows, and parade starting points.

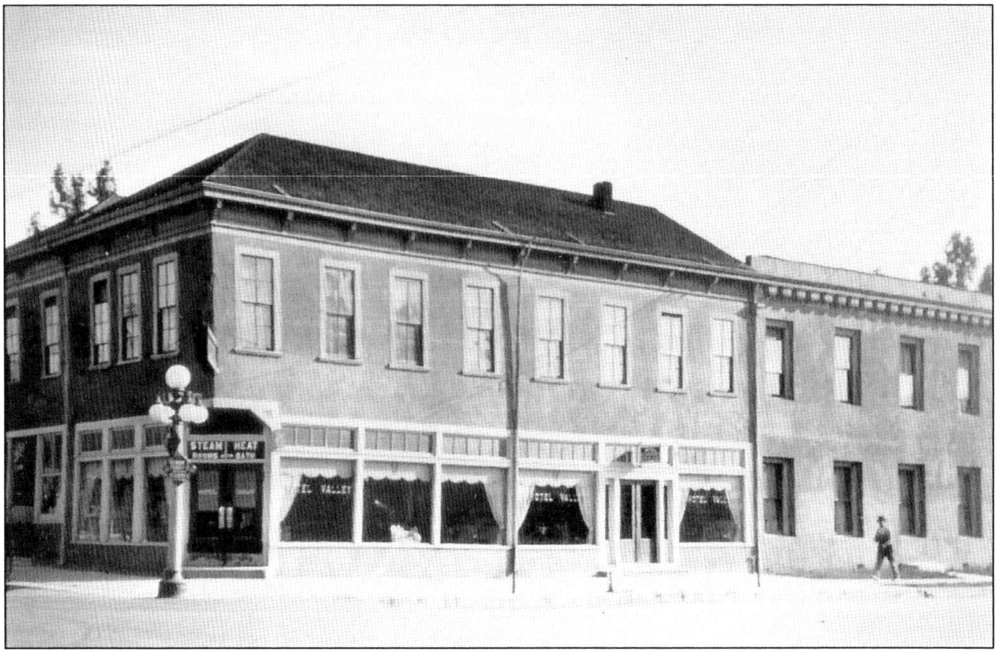

The Valley Hotel, located at the corner of L Street and First Street, was originally known as the Morning Star when it was built by Frank Grassi in 1872. When Patrick M. O'Donnell acquired the property in 1911, he renamed it the Valley Hotel. Two years later, O'Donnell increased the number of accommodations by building a concrete addition.

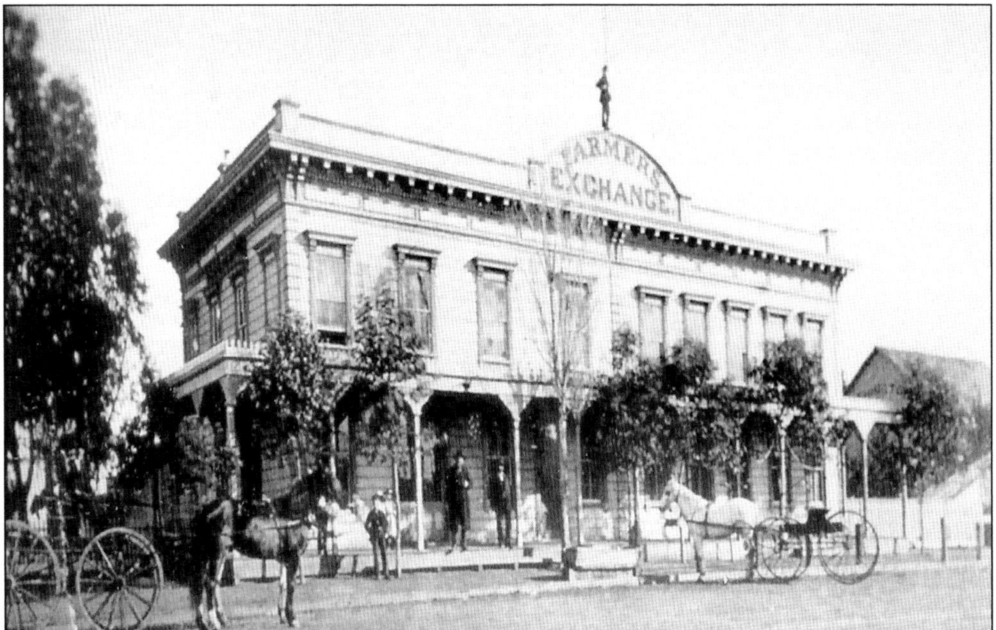

The Farmers Exchange Hotel, located on L Street, opened its doors in 1873. It enjoyed a good business, being about 150 feet from the railroad depot. Later, after extensive remodeling, the building would become the Greyhound bus depot.

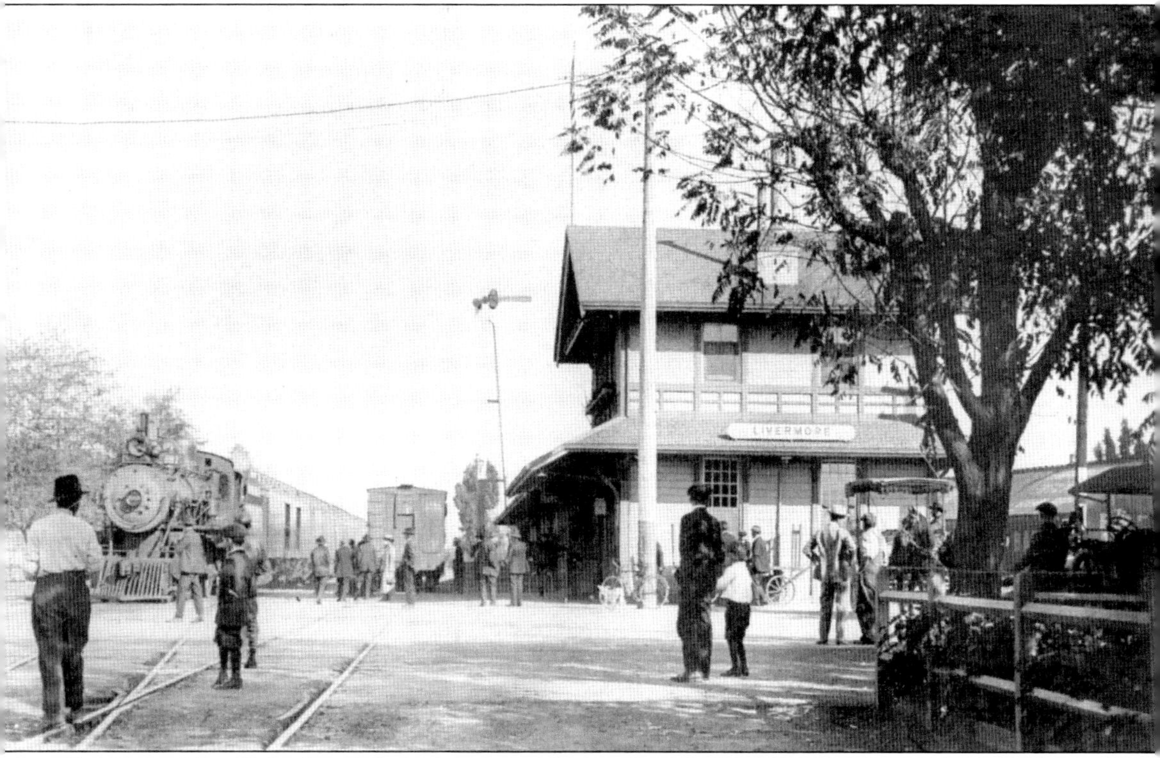

The Central Pacific Railroad (later to become the Southern Pacific) finished the tracks through Livermore in the summer of 1869 and established the first depot west of L Street. When that building burned in 1891, its replacement was constructed on the east side of L Street, south of the tracks. The building is still standing. Underpowered 19th-century locomotives with heavy loads needed a "pusher" engine to negotiate Altamont Pass east of Livermore. A turntable was located a short distance west of the depot where the westbound locomotive engineer, having "pushed up" a train from the east side of the Pass, could turn around to push up the next eastbound train.

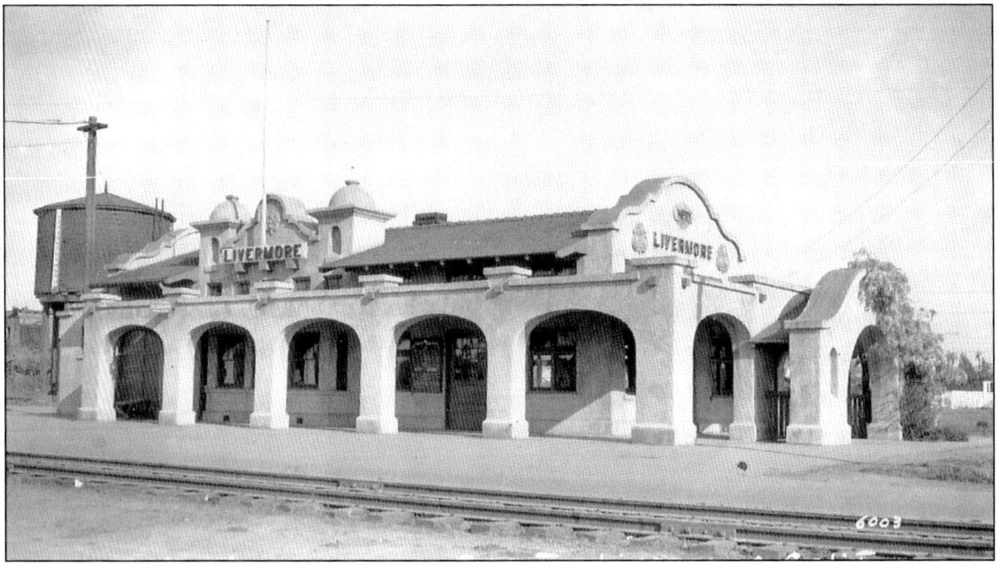

The first passenger train on the new Western Pacific Railroad came though the valley in August 1910. Eight months before, the line had been begun transporting freight. The depot was sited immediately south of the current tracks between K and L Streets, north of Railroad Avenue. The freight house for the station was located across the tracks to the north, opposite the passenger station. It was later moved to a location on Vasco Road, where it is now a warehouse.

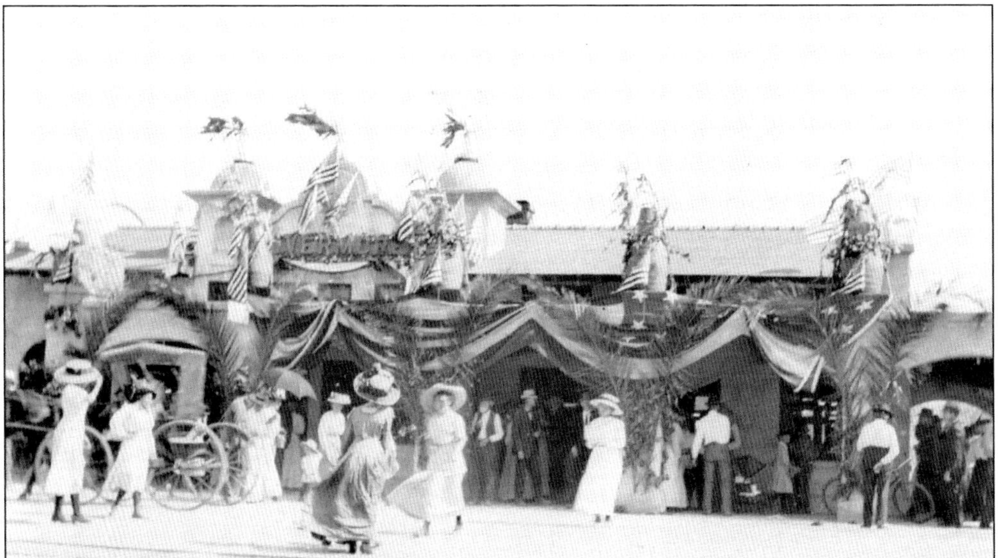

The first public use of the WPRR depot building was an ice-cream social two months earlier, hosted as a fund-raiser by the Christian Endeavor Society of the Presbyterian church.

Four

SCHOOLS

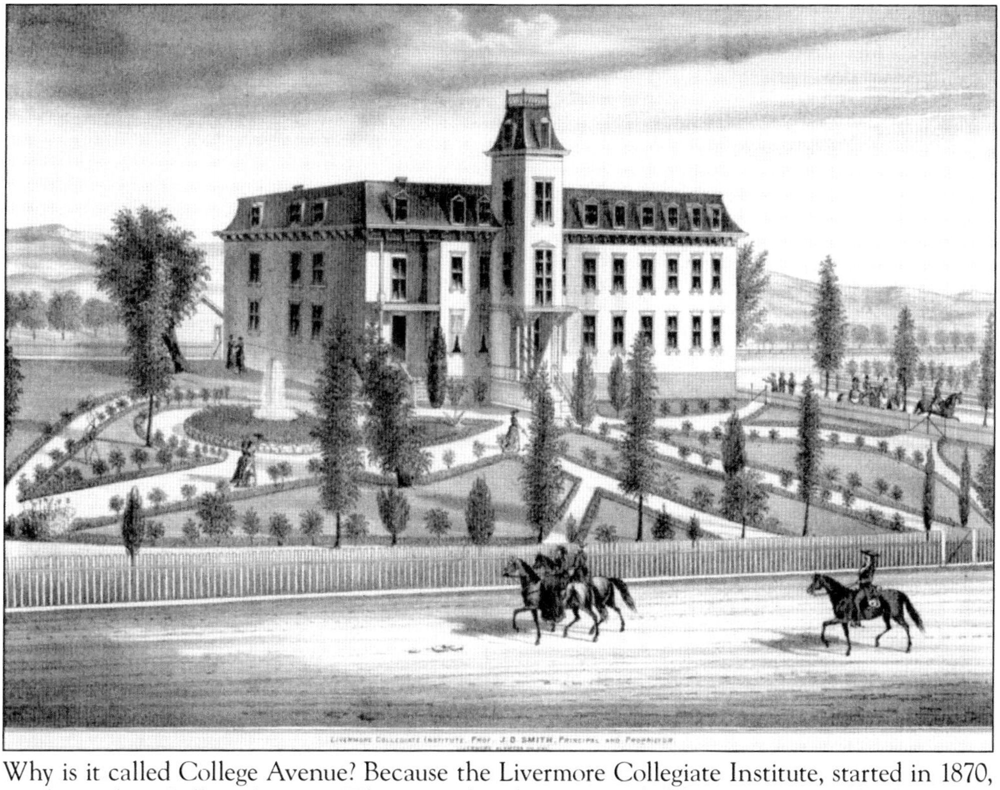

Why is it called College Avenue? Because the Livermore Collegiate Institute, started in 1870, was located on College Avenue. When state legislation provided for tax-supported high schools, boarding schools such as Livermore College were no longer financially feasible. Dr. John Robertson took over the old school building in 1896 for his Livermore Sanitarium. Later the building was sold to John McGlinchey, who remodeled it from 40 rooms to 20 to accommodate his large family. The building burned in 1931. This illustration appeared in Thompson and West's 1878 Alameda County Atlas.

CLASS STANDING OF EIGHTH GRADE—MAY, 1902.

NAMES.	Drawing	Word Analysis	Physiology	Spelling	English	Geography, No 1	Geography, No 2	Grammar	History	Defining	Arith & B. K.	Writing
Allen, Agnes	82	95	84	95	85	88	90	90	83	90	85	9
Atkinson, Frances	85	96	93	95	90	86	88	90	90	92	90	9
Beazell, Frank	85	95	88	95	95	88	90	90	91	95	86	8
Beck, Roy	65	82	80	90	85	80	82	73	80	90	82	8
Blackford, Clyde	92	92	90	95	95	86	88	88	90	95	90	9
Brooks, Florence	90	90	86	94	90	92	94	92	90	91	88	9
Casey, Joe	84	90	86	95	85	79	81	85	85	95	89	9
Concannon, Joseph	79	71	76	90	85	78	80	74	85	85	80	8
Concannon, Sadie	90	88	88	90	90	82	84	88	82	92	87	8
Enos, John	80	95	86	92	90	83	85	87	83	90	86	9
Fink, Rose	90	95	88	95	90	88	90	88	85	90	85	9
Flanagan, Annie	80	85	85	90	85	85	87	85	80	93	85	9
Fitzgerald, Frank	70	88	75	93	88	79	81	80	83	90	90	8
Hansen, Rasmus	90	95	82	92	85	88	90	83	90	95	90	9
Holm, Arthur	85	95	80	94	83	83	85	84	83	90	85	8
Kelly, Mary	80	90	82	95	83	76	78	84	73	95	79	8
Knox, Arthur	84	88	90	95	90	86	88	82	83	88	88	8
Leal, Antone	85	71	70	92	82	81	83	72	80	85	87	8
Langan, Chester	98	75	73	95	90	88	90	71	80	90	90	8
Meyn, Minnie	85	98	90	95	92	93	95	95	90	95	93	9
Mohr, Herman	84	87	84	92	85	83	85	87	80	90	88	9
Ramke, Rebecca	90	95	85	95	86	83	85	88	82	92	90	9
Reimers, Lillie	75	80	75	93	82	78	80	78	83	90	85	8
Sanderson, Olive	80	93	85	95	83	80	82	87	80	95	83	9
Stanley, York	75	80	80	90	85	78	80	75	75	83	83	8
Wagoner, Willie	85	93	92	95	96	88	90	90	90	90	90	9
Wente, Carrie	88	90	85	95	92	88	90	92	95	95	90	9
Wente, May	95	98	90	95	90	88	90	90	85	95	90	9
Young, Mattie	88	93	80	93	90	88	90	90	85	95	80	9

A full curriculum was required of children graduating from the Livermore Grammar School eighth grade in 1902. Several people on this list would later become prominent in local affairs. Note that there are two Concannon children and two Wente children listed. It must have been a long walk to school for those children. Joseph Concannon took over management of the Concannon Winery after his father's death in 1911. Arthur Knox was the son of the mayor. Rasmus Hansen later became a prominent businessman in the community. The first school building in the eastern end of Livermore Valley was built a short distance west of Robert Livermore's home place in 1866. There were 13 children in the first class. With the increase in population following the establishment of Mendenhall's new town, the schoolhouse was moved to what is currently the Livermore High School football field (hence, School Street). A second building was constructed. Again a larger building was needed. On land donated by William Mendenhall, a fine two-story school building was constructed on Fifth Street in 1877. In 1885, there were five teachers and a principal. The school census reported 597 children between the ages of 7 and 17. That building was replaced in 1922, but on the same site.

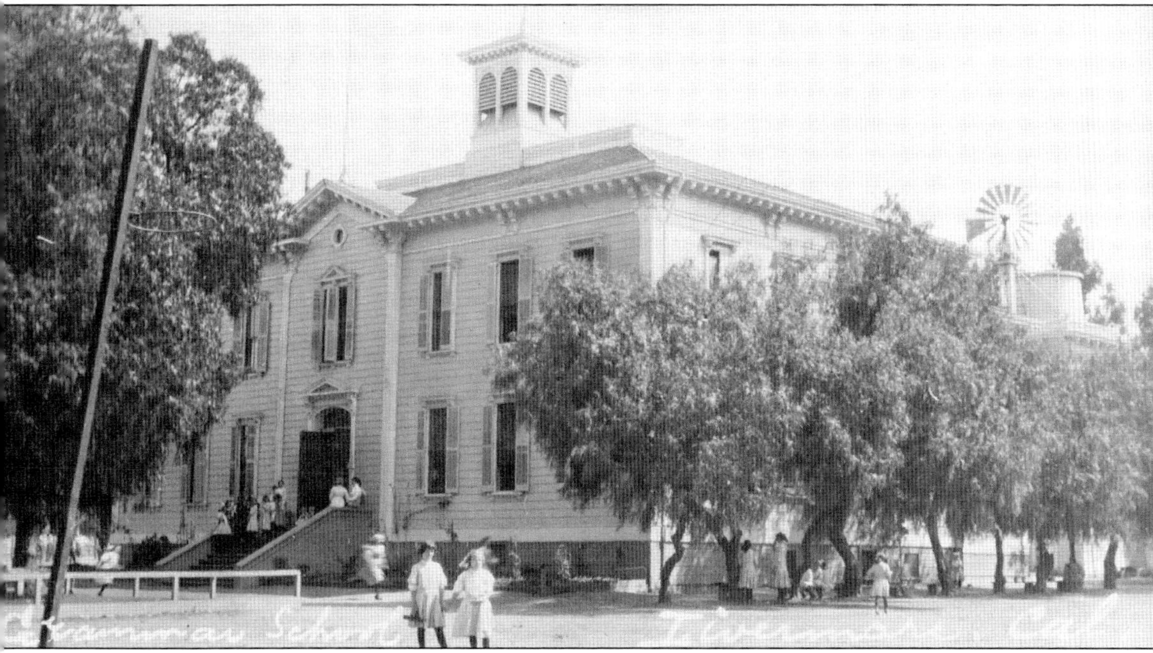

The Livermore Grammar School was constructed in 1877. Initially only four rooms on the first floor were furnished. When the student body exceeded 200 pupils, the board of trustees was urged to finish the second-floor rooms, at a cost of $500, so that there would be some relief to classroom crowding in 1880.

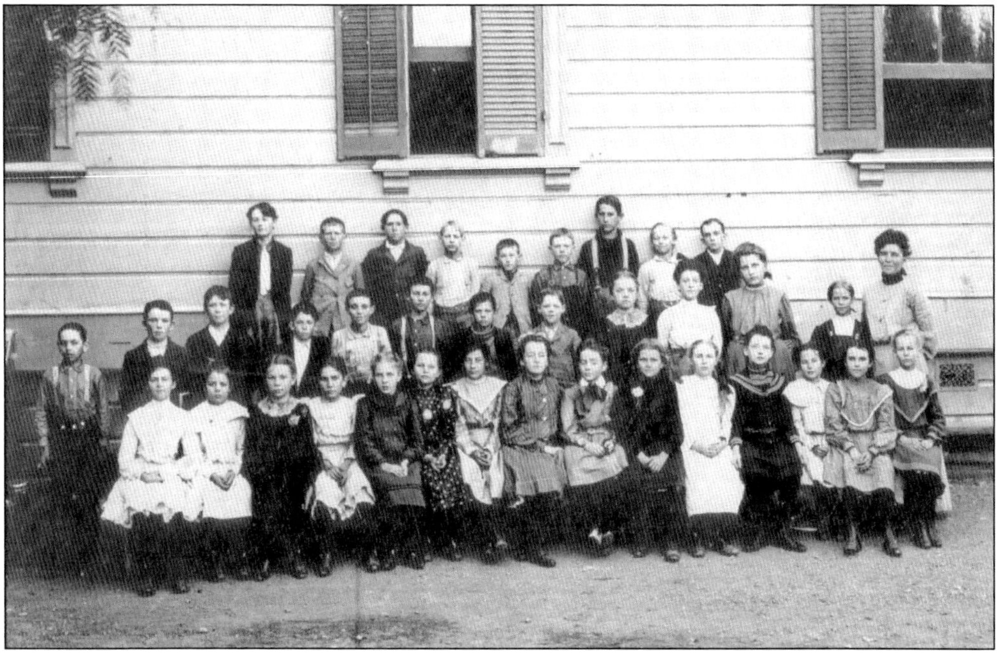

In 1905, Margaret McKee's fifth-grade class included 35 children. Pictured, from left to right, they are (first row) Emma Hansen, Adeline Fitzgerald, Alice Gallagher, Ruth Howard, Emma Twisselman, Hazel Peterson, Muriel Hayes, Henrietta Wagoner, Josephine Damas, Katie Nienberg, Edna Vagts, Mabel Sachau, Clara Anderson, Grace Twombley, Sophie Jorgensen, and Margaret McKee; (second row) Hazel Hansen, Edith Connell, Ruth Carter, Mary Anderson, Dan Winegar, Alfred Inman, John Nienberg, Simon Foscalina, Leslie McVicar, Herman Lienau., Francis Kelley, and Cornelius Biel; (third row) Harold Madden, Raleigh Badgley, Carl Mauchley, Rex Mueller, Neil Gilchrist, Clyde Badgley, Joe ?, Peter Winfield, and Joe Gallagher.

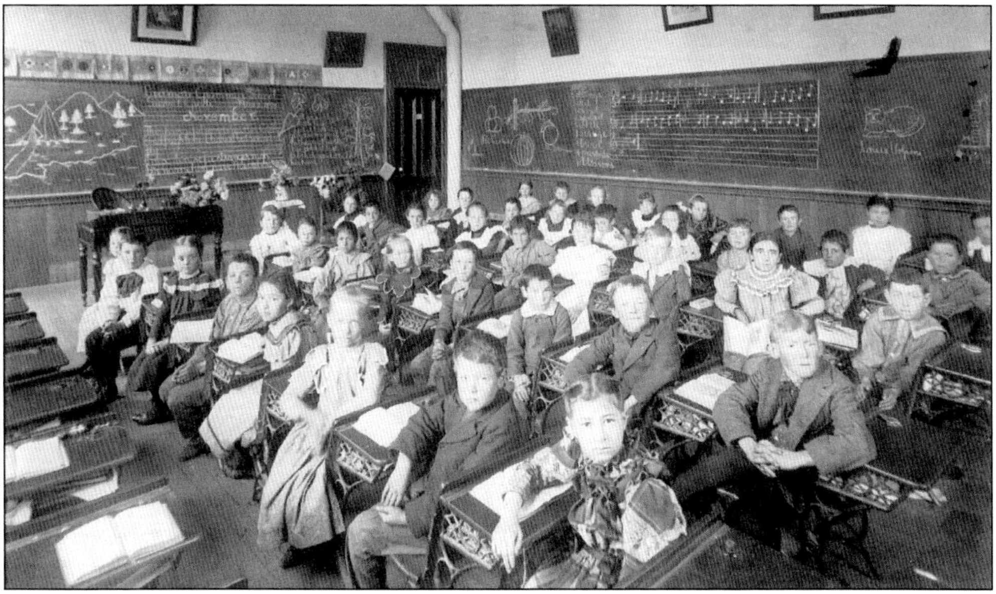

Nellie Boston was the teacher of these second-grade children at Livermore Grammar School around 1896.

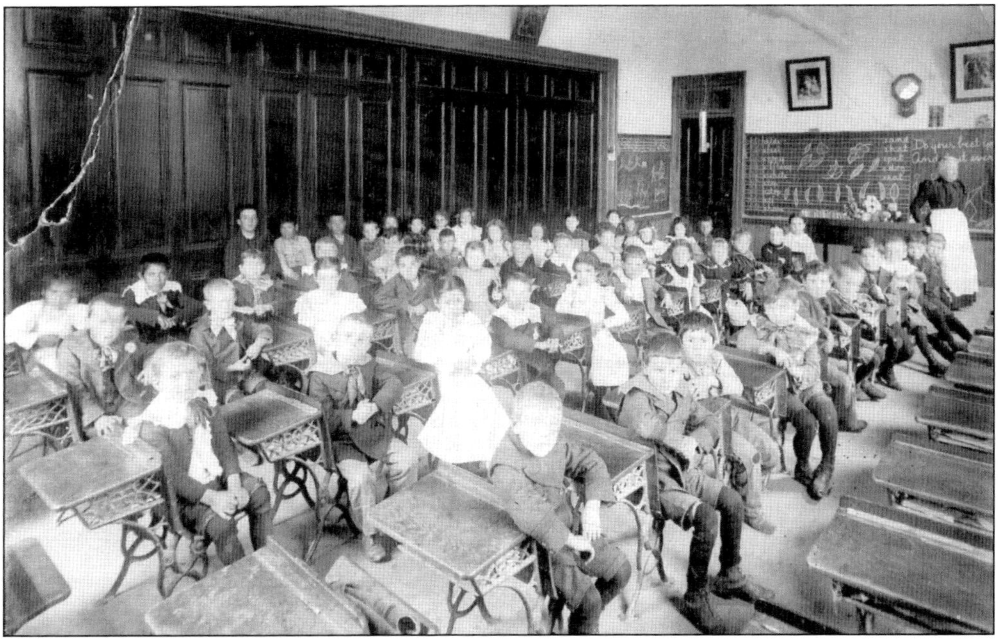

Classrooms at Livermore Grammar School were often populated by 35 and 40 students in each room. It is amazing how much children learned in such an environment.

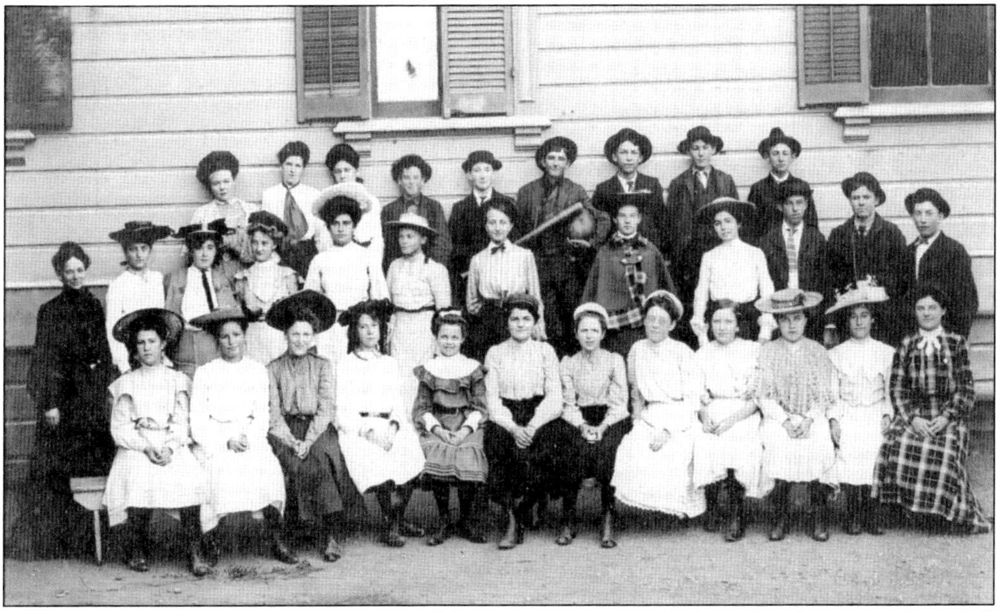

The eighth-grade students that graduated from Livermore Grammar School in 1904, from left to right, are (first row) Gertrude Cardoza, Emma Hansen, Edith Monaghan, Margaret Mack, Ruby Hendriksen, Myrtle Osbourne, May Berlin, Genevieve Beck , Jane Teeter, Grace Faragher, Lizzie Larripa, and Lillie Johnson; (second row) Miss Dougherty (teacher), Effie Wilder, Kathryn Taylor, Ethel Bagley, Amelia Altamarano, Martha Nienberg, Marguerite Leonhardt, Vivien Thomas, Victoria Beale, Willie Anderson, Dale Anderson, and Harold Rees; (third row) May Kelley, Hazel Dutcher, Addie Anderson, Joe Connelly, Leo Burns, Dee Lefever, Ernest Wente, Dan Gallagher, and Carl Jorgensen.

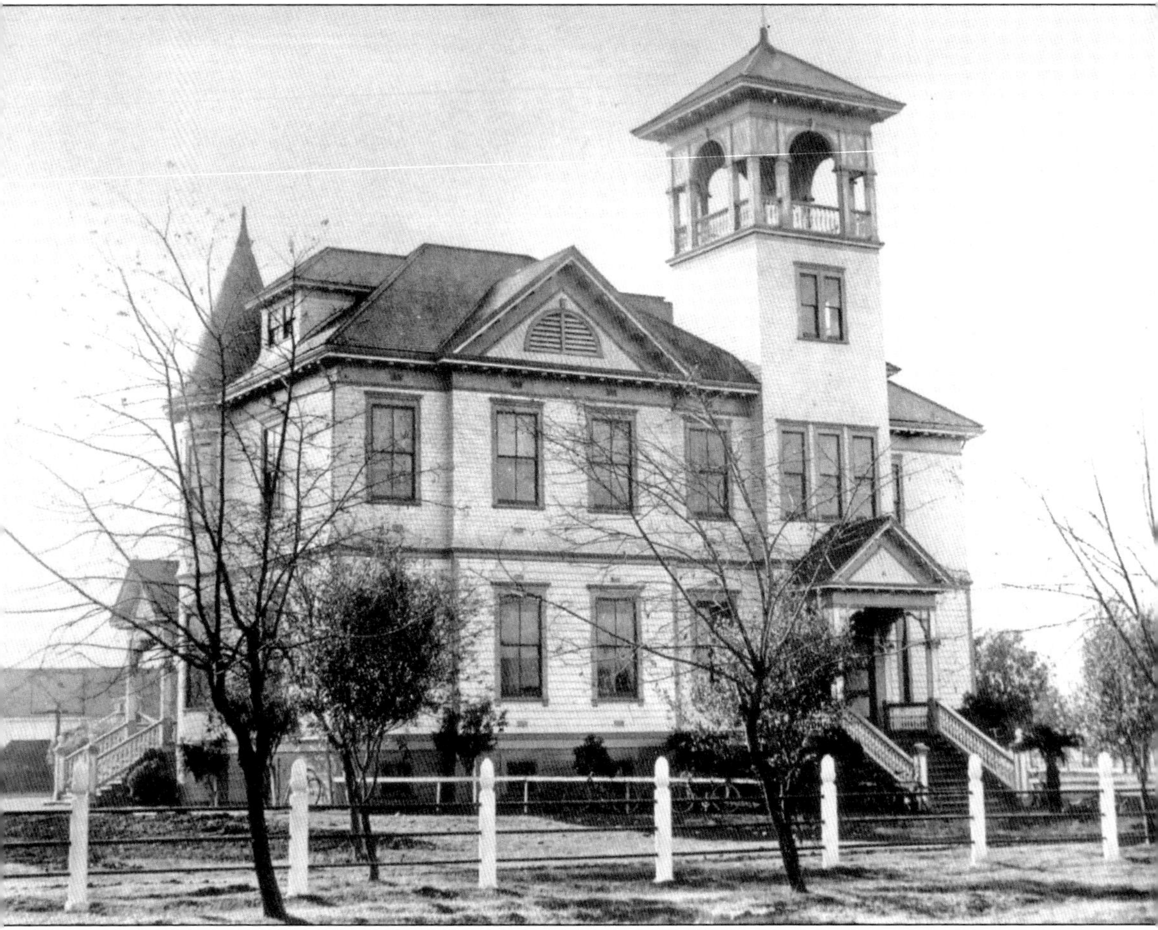

The act providing for the establishment of Union High Schools in California was introduced in the legislature by Livermore's representative, Frank Fassett. It was passed on March 20, 1891. Consequently Livermore became Union High School District No. 1 in the state. A local election in 1892 to provide funds for the high-school building passed by a strong majority. The contract was let to J. F. Meyers late that year to construct the school building, and it was completed in time for the opening in August 1893.

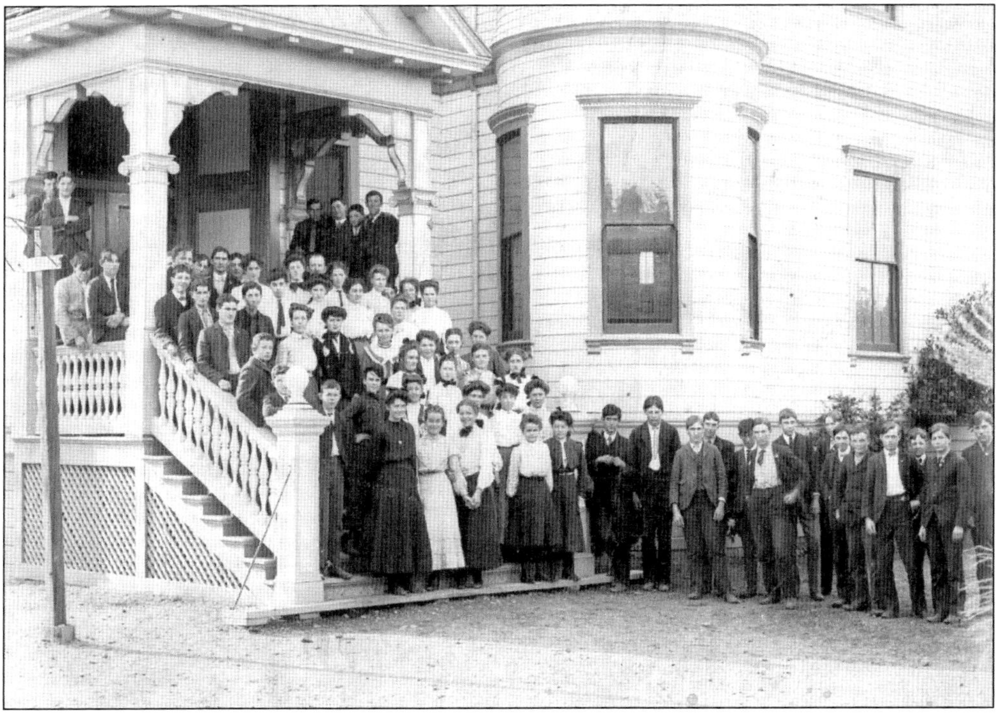

The entire student body of Livermore High School turned out for this picture in 1904.

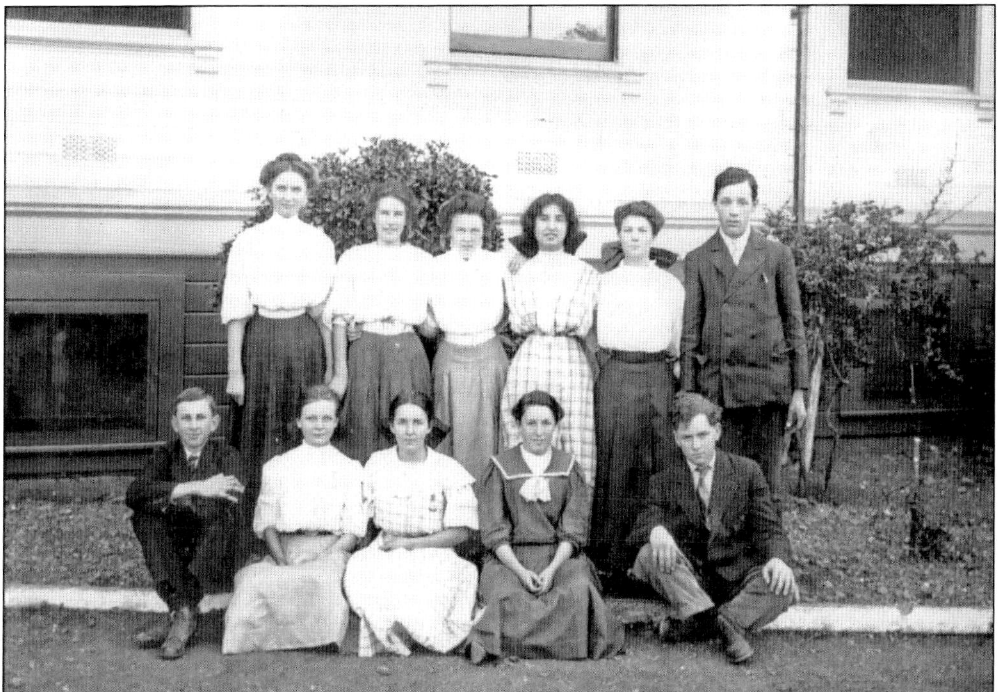

Graduating from Livermore High School in 1911, from left to right, are (first row) Ray Lamb, May Ormand, Nellie McDonald, Bess Monaghan, and Desmond Teeter; (second row) unidentified, Alma Christensen, Dorothy Mess, Hazel Verue, Oliver Barker, and Herman Wente.

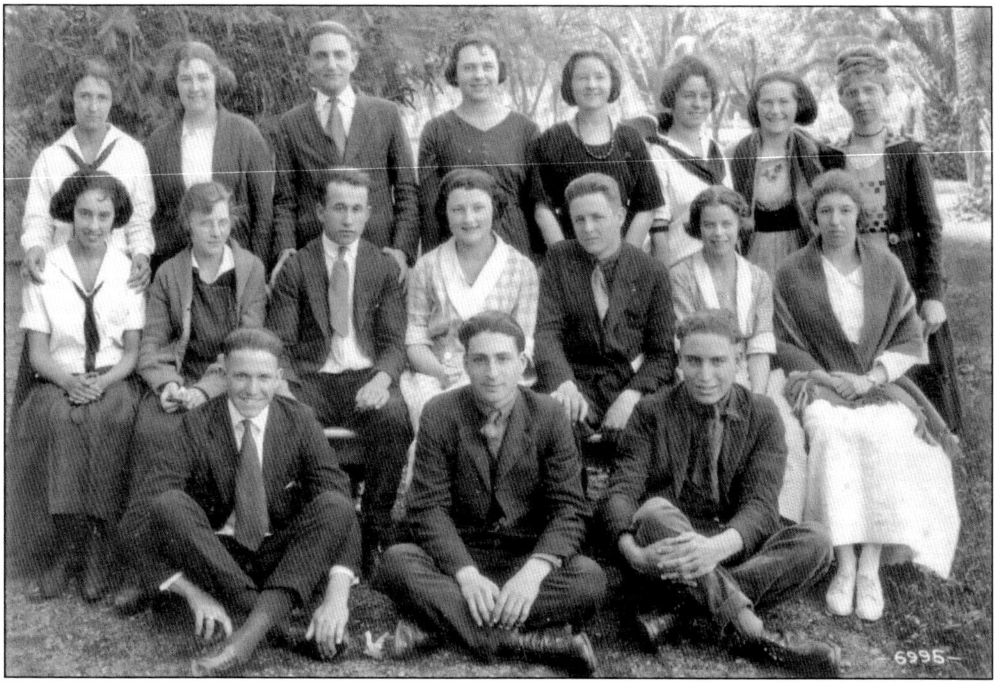

In 1921, graduates of Livermore High School, pictured from left to right, are (first row) Ernest Hall, Angelo Bosso, and Billie Kaiser; (second row) Olive Rose, Grace Gunderson, Arthur Mendonca, Margaret Martin, Richard Callaghan, Kathleen Cope, and Katherine Stuchell; (third row) Anna Beigbeder, Edna Smith, Peter Perata, Cora Senkenberg, Nellie Armstrong, Anna Ibarolle, Imelda Martin, and May Nissen, the teacher. Not present were Edna Prall, Helen Smith, Havana Hansen, and Hilma Wente.

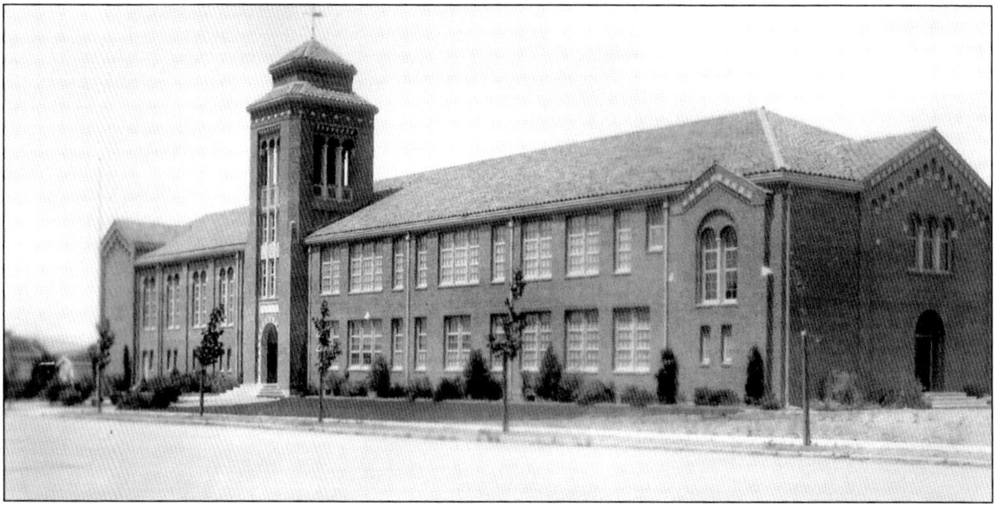

After the first high school was found in the late 1920s to have serious safety problems, the school board selected a site on Maple Street on which to erect a new facility. The main building was first occupied in April 1930, when this photograph was taken. Following the 1933 earthquake in Southern California, the state legislature passed building code changes that required reinforcement of the main building and two others. That reinforcement activity changed the facade of the building from brick to stucco by 1937.

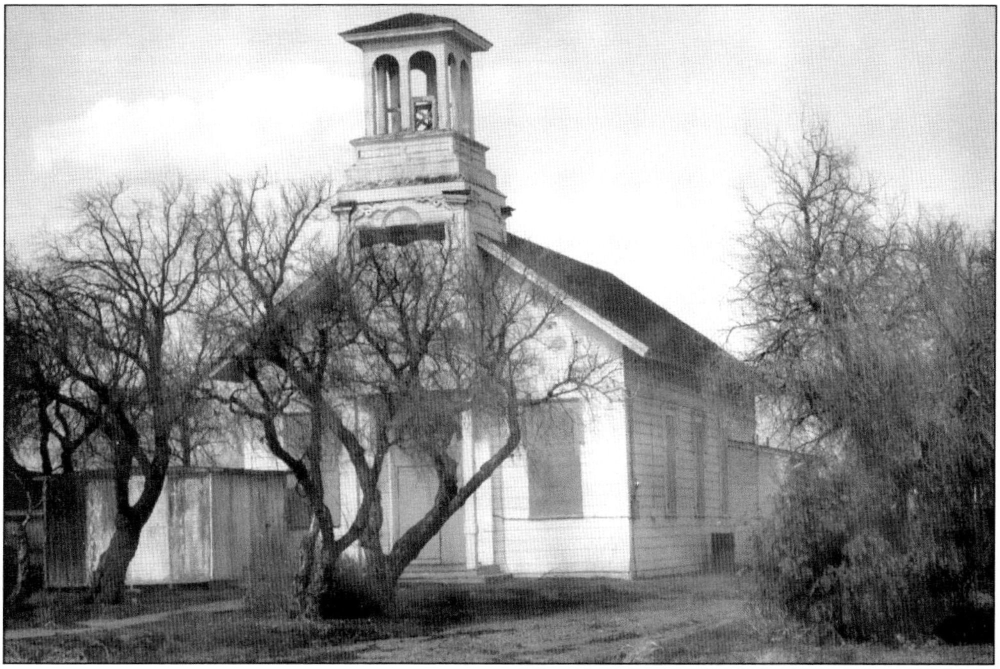

The May District, organized in 1869, was named for George May, who held extensive farming land in the north valley. In 1887, a dance was held at the school to raise money to purchase a bell. The district was annexed to the Green District in July 1960 because of reduced attendance. The building was then used for several years by Cask and Mask, a local little theater group. The Heritage Guild made some attempt to stabilize the structure, but vandalism and finally arson took down the school building in January 1980.

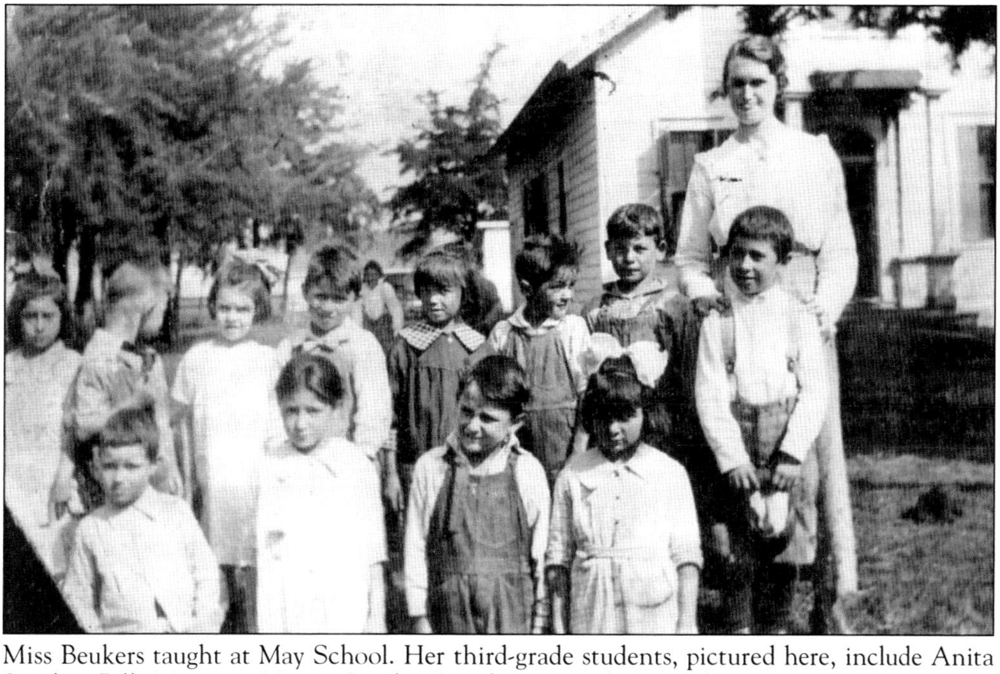

Miss Beukers taught at May School. Her third-grade students, pictured here, include Anita Stankey, Billy Manning, Norma Stanley, Joseph Rose, and Ida Cardoza.

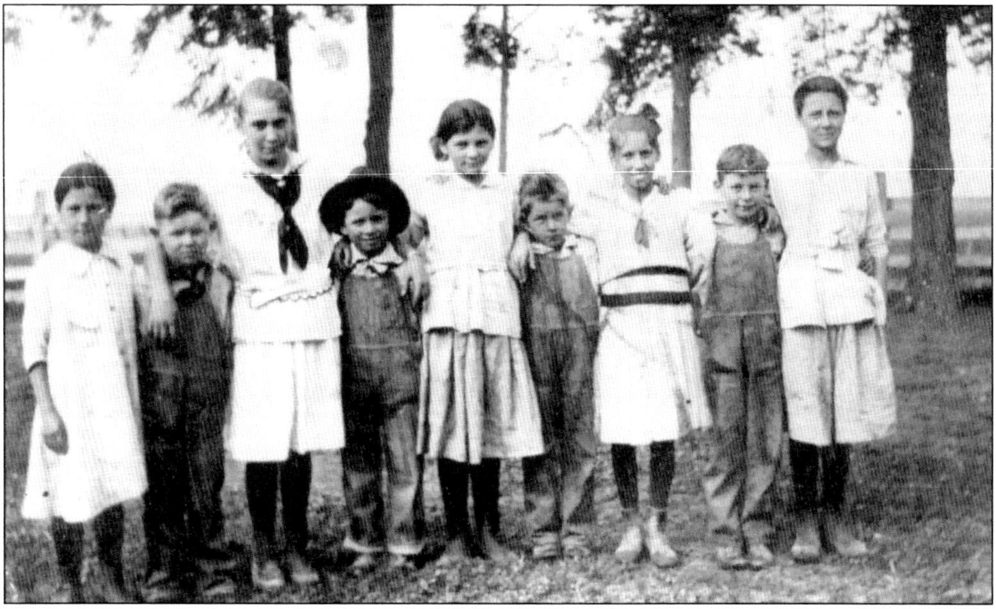

Students at May School during World War I included Rosalind Raymond (Ratti), Billy Manning, Helen Mondot, Joseph Rose, Margaret Raymond (Brown), William Mondot, Mabel Rose (Meyers), John Fannuchi, and Edith Raymond (Rasmussen).

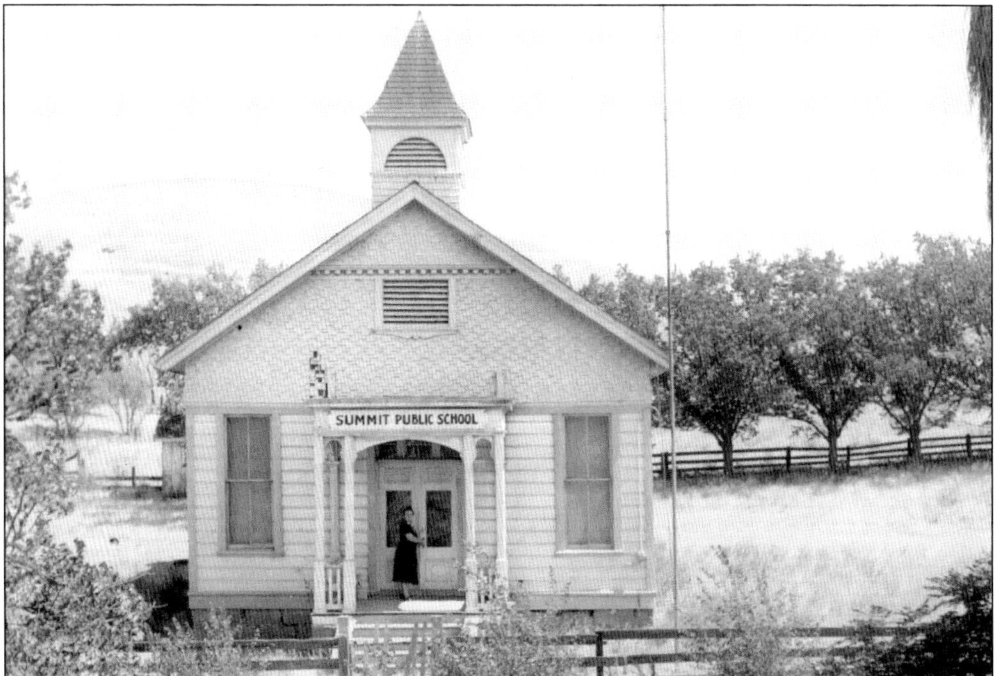

In the village of Altamont, the Summit School District was organized in 1869 while the Central Pacific Railroad was under construction through the valley. When the building was under construction in 1894, it was found that no provision had been made for a bell tower and a bell. The village collected $75 among themselves to correct the omission.

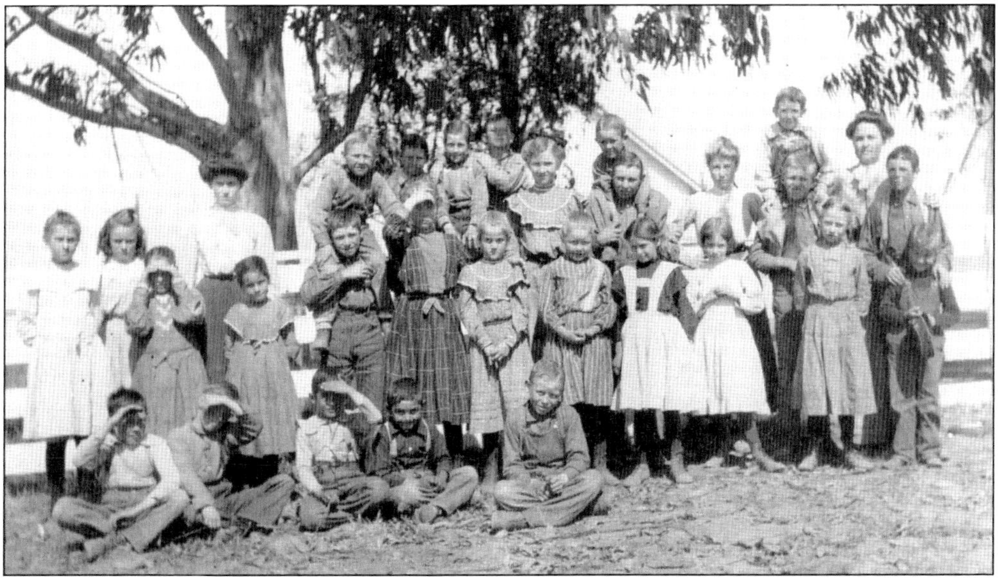

The Green District, named after Thomas Green, who had a store nearby, was organized in 1875. The school building was located at the western end of the Altamont Pass. In 1906, these children, from left to right, attended Green School: (first row) Frank Garaventa, Joe Mannix, Robert Livermore, Joe Livermore, and Hennie Peters; (second row) Annie Getchell, Maude Regan, Dora Kalkey, May Stanley, Walter Clausen, Alma Anderson, Ada Christensen, Anna Kalkey, Nora Mannix, Enid Peters, and Carl Edgar; (third row) Marcella Regan, Oscar Teel, Otto Amerine, Andrew Christensen, Harold Anderson, George Peters, Bill Teel, Martha Anderson, Hennie Teel, Clarence Brown, unidentified, Amelia Hartman (teacher), and Jack Regan.

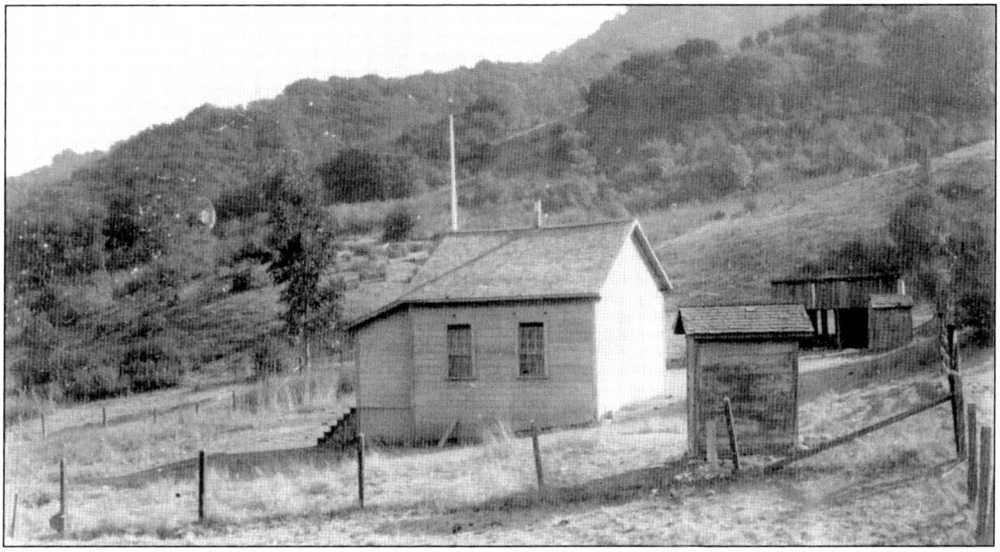

The Antone District had difficulty deciding whether or not it was a part of the Inman District. In 1912, two candidates for school trustee were to be voted on in five of the districts. One of those was Inman. Voters from Antone District, six in 1916 and three in 1919, voted in the Inman election, even though their children attended the Antone school. Was the Antone District in or out? Even the county school superintendent's office does not know. By 1922, when the Amador high-school district was formed, Antone became a part of that district.

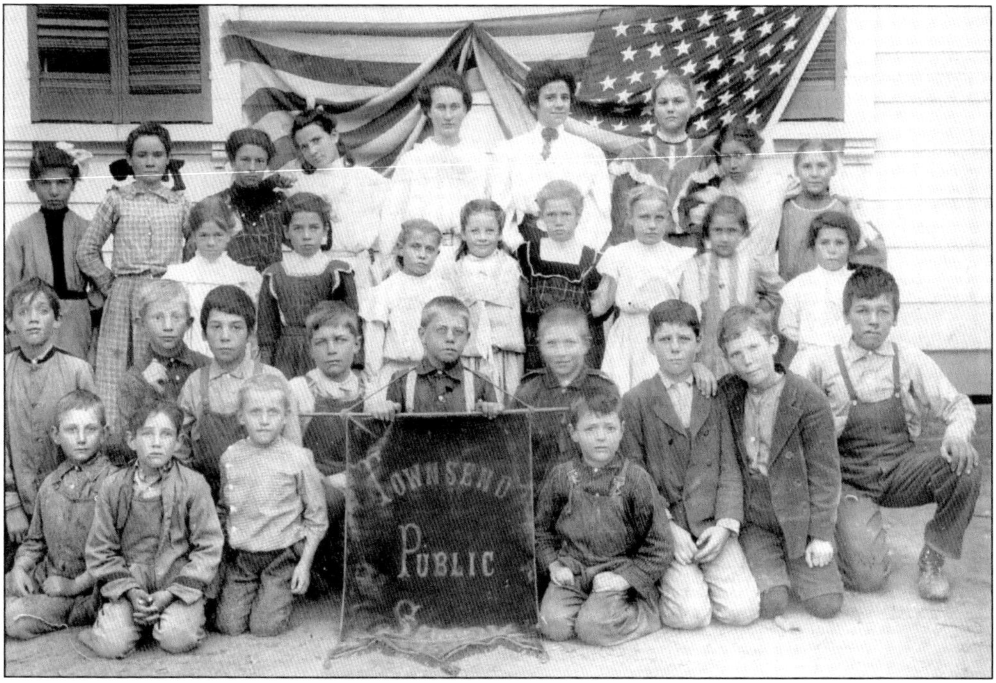

Townsend School was located about one-half mile east of the Tesla-Greenville intersection. The district was organized in May 1869. Like most other country schools, it also functioned as a social center. In 1908, the teacher was Agnes Wallace, later Agnes Dutcher Rees. After the Townsend District was annexed to Livermore, the schoolhouse was moved to Scenic Avenue, where it is now a private residence.

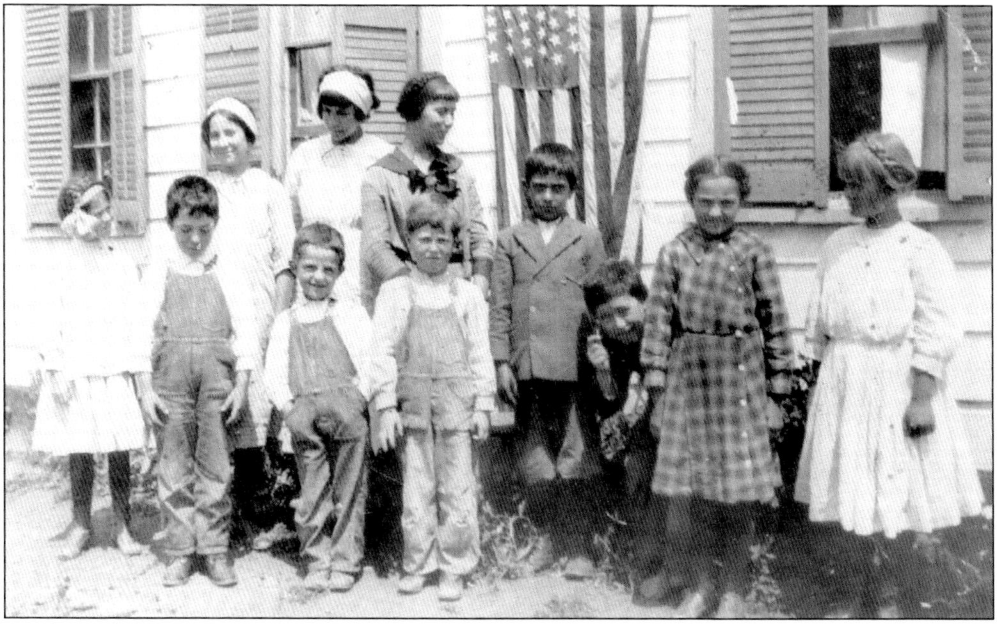
Mocho School was located on Mines Road, southeast of Livermore. It was established in 1890 after the old Wilson District farther down the road had lapsed. The third child from the left in the front row is Manuel Duarte, who later became a prominent pharmacist in the community.

Five

Civic Activities

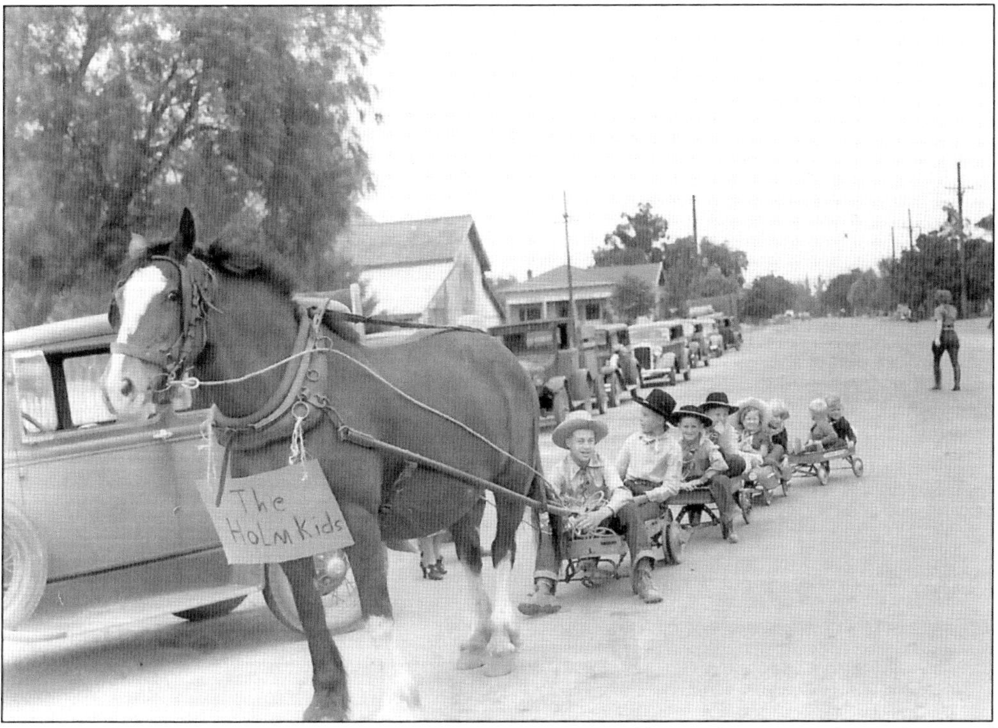

Livermore has always been known for its civic activities, and horse shows, parades, rodeos, and other events have been a part of the town's culture since the beginning. "The Holm Kids," pictured here on June 15, 1937, are in wagons being pulled by a horse. They are, from left to right, Leslie Holm, Bobby Holm, Frank Holm (twin brother of Tillie Calhoun), Carl Stebbins, Shirley Miller, Merilyn Holm (now Tillie Calhoun), Richie Holm, and Jimmy Holm.

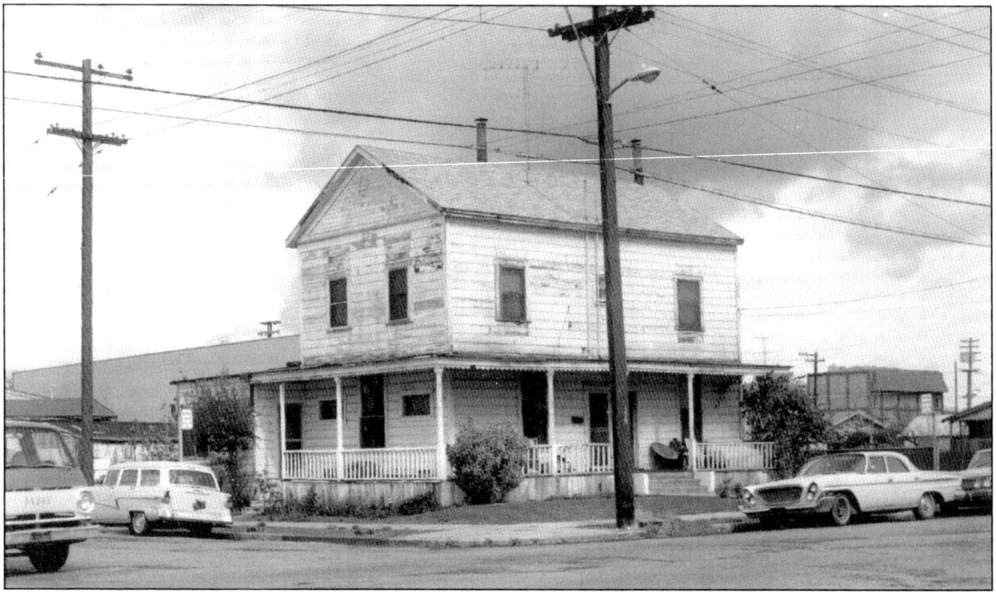

Even before Livermore was incorporated in 1876, the town had two volunteer fire companies—the Livermore Hook and Ladder Company and Niagara Fire Company No. 1. In 1873, this first firehouse was located on Second Street between K and L Streets (now the Wells Fargo parking lot) and later moved to Third and K Streets where it was used as a private residence.

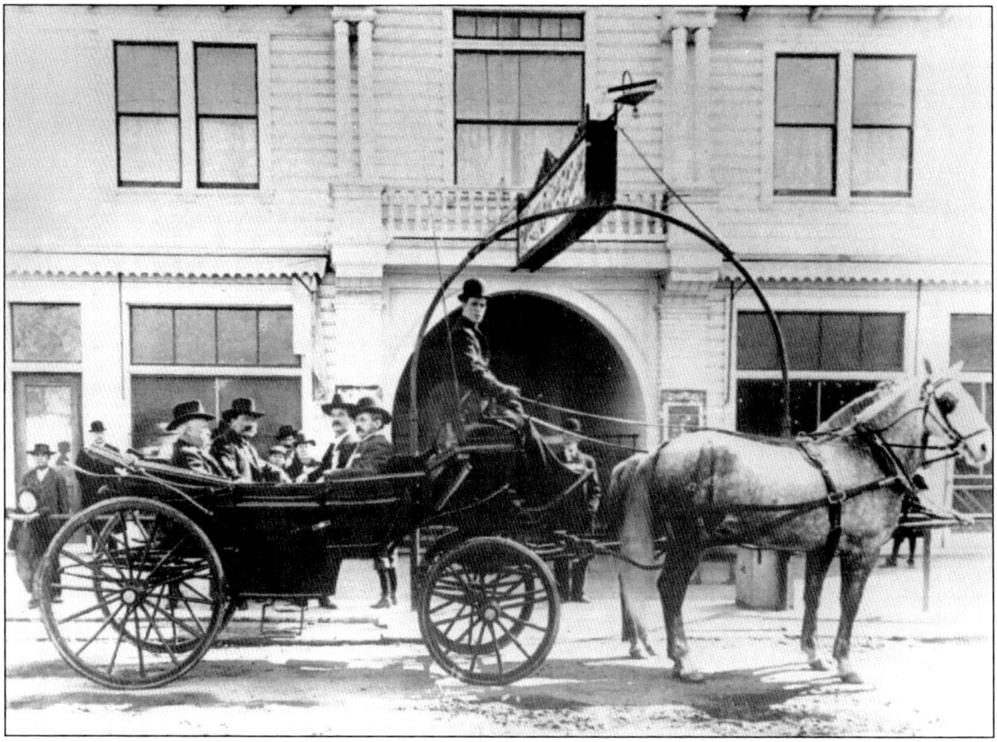

Horse shows were a part of Livermore's agricultural legacy. In 1908, show judges D. G. McNally, Hans Christensen, Max Berlin, and Theo Gorner were passengers in a carriage driven by Eugene Day.

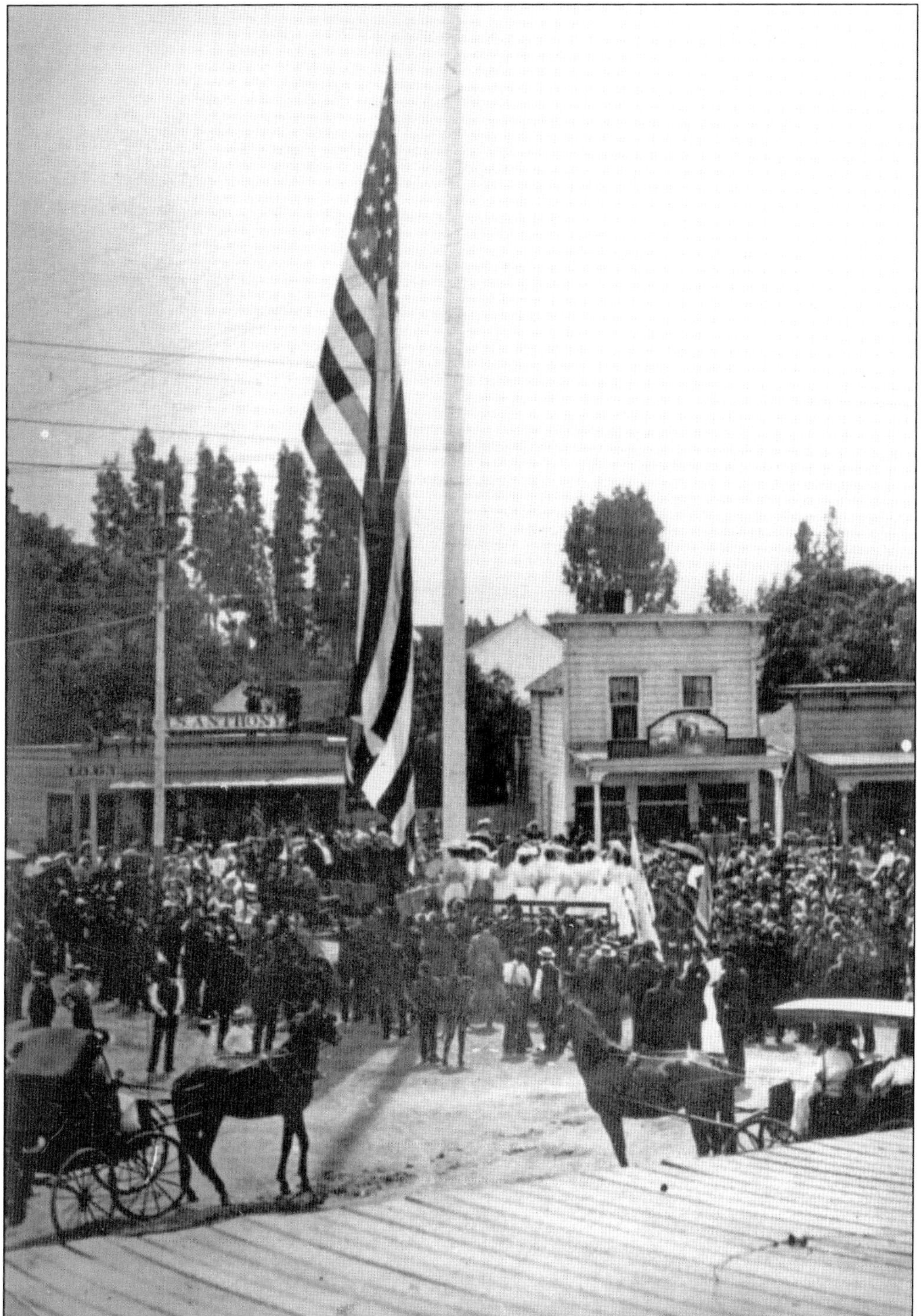

The streets at the intersection of Livermore Avenue and First Street were crowded on September 9, 1905, when the town's new flagpole was dedicated. After 99 years of service as a landmark, it was replaced by a new pole.

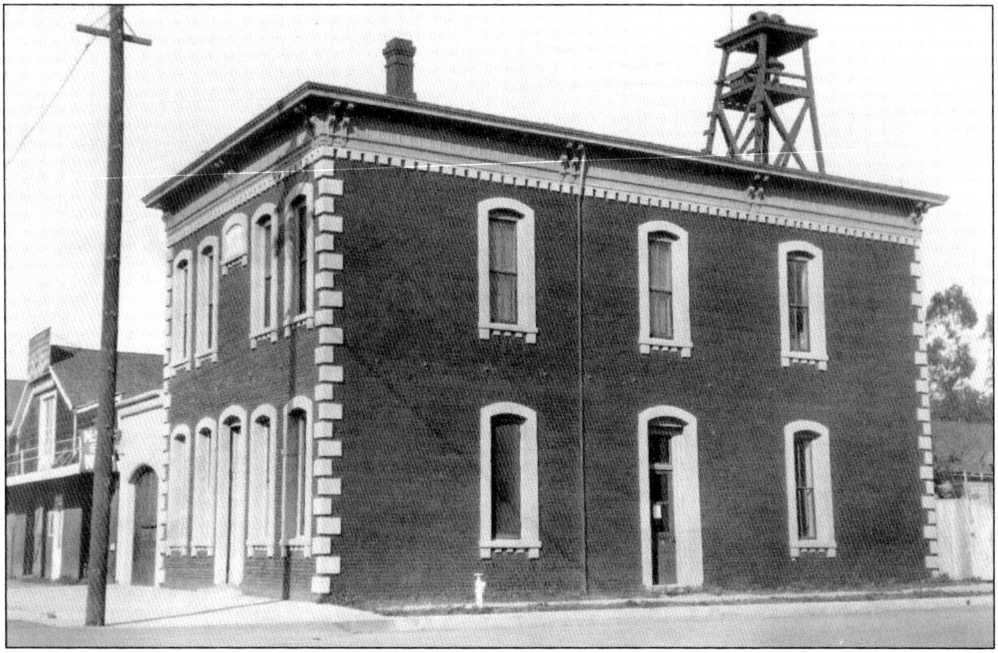

The town fathers purchased the old Bank of Livermore at First Street and McLeod in 1903. It replaced the old town hall/firehouse on Second Street. The new civic building was purchased for $3,000; the town fathers paid it off at $1,000 a year.

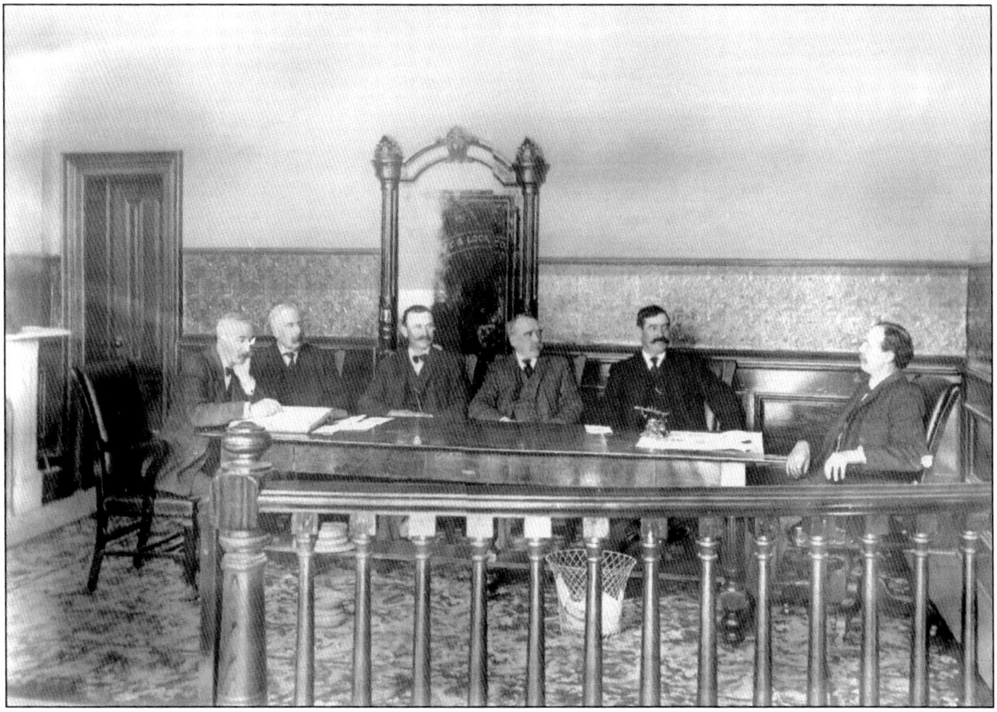

In 1905, the town's governing body, pictured here from left to right, was made up of W. H. Wright, city clerk; John Ryan; Daniel Murphy; Hans Matthiesen; Charles Beck; and A. W. Feidler, mayor.

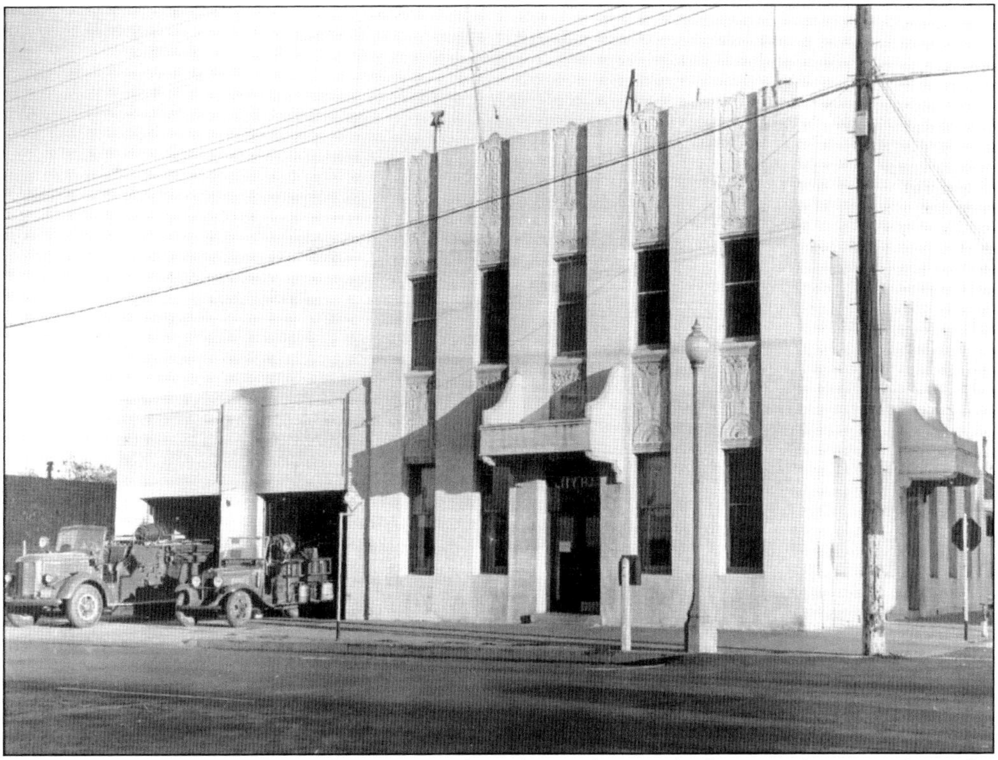

In 1937, the town hall received a new art deco face. The city had received a grant from the government for this WPA project.

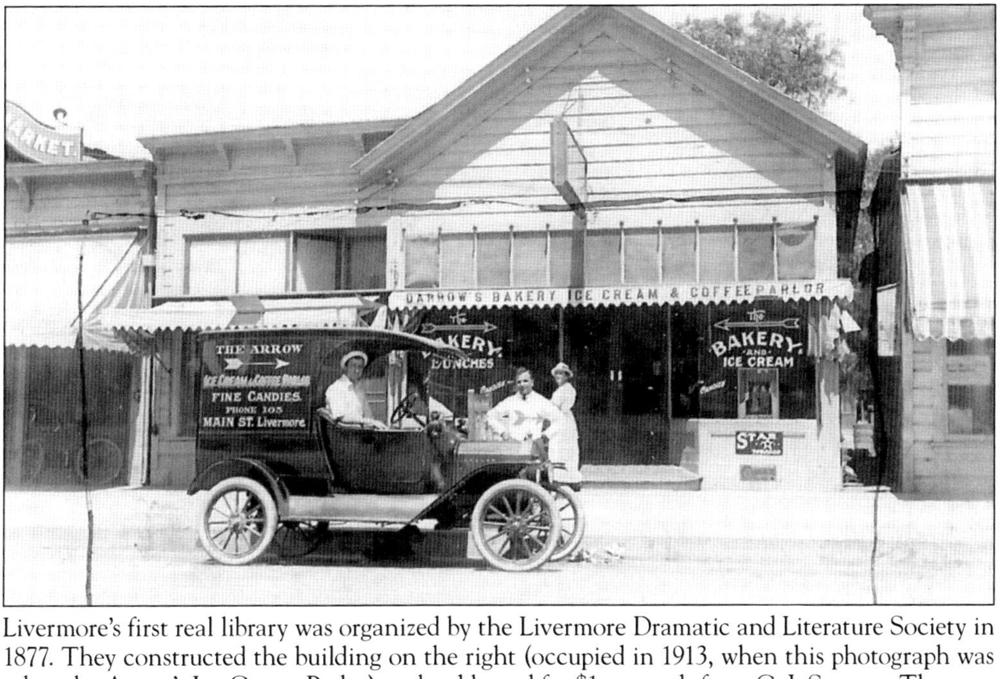

Livermore's first real library was organized by the Livermore Dramatic and Literature Society in 1877. They constructed the building on the right (occupied in 1913, when this photograph was taken, by Arrow's Ice Cream Parlor) on land leased for $1 a month from C. J. Stevens. The men pictured are Aqualino Paul "Joe" Caratti and John "Jack" Caratti.

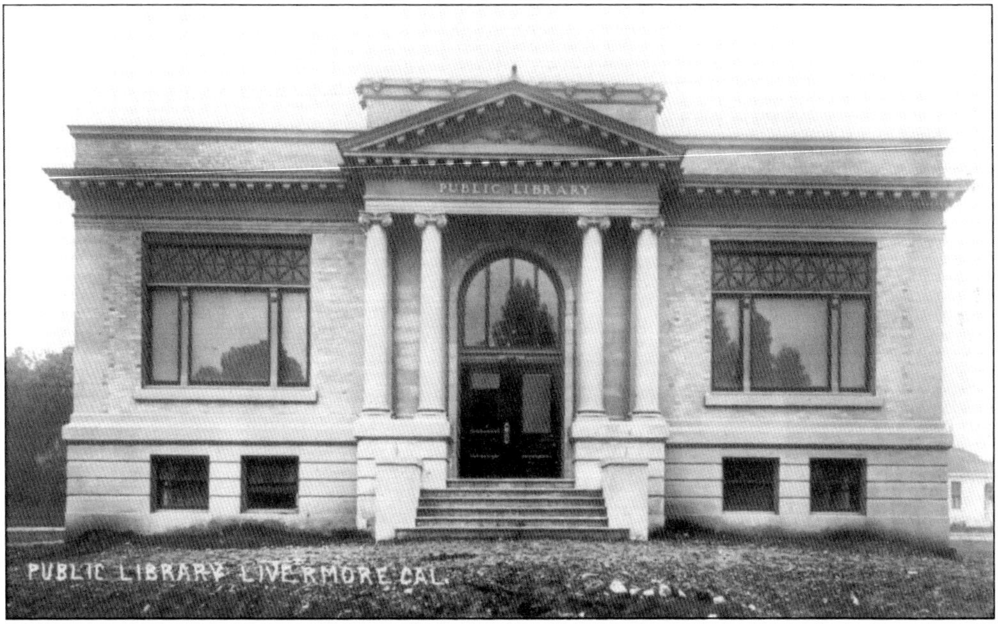

The Livermore Women's Improvement Club was successful in obtaining a grant from the Carnegie Foundation to provide the library in 1911. Livermore became the first city its size in California to have a tax-supported library.

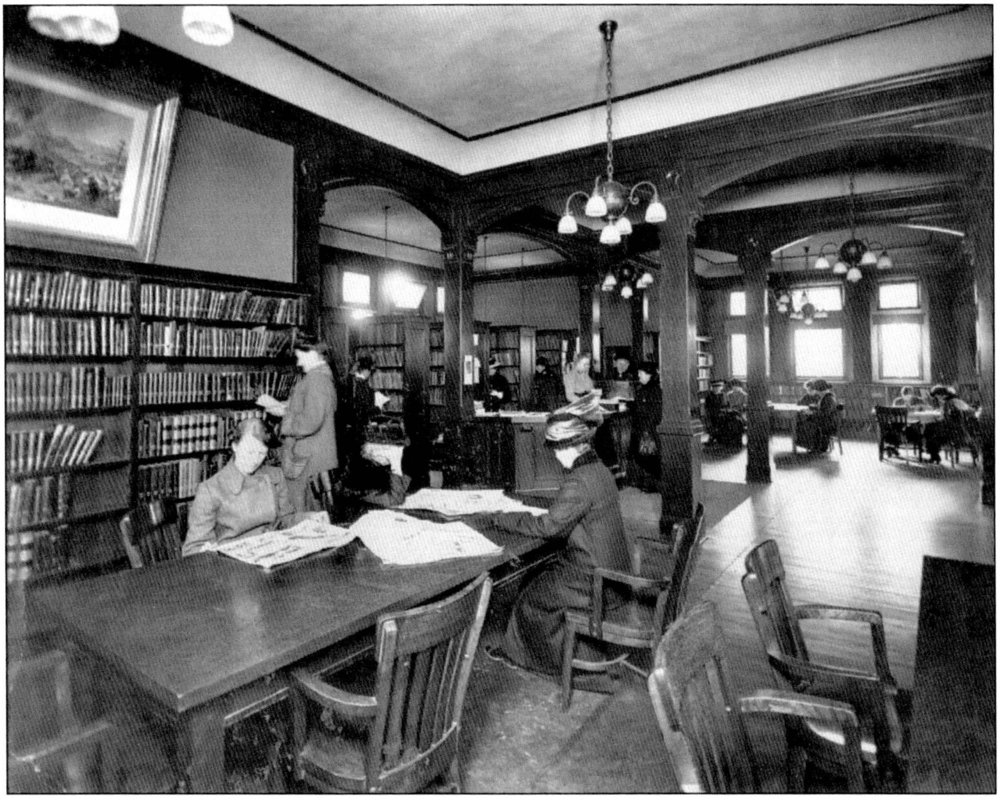

The warmth of the new library reading room attracted a number of visitors.

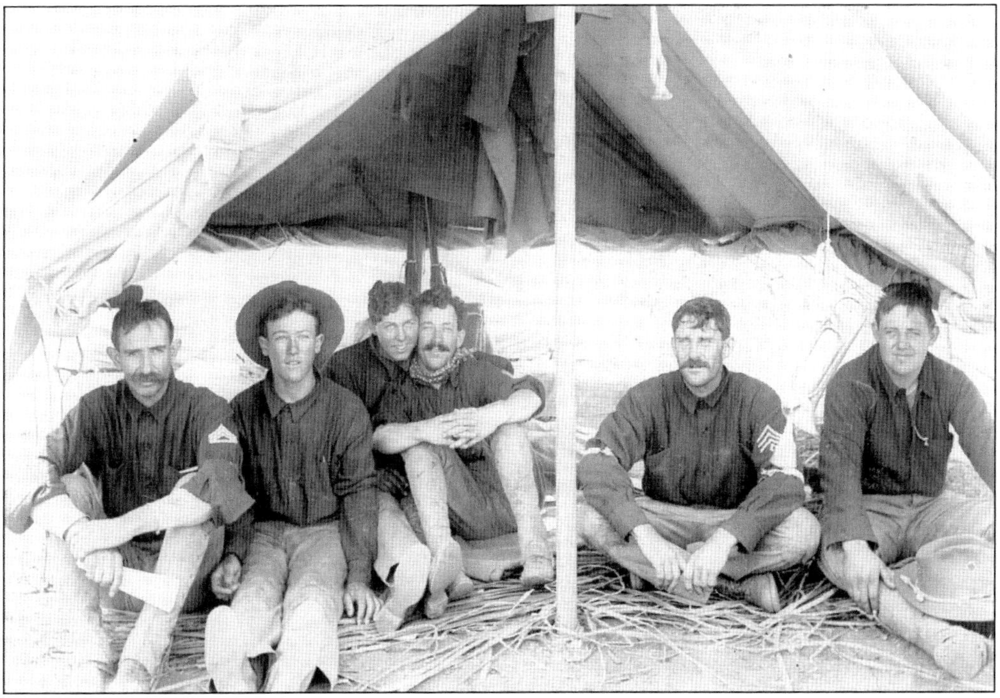

In 1904, the 5th California Infantry, Livermore's Company I, was sent to Atascadero for training. Members included Ken Madden, Joe Callaghan, Arthur Knox, Mark Sanderson, Ben Carroll, Dewitt Dutcher, and John (Jack) Jensen.

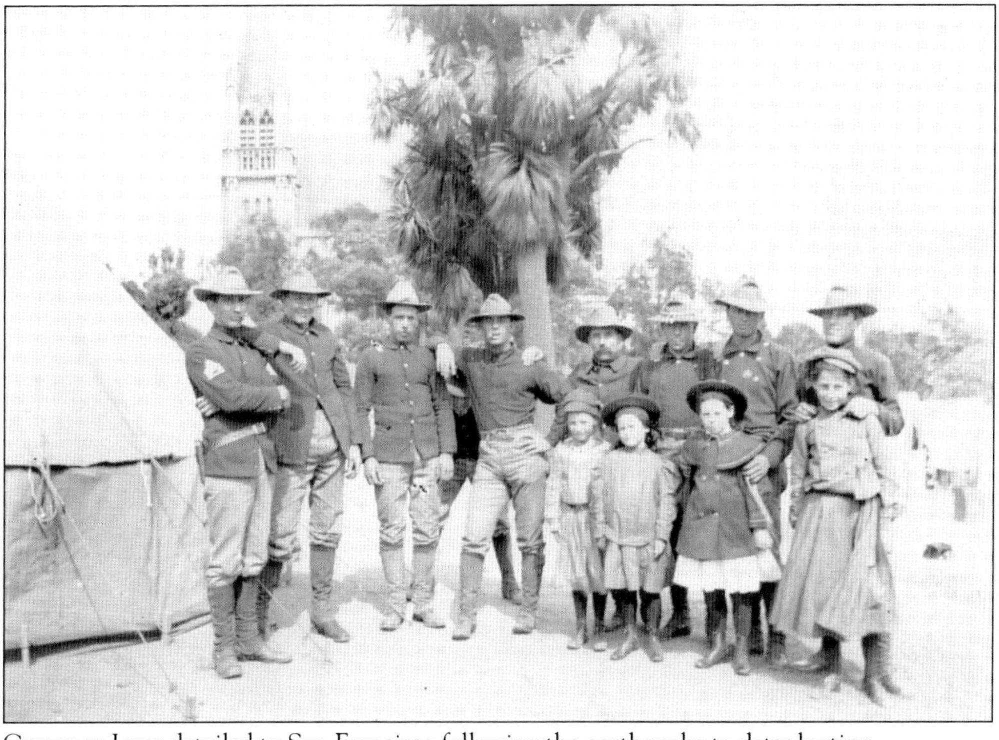

Company I was detailed to San Francisco following the earthquake to deter looting.

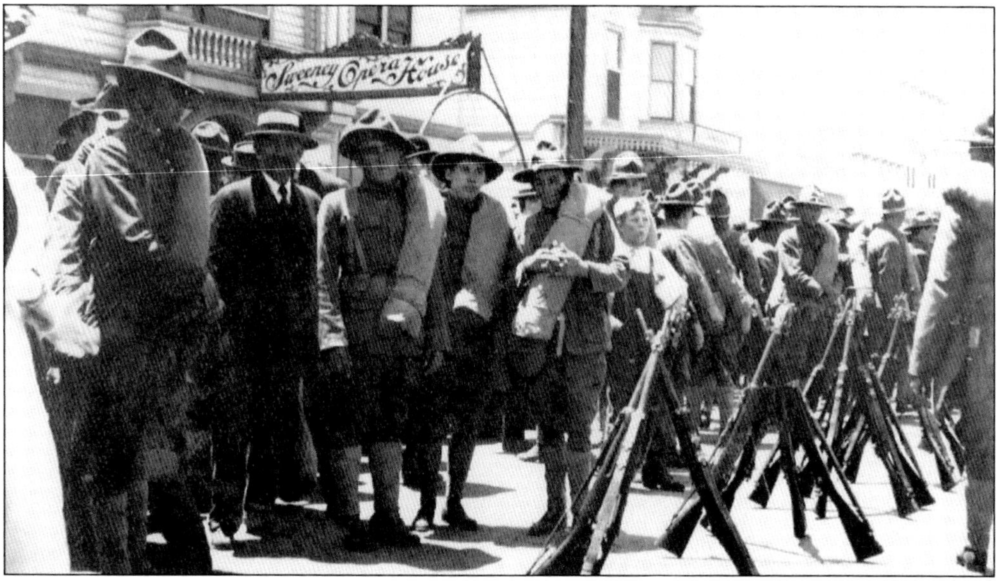

Members of Company I assembled at Sweeney's Opera House on East First Street before leaving for duty on the Mexican border in 1916. As a National Guard unit, Company I could not follow regular army troops under General Pershing into Mexico to pursue Pancho Villa and his army. Their duties were limited to preventing Villa's troops from reentering the United States.

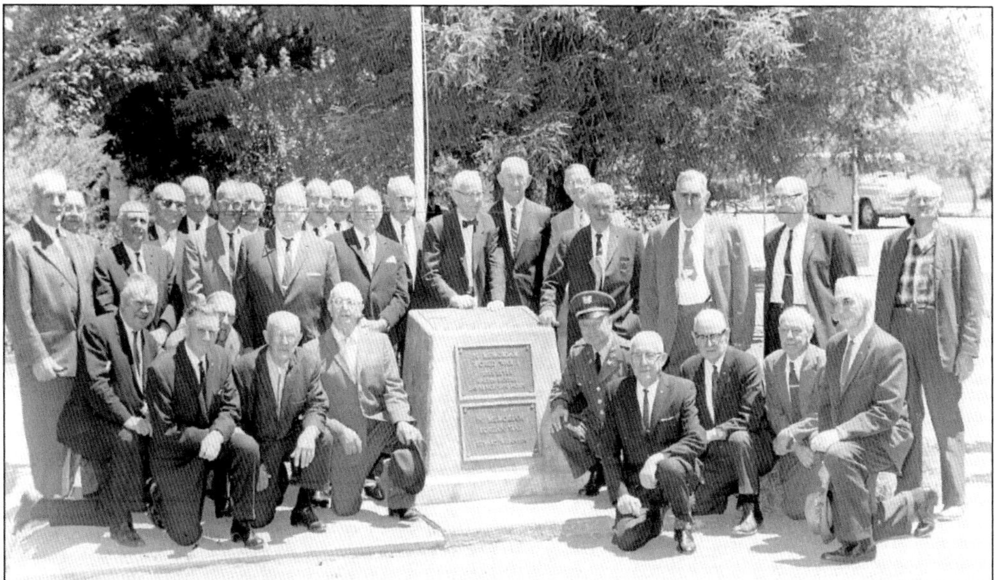

A reunion of Company I members was held in 1967 at the Carnegie Library park.

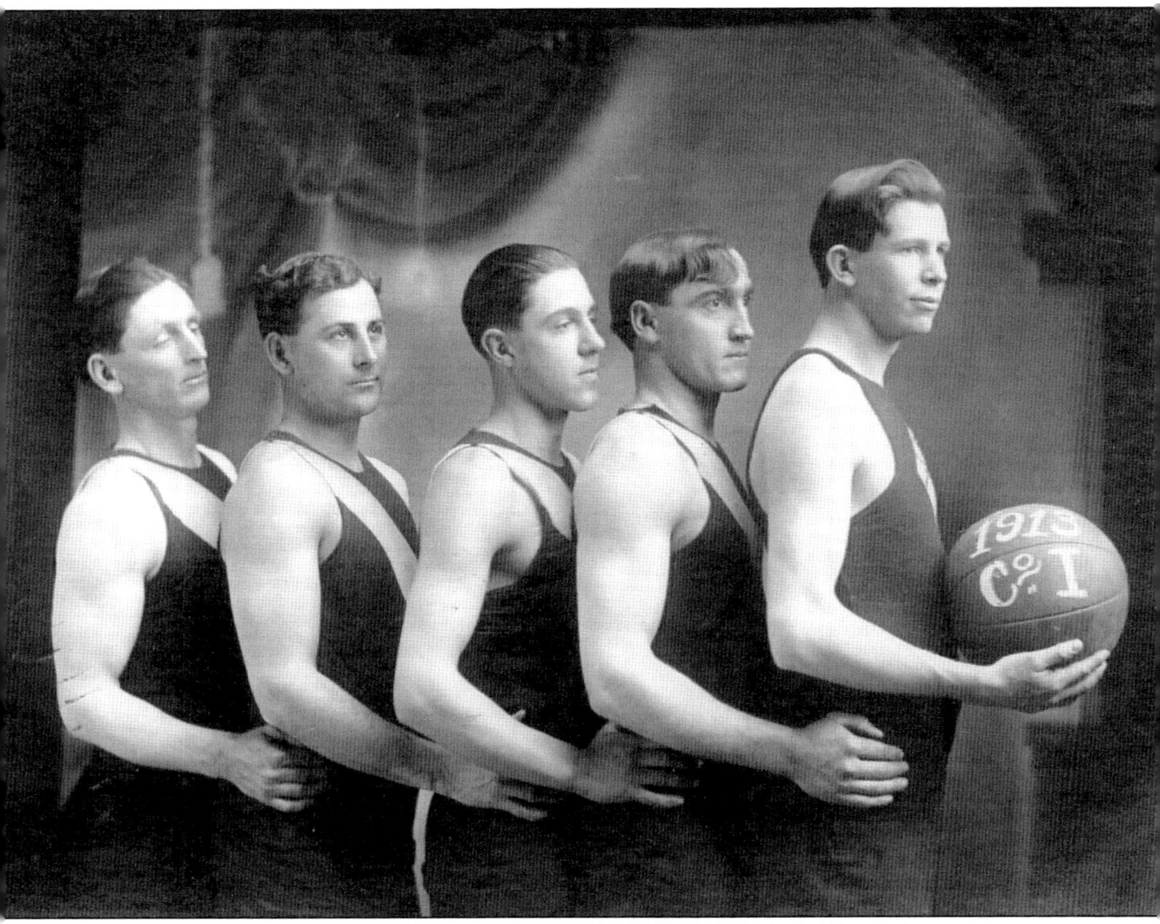

Company I was also active in local sports. Their basketball team included Dick Moore, ? Smith, Norman Sangmaster, Herbert Sweet, and Anthony O'Donnell.

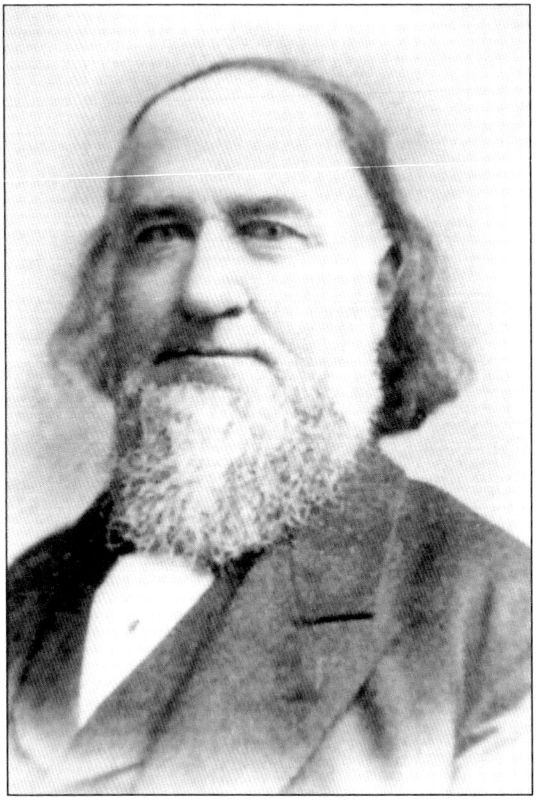

Livermore's First Presbyterian Church was organized in February 1872 by missionary William Wallace Brier. Initially 13 communicants made up the small congregation. Brier had a long history of establishing Presbyterian churches in California before the Livermore church was organized. The Livermore church was his 14th, and the Presbyterian church in Pleasanton was his 15th. He also organized eight Presbyterian churches in Nevada between the years 1860 and 1874. In the first election for officers after Alameda County was created in 1853, William Wallace Brier became the first county superintendent of schools.

The Presbyterian sanctuary at Fourth and K Streets was dedicated in 1874. This photograph shows the addition to the sanctuary finished in 1893. Later changes moved the pulpit to the opposite end of the building. The chapel is currently used for small weddings.

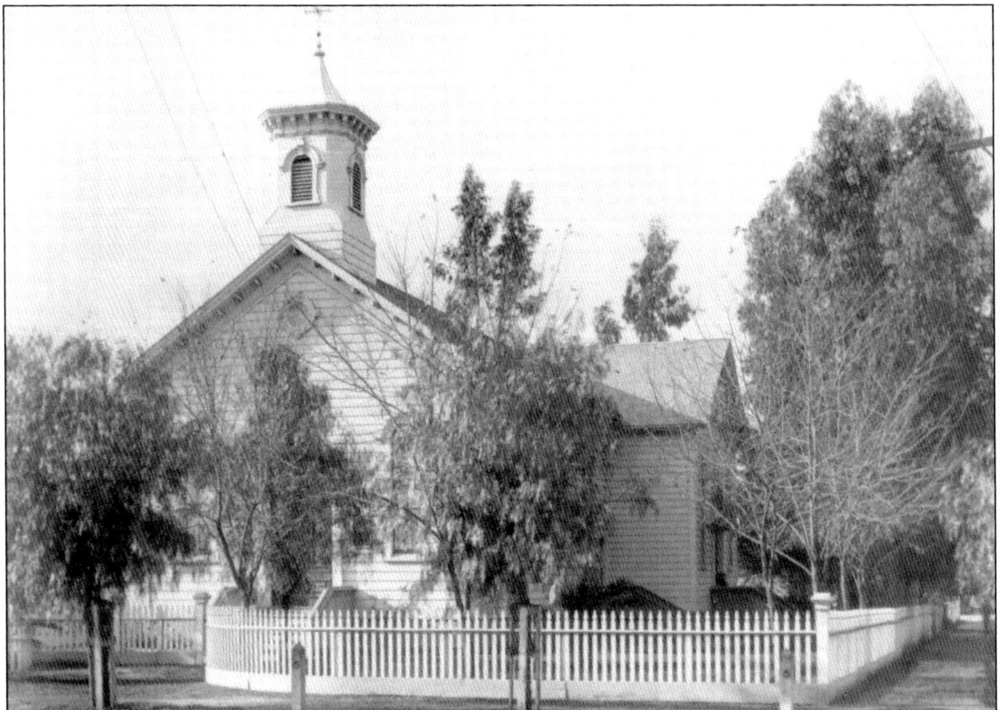

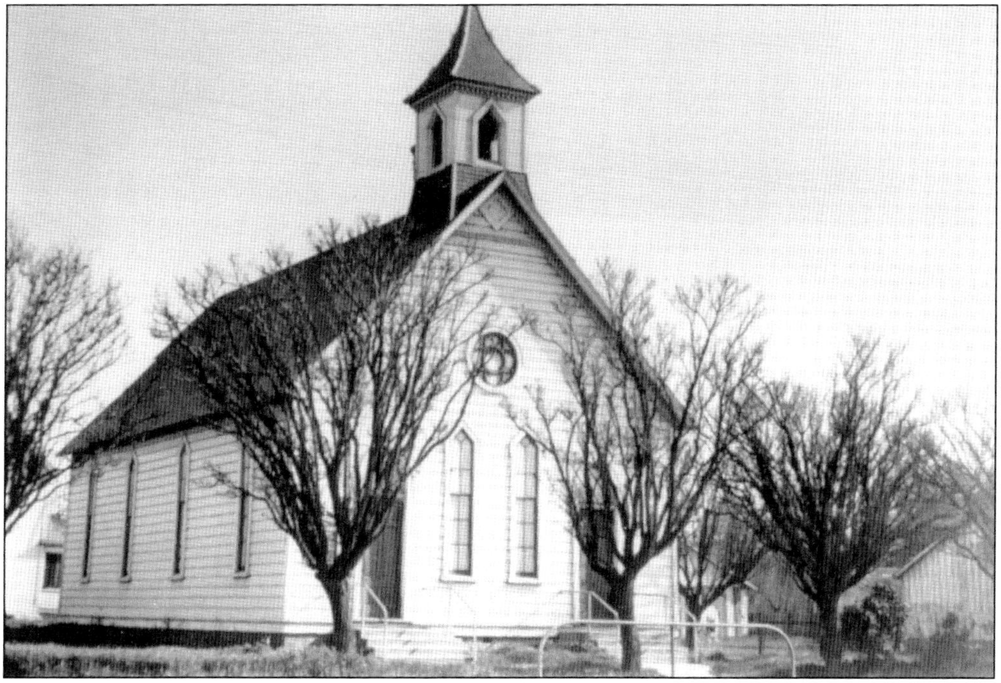

The Methodists came early on the scene in Livermore's history, but members were not able to finance a sanctuary until 1885, when they built this house of worship at Third and I Streets.

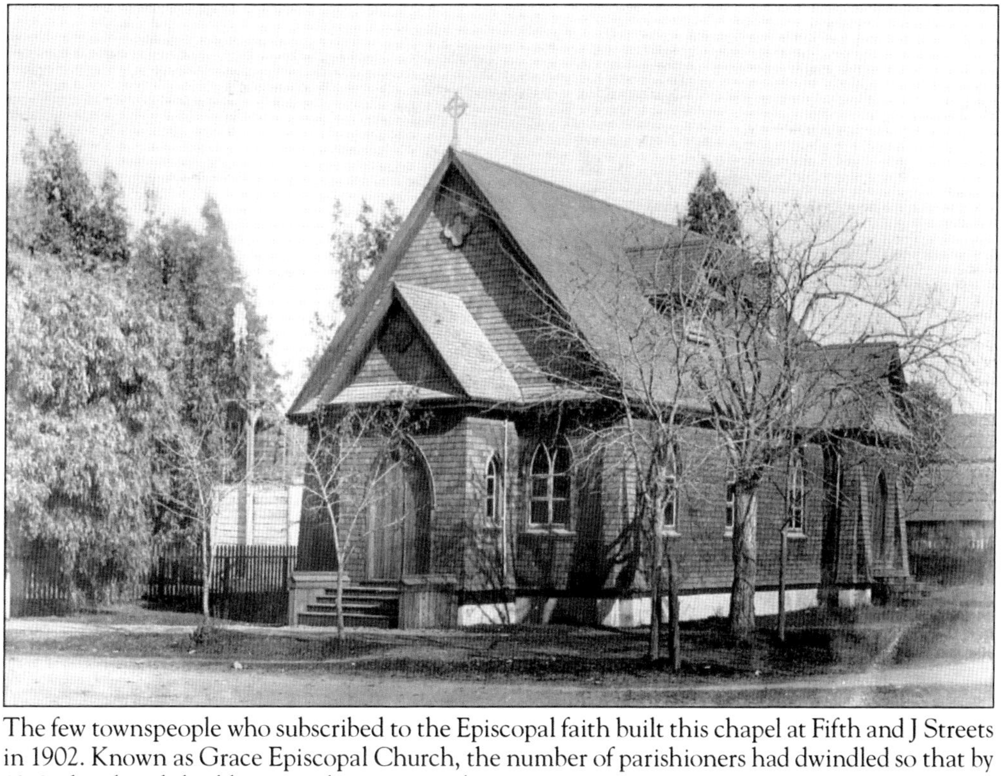

The few townspeople who subscribed to the Episcopal faith built this chapel at Fifth and J Streets in 1902. Known as Grace Episcopal Church, the number of parishioners had dwindled so that by 1919, the church building was deconsecrated.

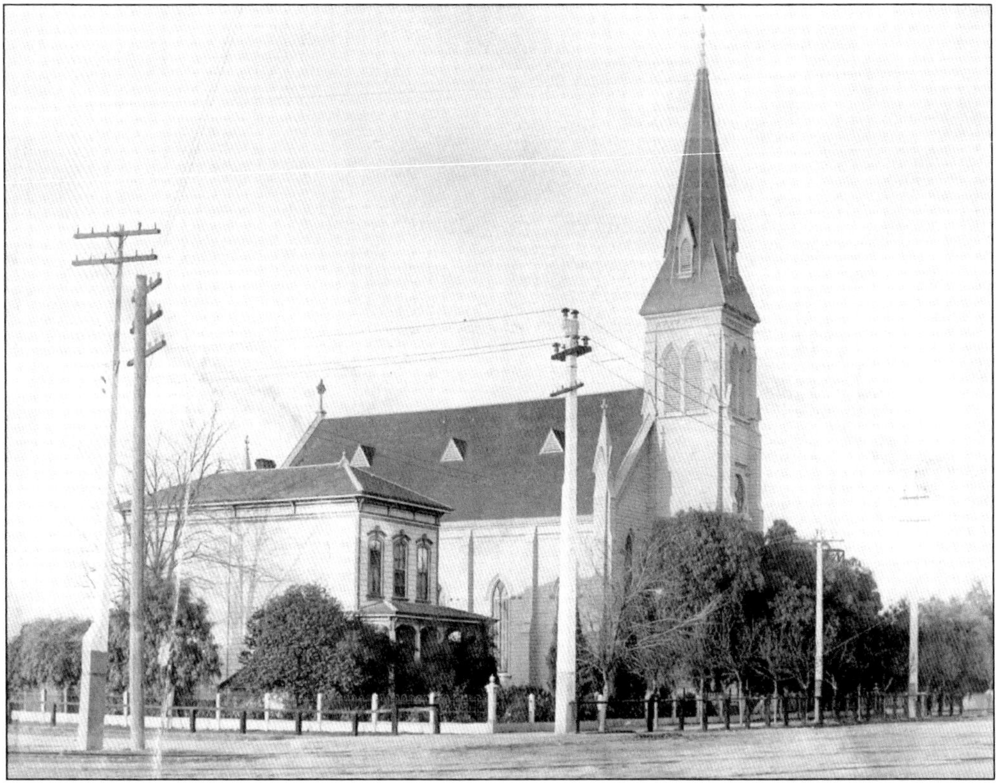

The first Catholic services were held in Bardellini's hotel in Laddsville. The first Catholic church was constructed in 1872 on land donated by the Ladd family. St. Michael's Catholic Church, pictured here, was the spiritual home for many of Livermore's Irish, Italian, and Portuguese. Designed by Oakland architect Thomas R. Bassett, it was complete in March 1892 near the corner of First and Maple Streets. It was a magnificent wooden Gothic structure with a bell tower that rose 148 feet in the air. The church burned in a spectacular fire in the summer of 1916.

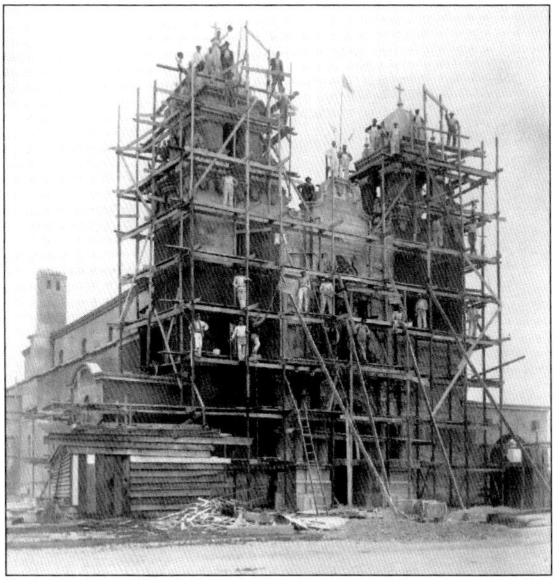

Soon a replacement Catholic house of worship was under construction at the corner of Fourth and Maple Streets. It was built from 1916 to 1918.

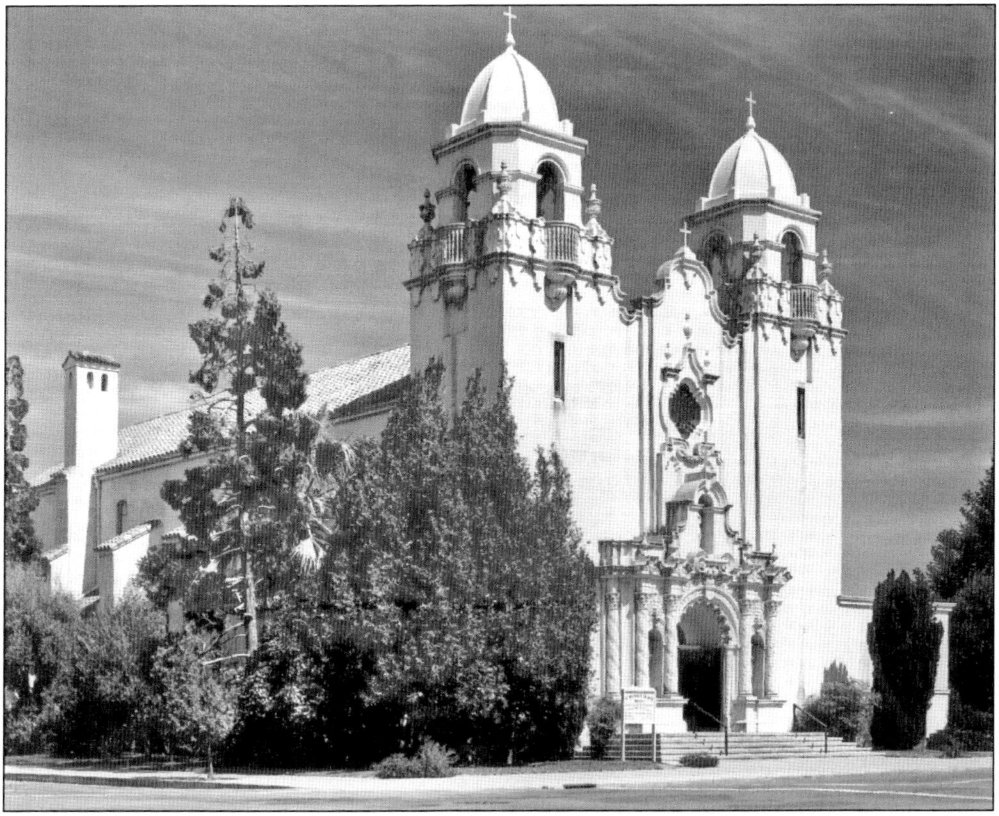

The new St. Michael's Catholic Church was dedicated on Sunday, June 9, 1918.

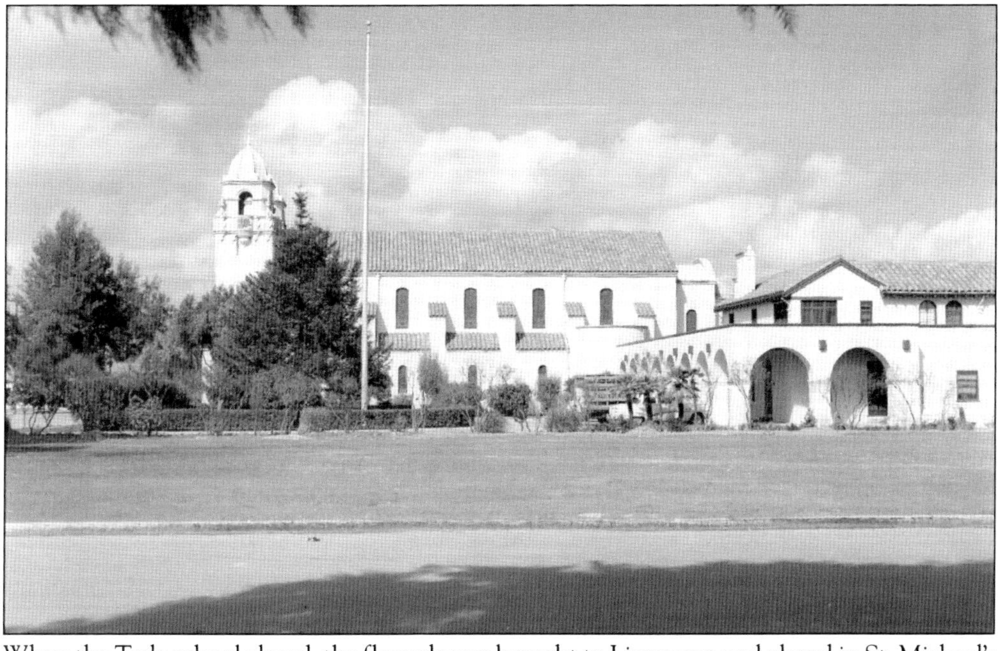

When the Tesla school closed, the flagpole was brought to Livermore and placed in St. Michael's rectory garden.

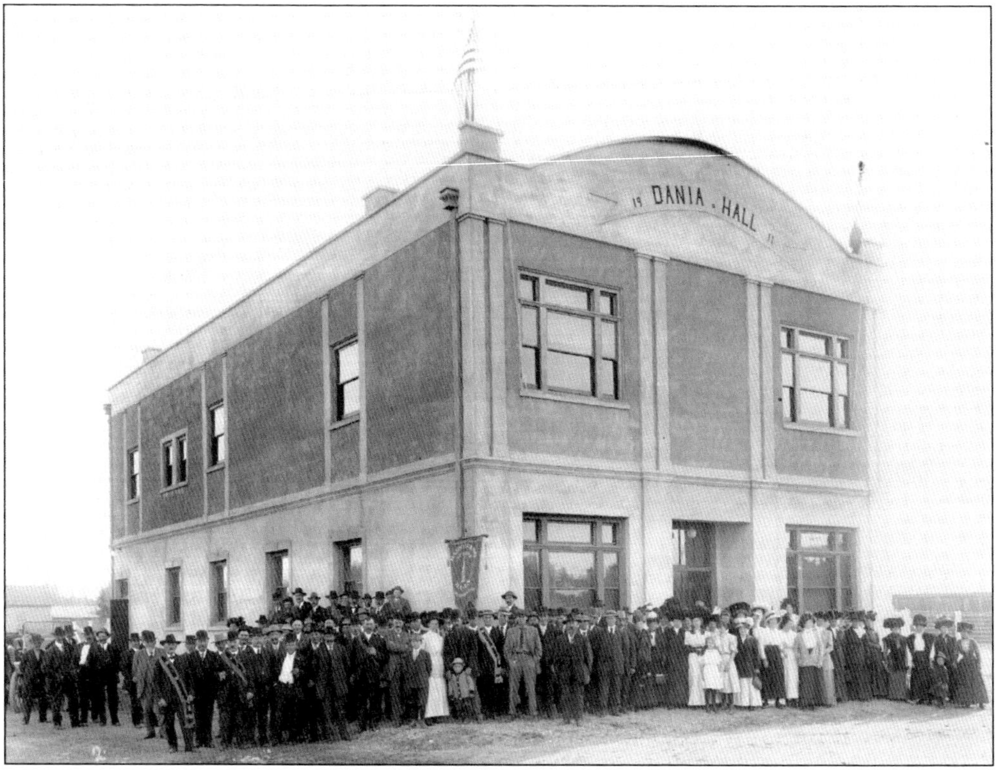

The completion of Dania Hall and its dedication in 1911 were cause for celebration for Livermore's Danish people.

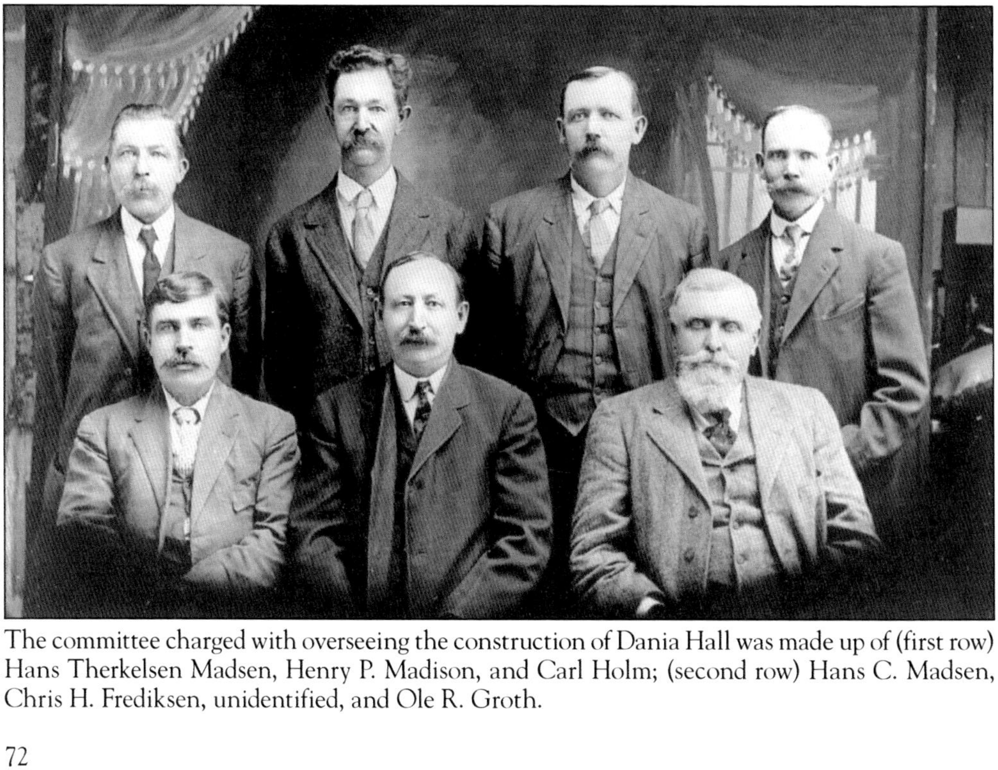
The committee charged with overseeing the construction of Dania Hall was made up of (first row) Hans Therkelsen Madsen, Henry P. Madison, and Carl Holm; (second row) Hans C. Madsen, Chris H. Frediksen, unidentified, and Ole R. Groth.

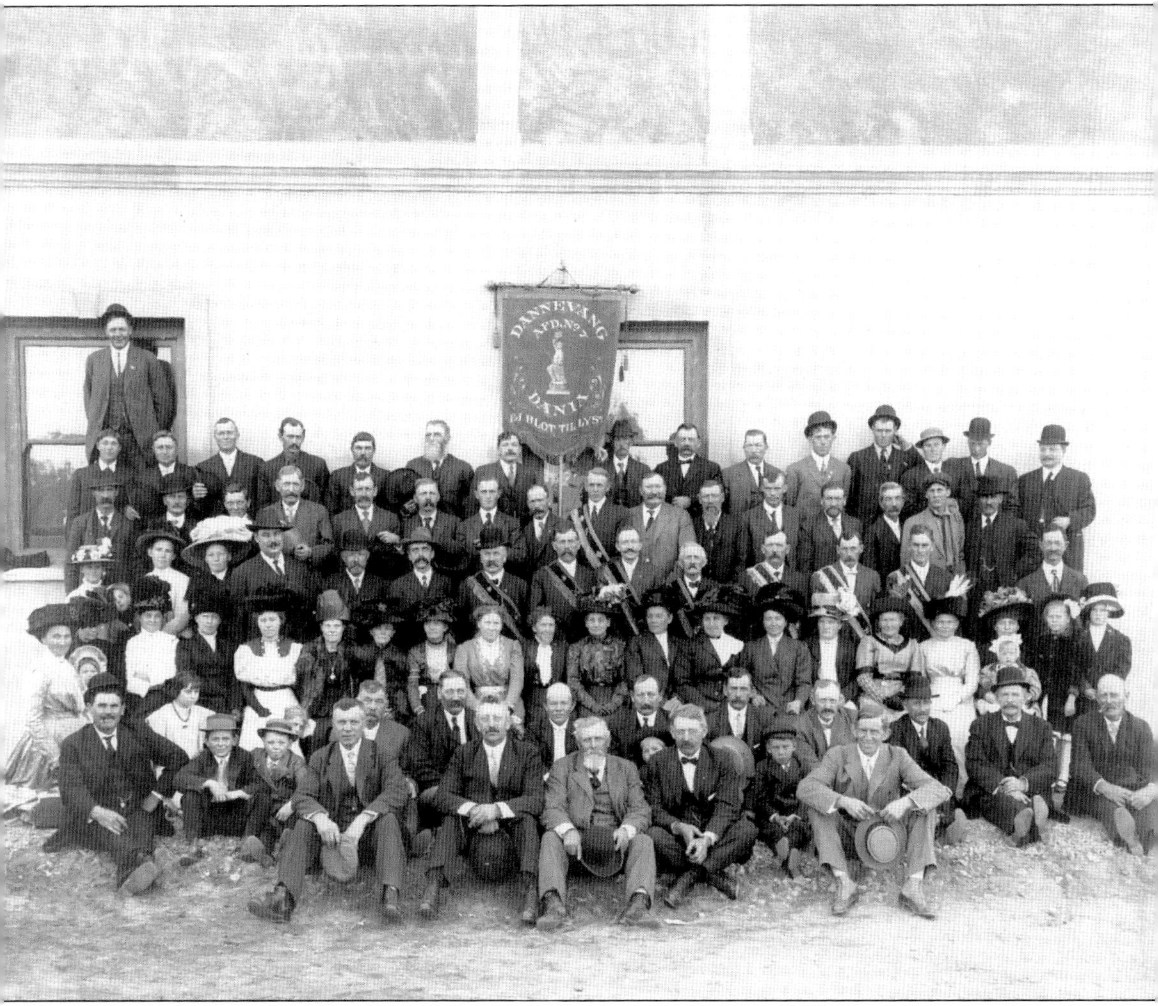

Members of Dania gathered for this photograph in 1911. The gentleman with the white beard in the front row was Carl Holm, who came to Livermore in 1872.

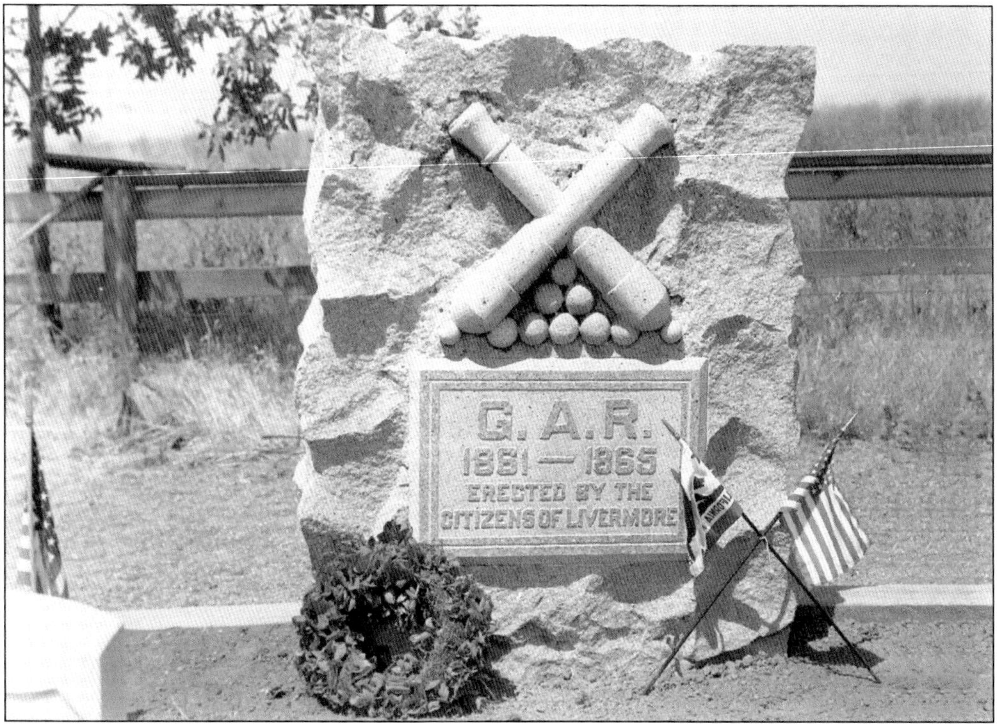

This monument in Roselawn Cemetery commemorates members of the local Grand Army of the Republic (GAR) organization.

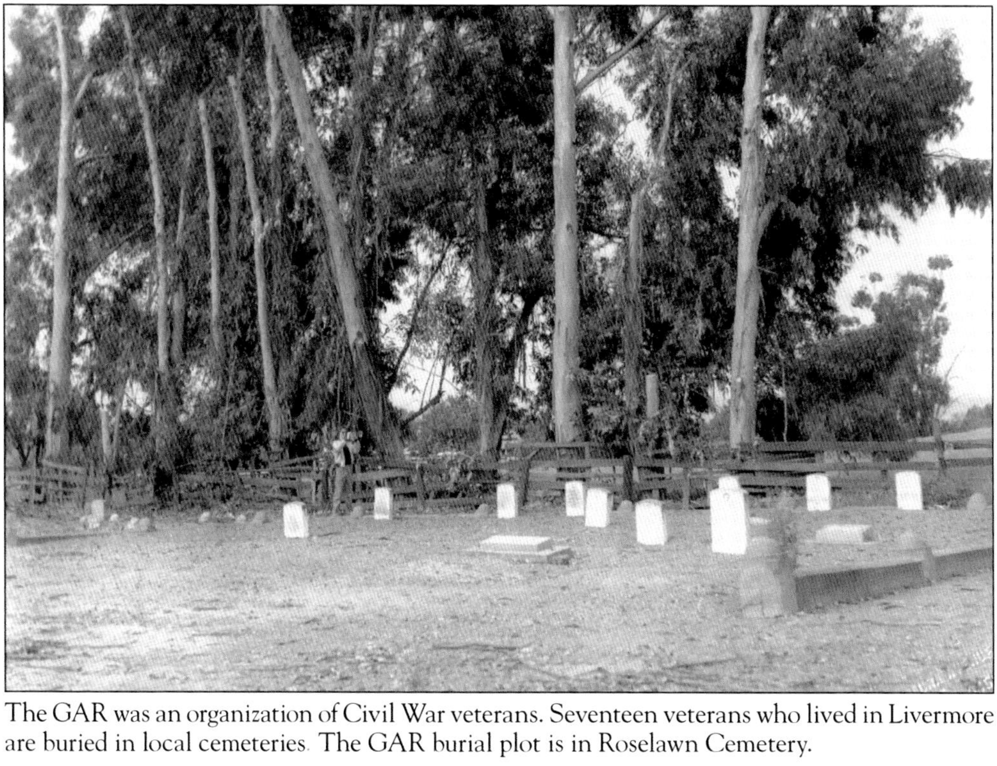

The GAR was an organization of Civil War veterans. Seventeen veterans who lived in Livermore are buried in local cemeteries. The GAR burial plot is in Roselawn Cemetery.

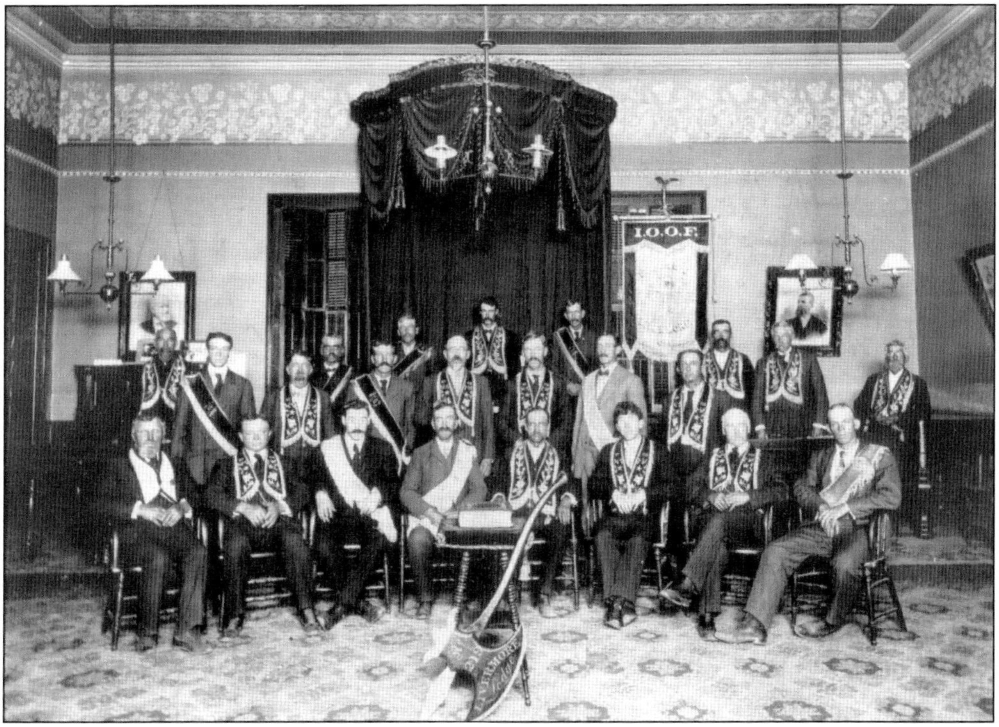

Elected members of the Odd Fellows lodge gather around 1900 for this formal photograph.

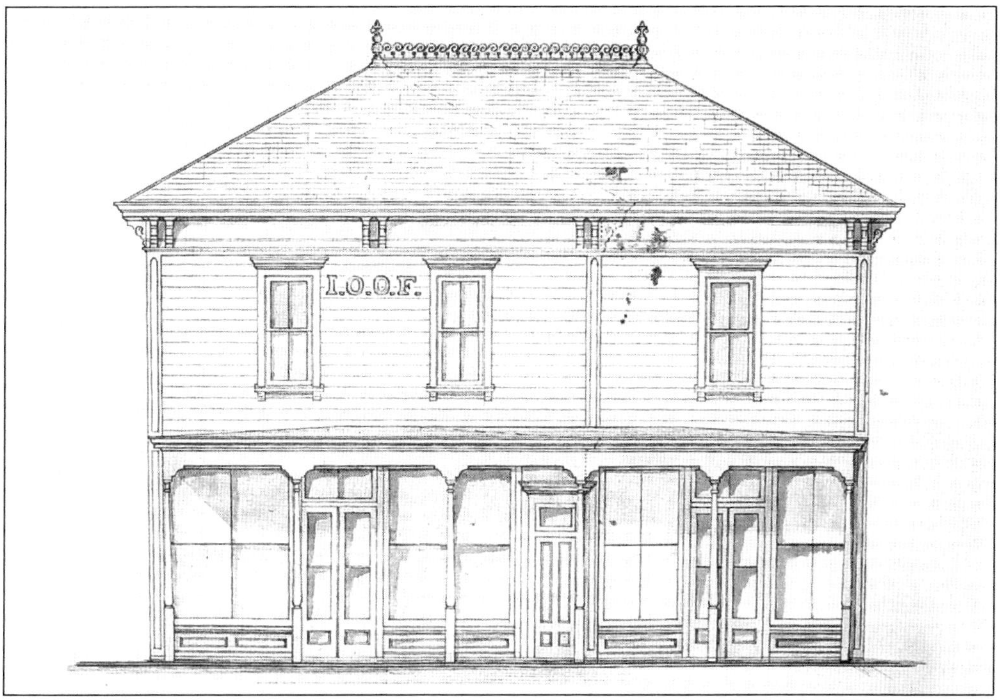

The International Order of Odd Fellows was the first fraternal organization in the community to erect a lodge hall. First built in 1872, it was enlarged in 1873 when an extension was added from the ground floor doorway to the right.

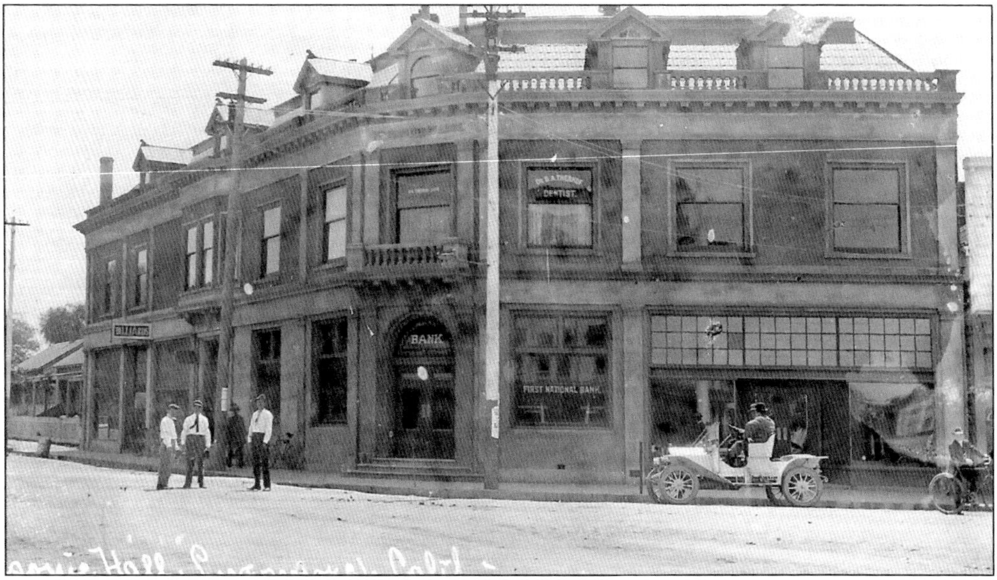

In 1907, a major community landmark was erected by the AF&AM Masonic Lodge at the intersection of First Street and Livermore Avenue. The Masons formed their lodge in 1871 in Pleasanton, there being no place in Livermore at the time that was suitable for such a meeting. Beginning in 1874, the group met in the IOOF building on First Street. When the McLeod building was constructed in 1886 at the northeast corner of First and Livermore, provision was made for the Masons to have the use of the third floor, which was initially occupied by banks. The second floor had some professional offices and the Masons' meeting room.

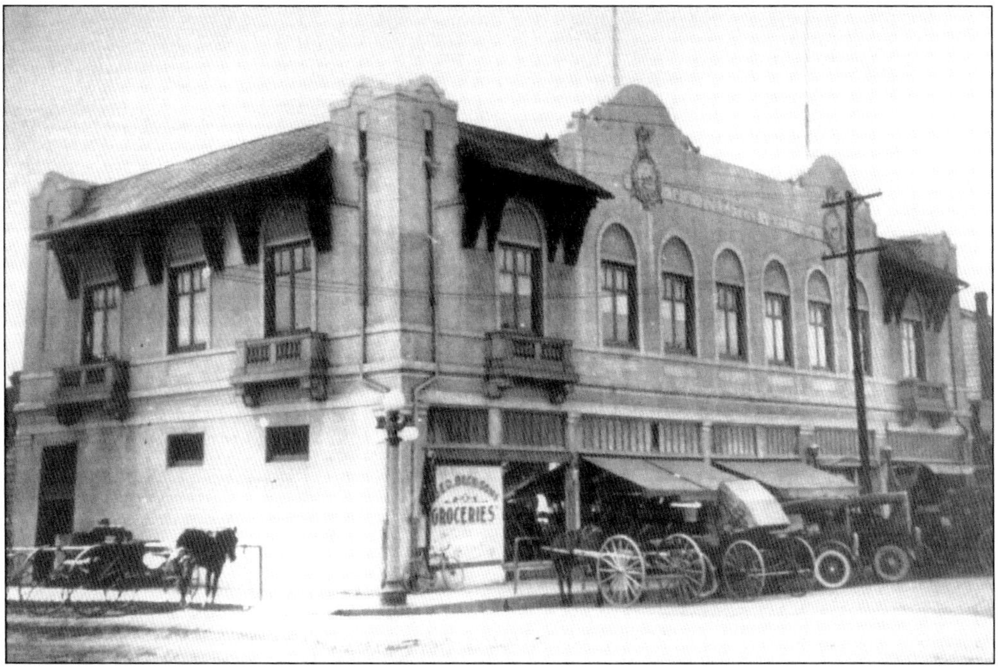

The Foresters Hall at Second and J Streets was completed in 1914. The lodge was organized in 1892; its early meetings were held in the Masonic rooms in the old McLeod building. The storefronts on the ground floor were rented out.

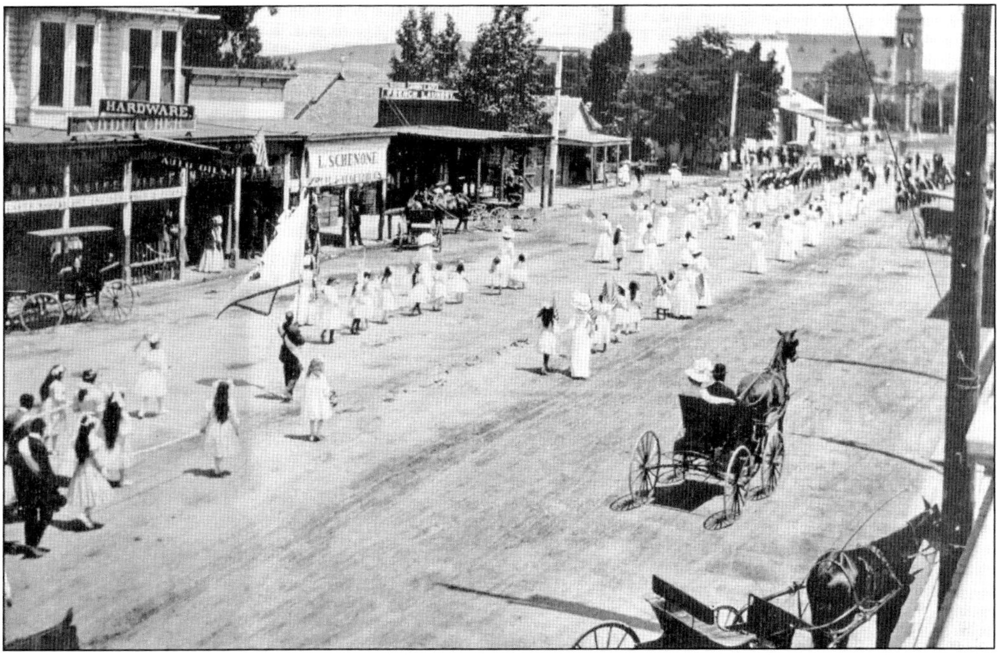

Many of Livermore's Portuguese residents were members of Irmandade do Divino Espiritu Santos (IDES), also known as the Holy Ghost Society. A part of their annual celebration, after the crowning of a queen, was a march from their hall on North Livermore Avenue to St. Michael's Church. This photograph commemorates the 1906 celebration.

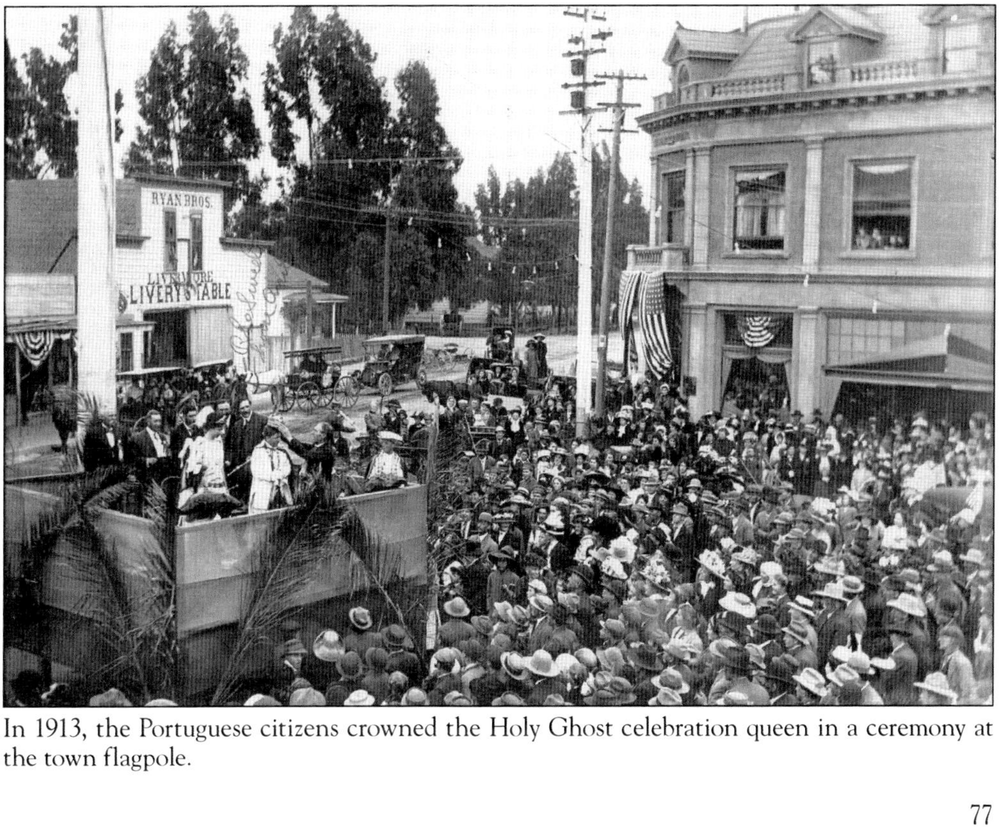

In 1913, the Portuguese citizens crowned the Holy Ghost celebration queen in a ceremony at the town flagpole.

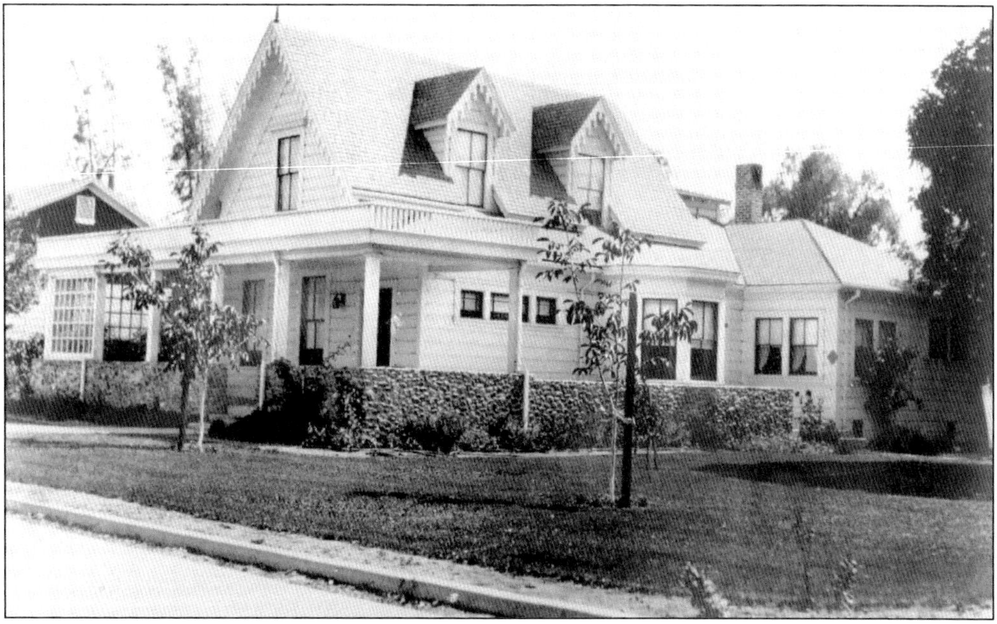

N. B. Holmes, one of Livermore's first settlers, built his home at Third and South L Streets before 1873. It was convenient to his blacksmith shop at Second and L Streets. The original Gothic architectural features have been compromised over the years. The porch, the stone wall, and kitchen addition in this photograph were added about 1926. This home was relocated seven miles out on Tesla Road in 1969.

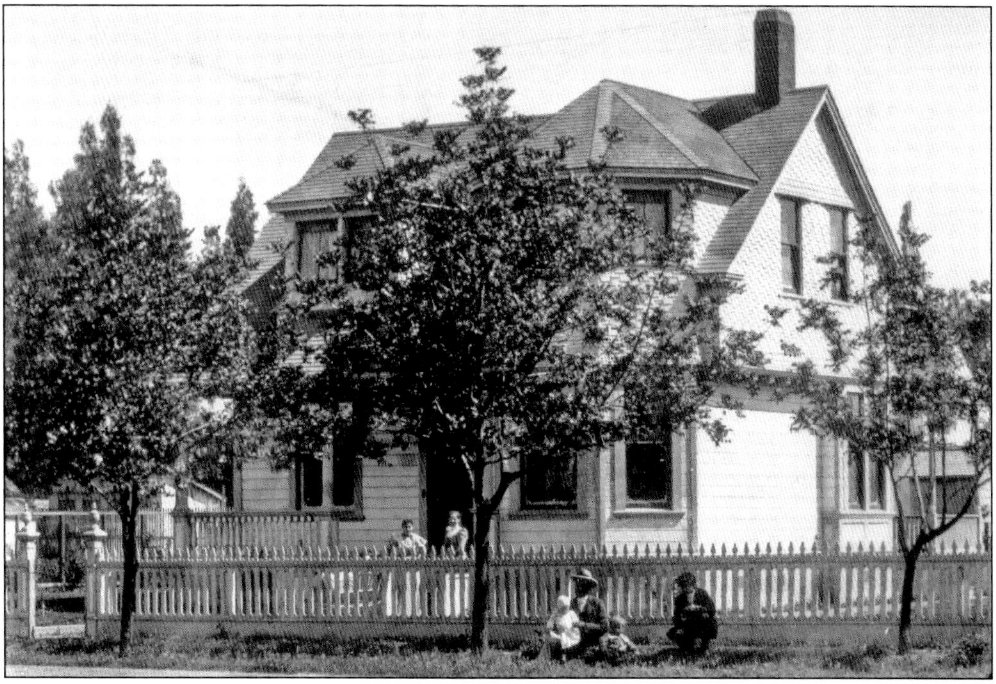

The Oscar Meyers home at 580 South L Street was completed in 1894. It was probably designed by family member and architect Henry Meyers. In 1904, it became the Presbyterian manse for the next 60 years.

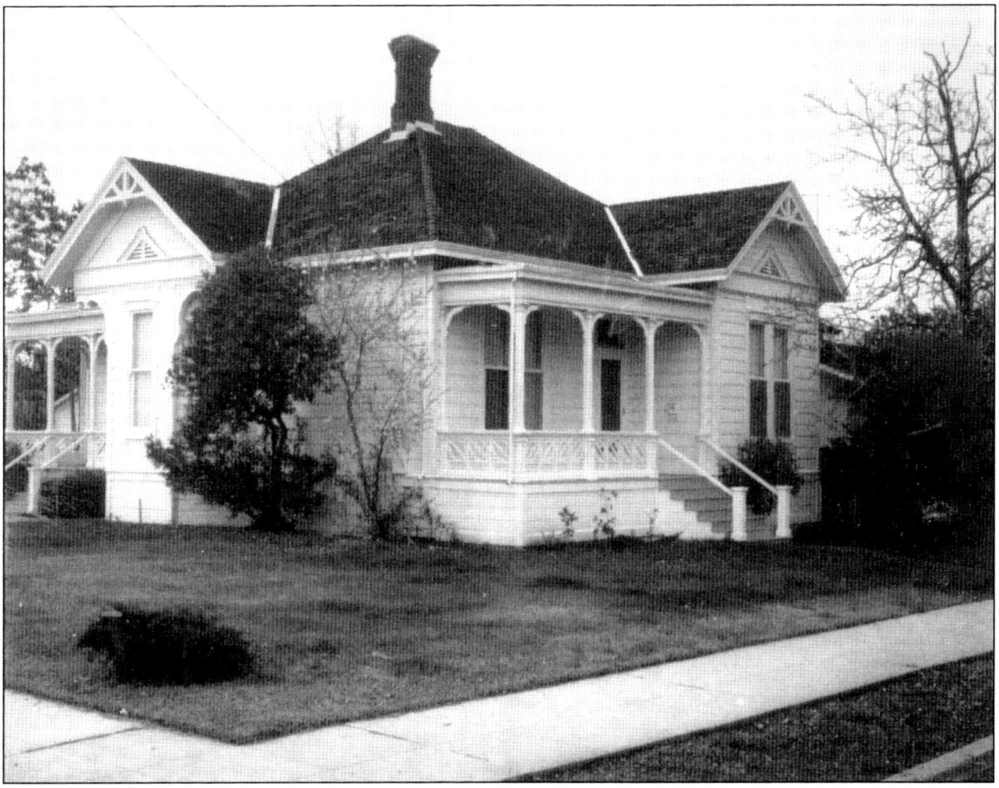

Frank Fassett, local farmer and legislator who wrote the bill for the unified school districts, built this house in 1888. The Eastlake influence is prominent on the facade. It is one of the few homes in the community that still has a carriage house.

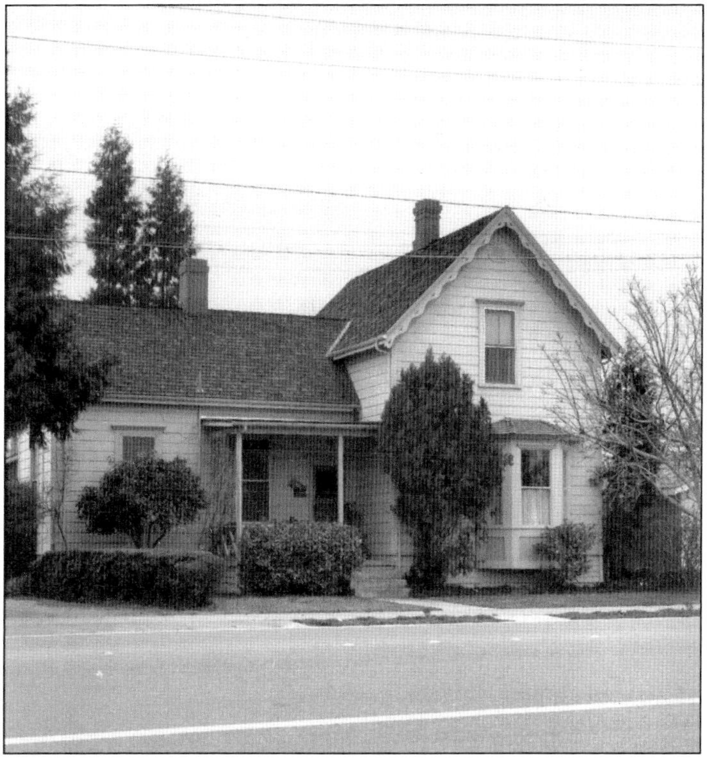

Byron Morrill was employed by Hiram Bailey to mind his property bounded by Seventh Street, K Street, College Avenue, and L Street. This house, built in 1884, was first located at the northeast corner of Seventh and L Streets. Many years later, it was moved to the back of the lot and now faces Seventh Street.

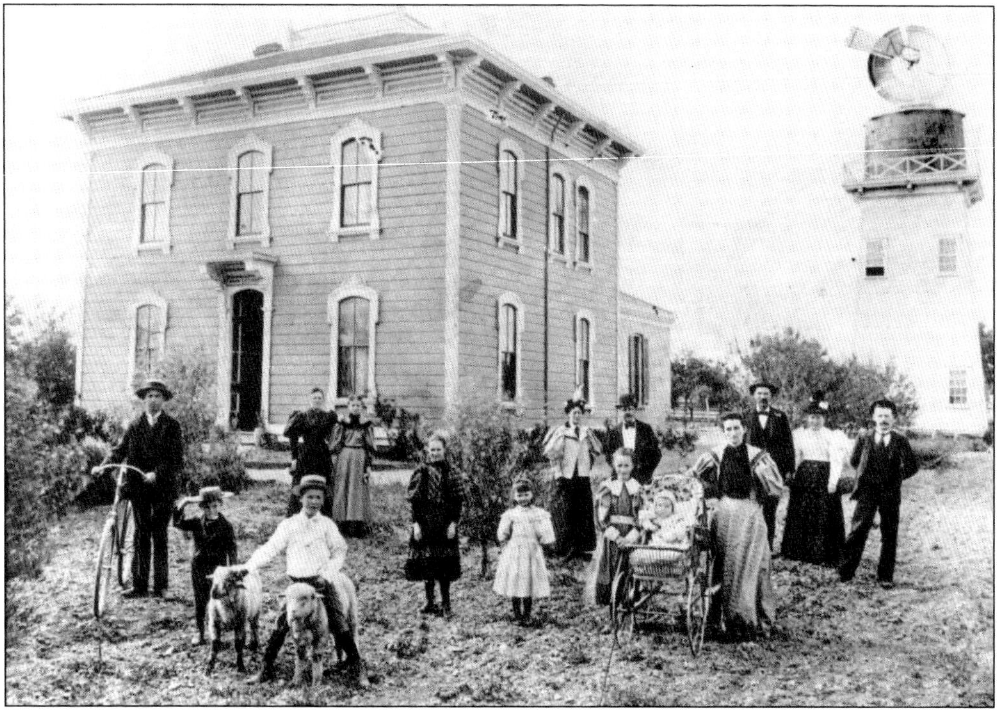

Henry Callaghan's 10-room house, dating from 1880, was located just east of the town boundary at 3101 East Avenue. His 35-acre vineyard extended to the east of his home.

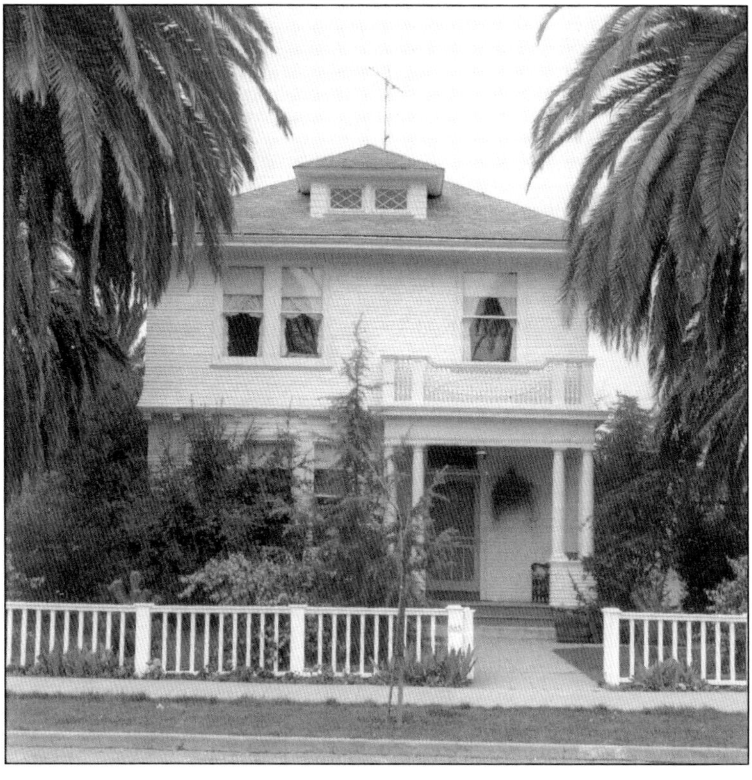

Local tradition says that Henry Meyers (later to become county architect) designed this home at 585 South L Street in 1897 as a wedding gift to his sister Lilly, who married Will Taylor, a local merchant.

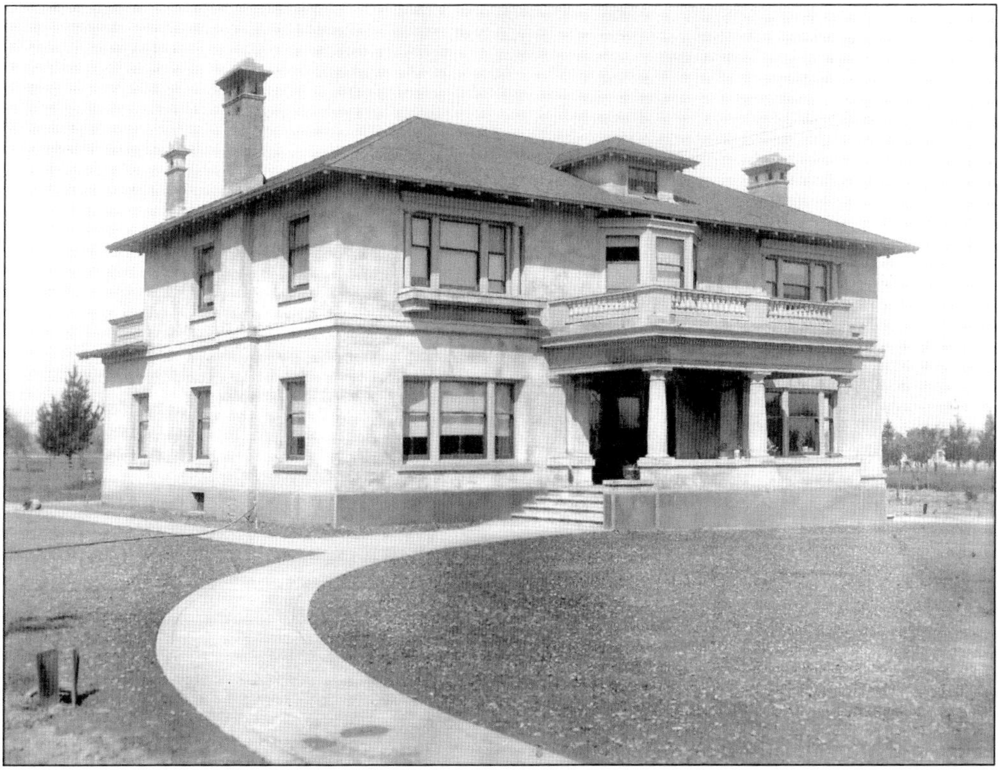

Beginning in 1908, Harry Winegar developed his property near Fourth Street and Holmes Street.

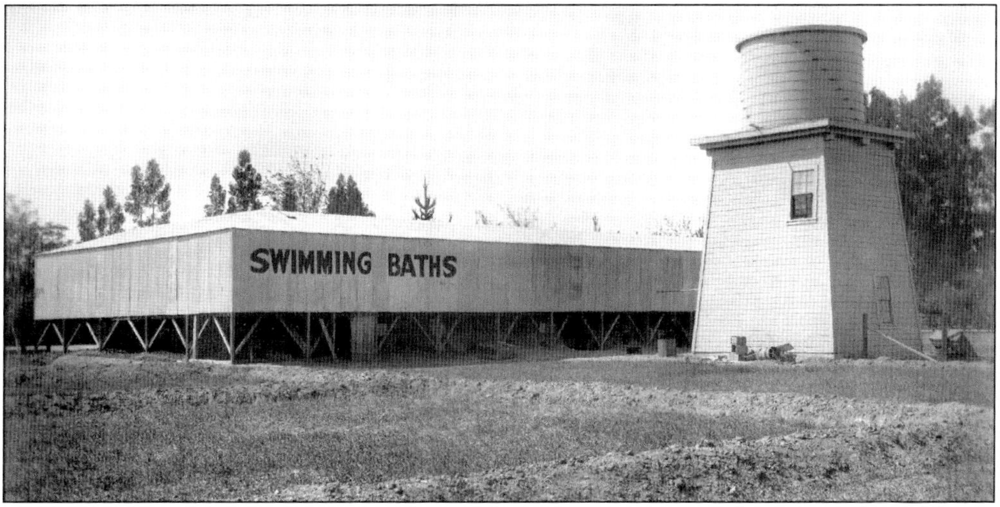

Winegar's estate included the town's first public swimming tank in 1908. It was 30 by 70 feet and held over 10,000 gallons. The tank was on West Fourth Street between R and S Streets. Winegar was a well-known baseball enthusiast, and during the same year, he had a "first class baseball diamond" built. He rallied support to bring professional league teams to winter here. In 1912 and 1913, the Oakland Oaks held their spring training in Livermore. Unfortunately, they did not return in 1914, and Winegar transformed the baseball park into an up-to-date poultry farm. The swimming tank continued to be used by the public into the 1920s.

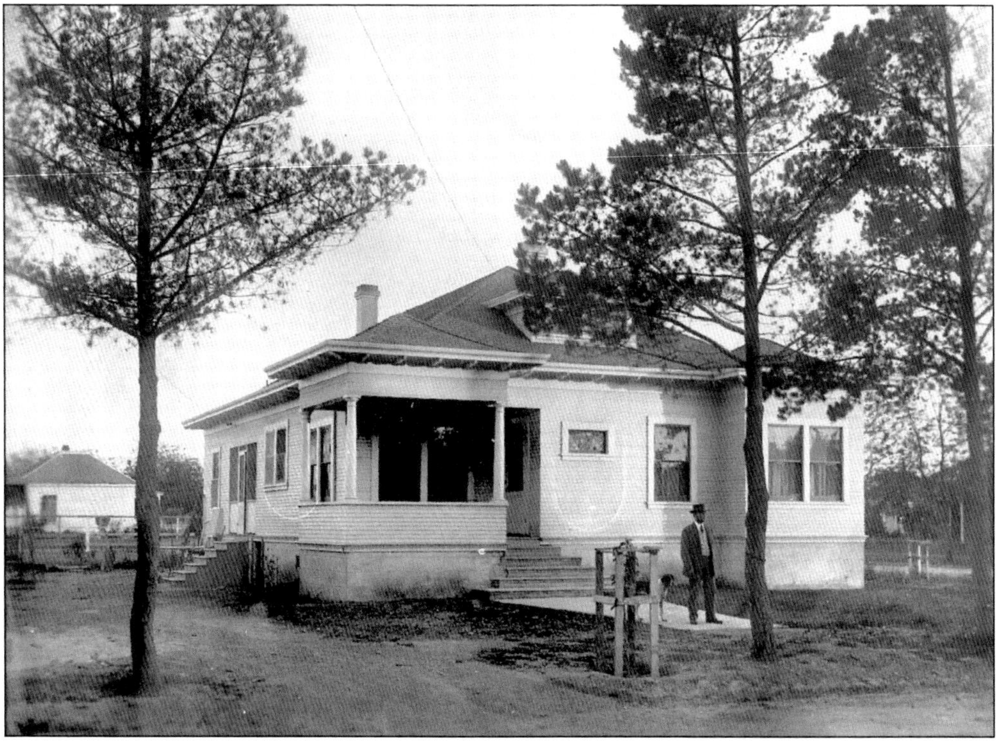

Dr. Frank Savage, a local dentist, lived at 2417 Sixth Street beginning in 1908.

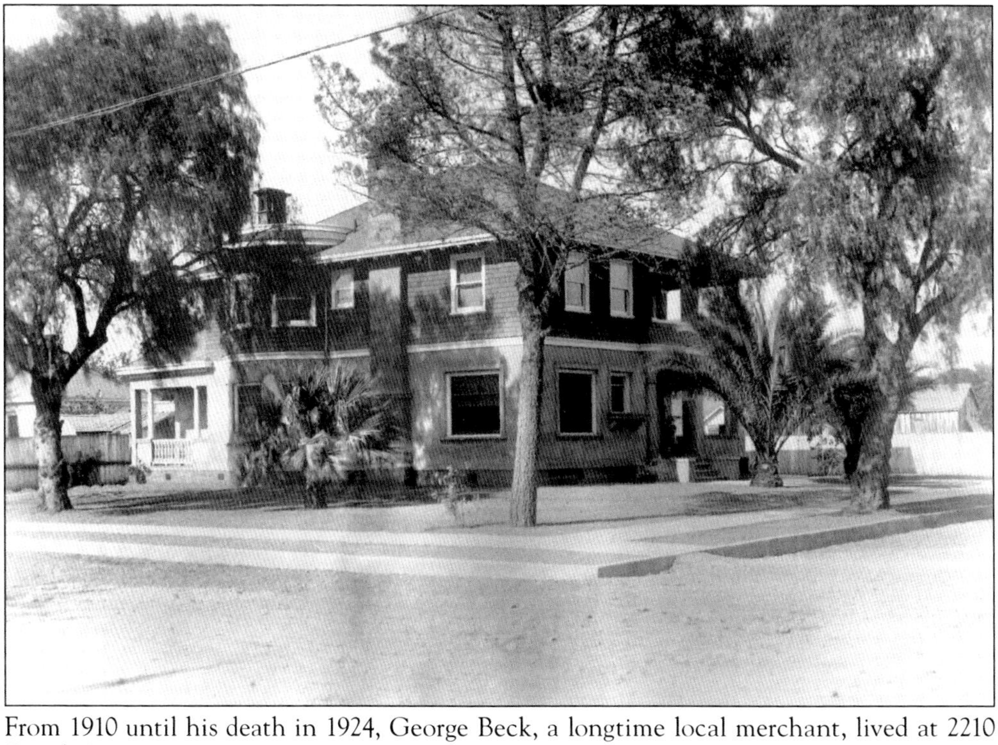

From 1910 until his death in 1924, George Beck, a longtime local merchant, lived at 2210 Fourth Street.

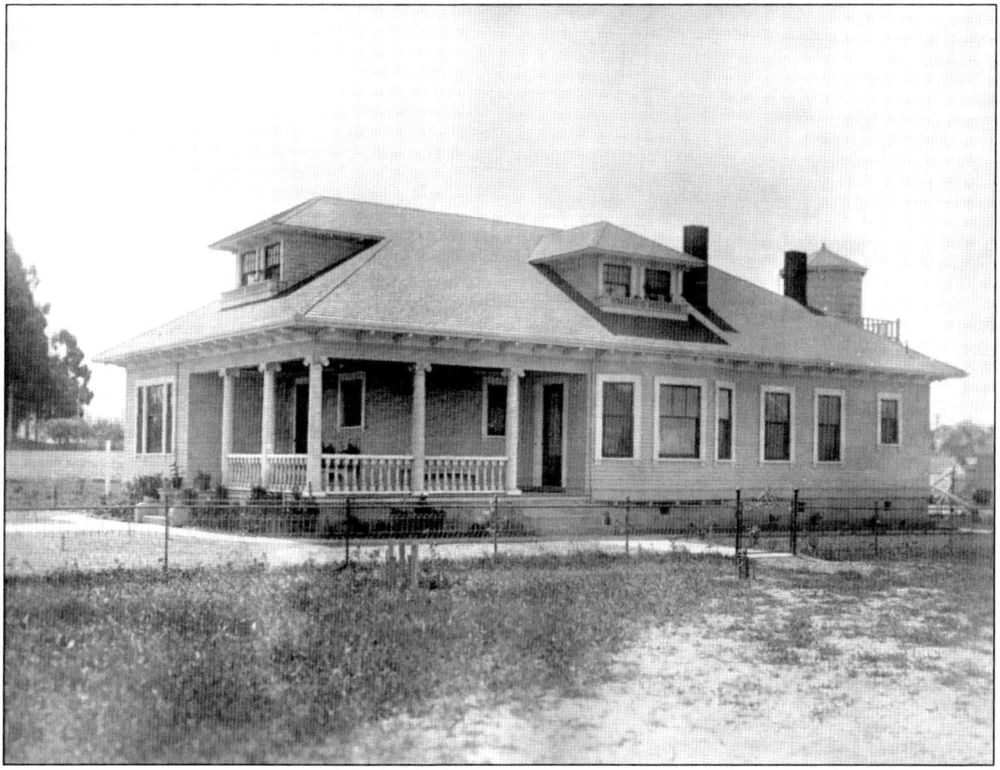

The home of Frank Gomez at 487 North Livermore and Walnut Street dates from 1908. Gomez was a retired farmer who had come to the valley about 1893.

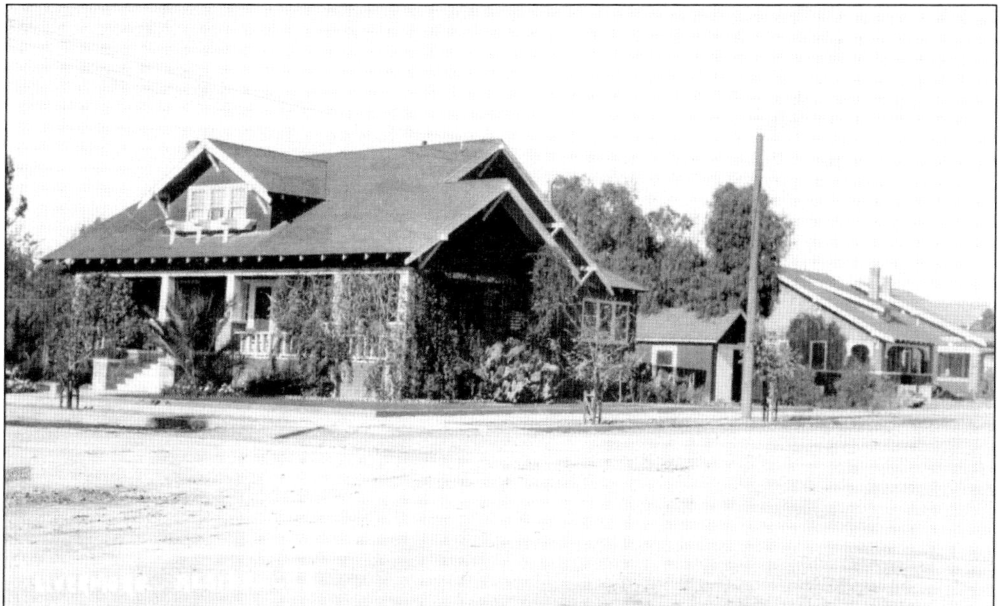

The home at 286 McLeod Street was built in 1910 for L. M. McDonald and his wife, who was A. J. McLeod's daughter. In 1922, it was purchased by the local American Legion Post. In 1931, Dr. Wallace Meyers acquired the property.

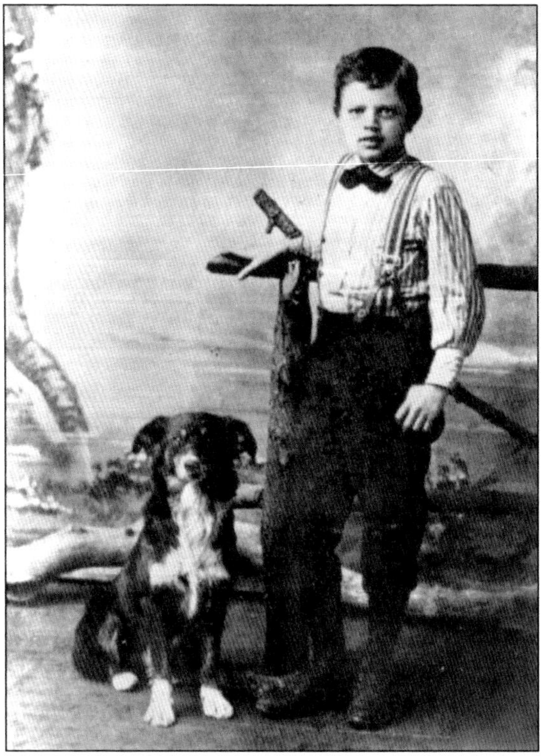

Jack London's family lived in Livermore from September 1883 until March 1886. He has written of his experiences here, saying, "One of the poor ranches on which I lived, there had been no books. In ways I was curious. I had been lent four books, marvelous books . . . One was Washington Irving's *Alhambra*, lent me by my school teacher. . . When I returned *Alhambra* to the teacher, I hoped she would lend me another book. But she did not. And because she did not . . . I cried all the way home on the three mile tramp from the school to the ranch."

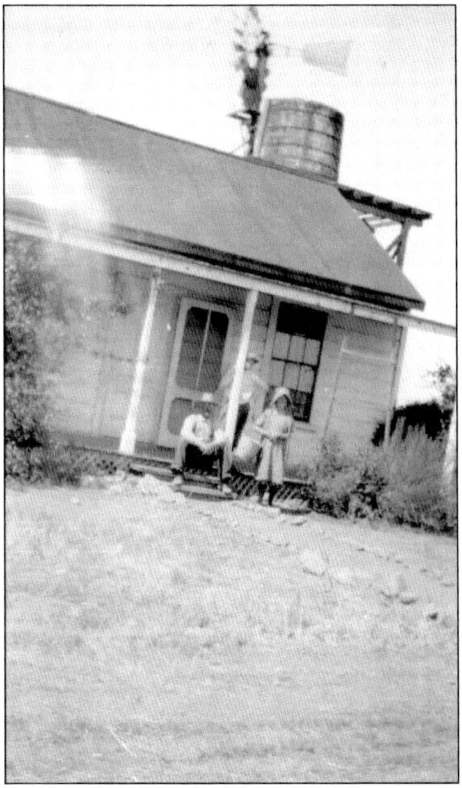

The London home was located on Alden Lane, west of town, a site since taken over by new residences.

Christopher Buckley was a San Francisco machine politician who used his home, Ravenswood, south of town on Arroyo Road, as a respite from his political wars during one of San Francisco's more corrupt political periods. Buckley was at the height of his power between 1887 and 1889. When malfeasance was charged, Buckley often came to his country residence until the matter blew over.

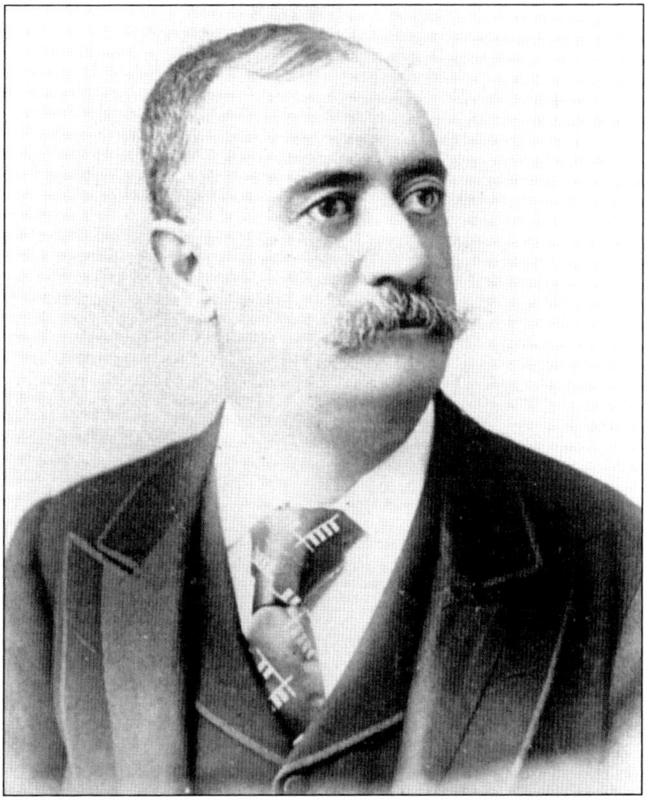

First to be built on Buckley's property was a "bedroom" cottage and a tank house, constructed in 1885.

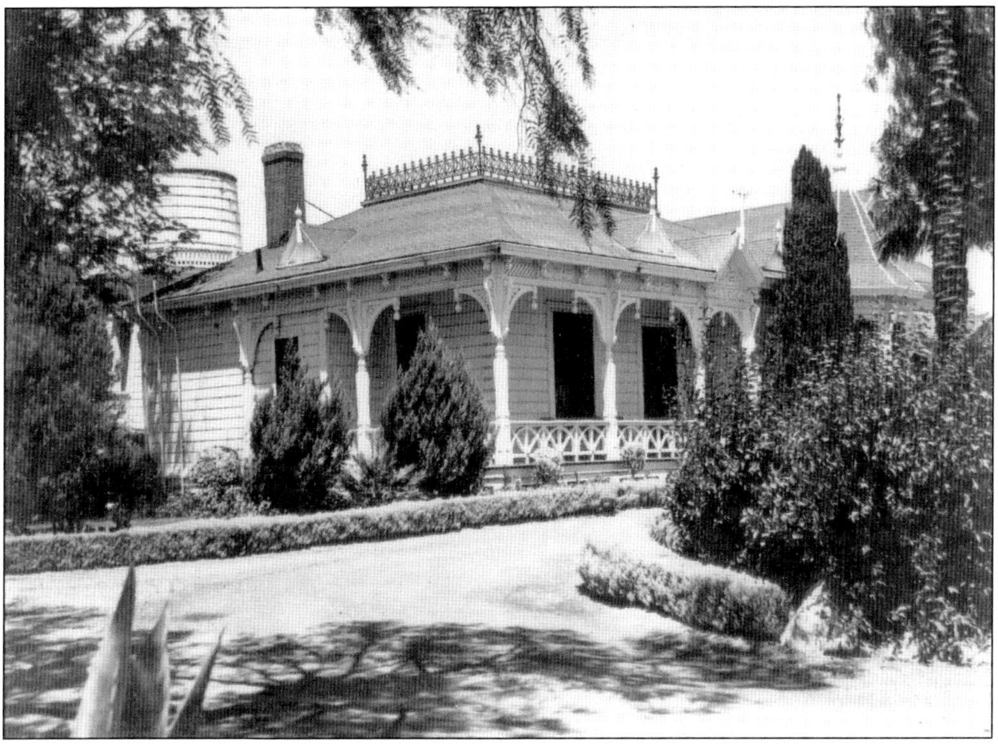

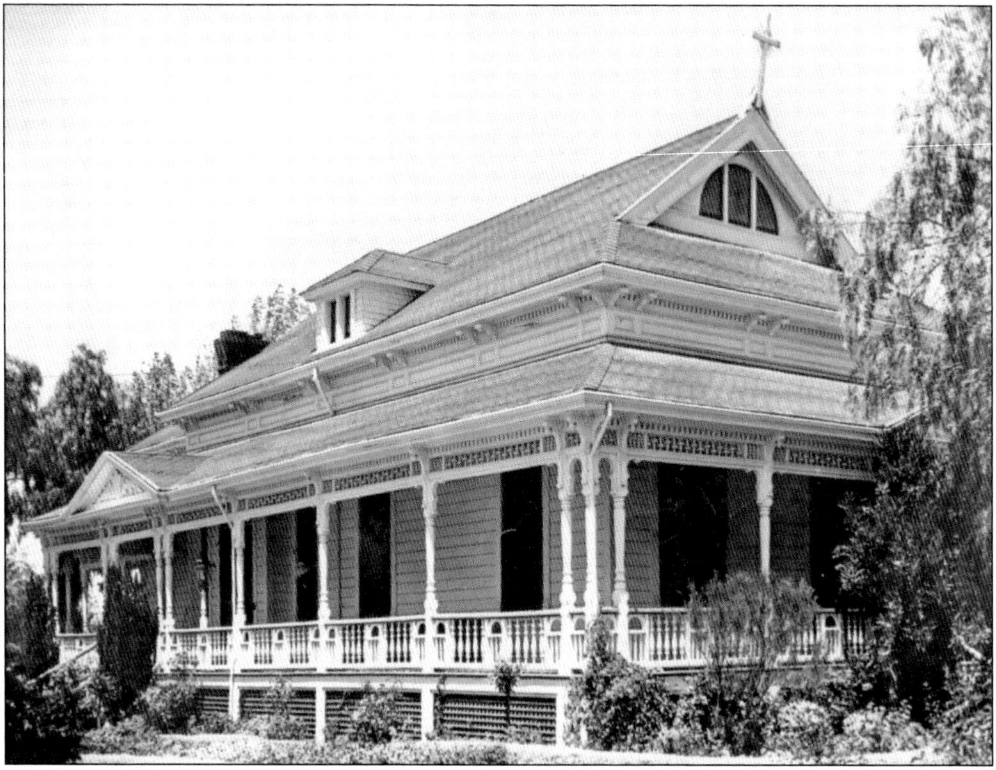

In 1891, Buckley had a larger house constructed where he could entertain his friends.

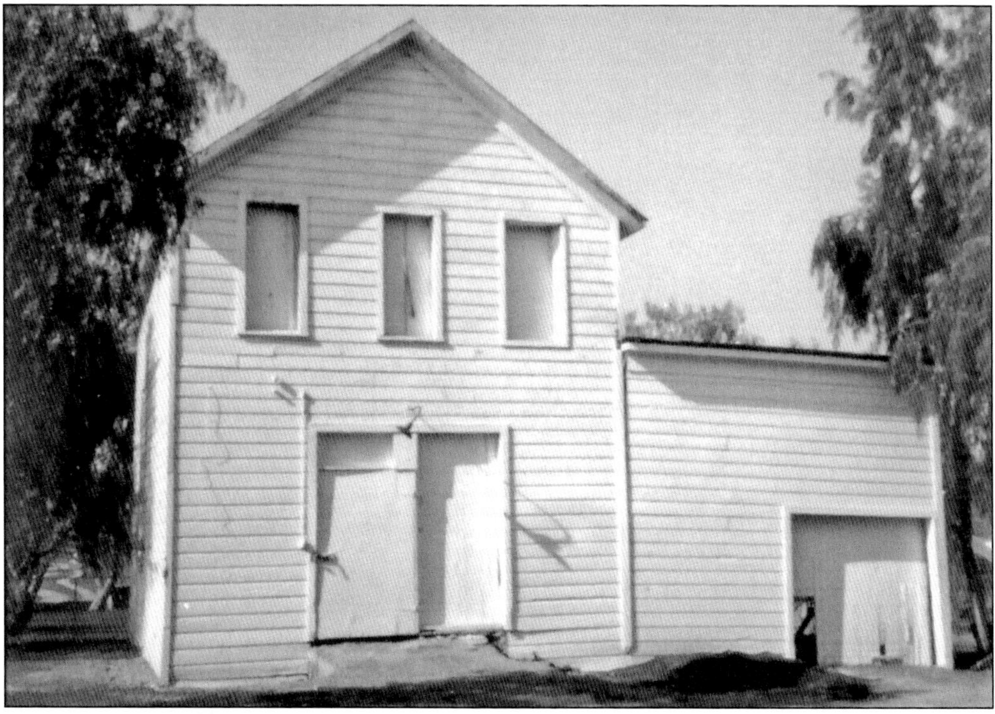

A necessity to Buckley's country estate was this carriage house, built in 1885.

Six

Health Care

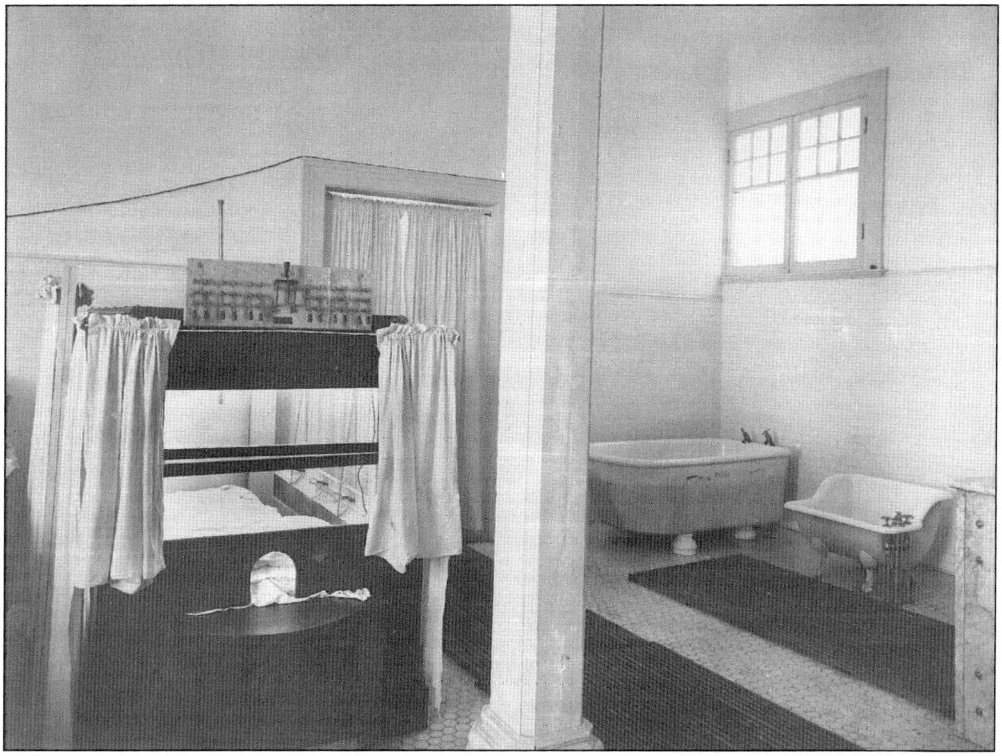

Livermore has a long history with state-of-the-art medical facilities. St. Paul's Hospital had the first incubator for premature babies in Alameda County, outside of Oakland. Pictured here is the electric treatment room in the Livermore Sanitarium. At the time, it was considered an advanced treatment for mental illness.

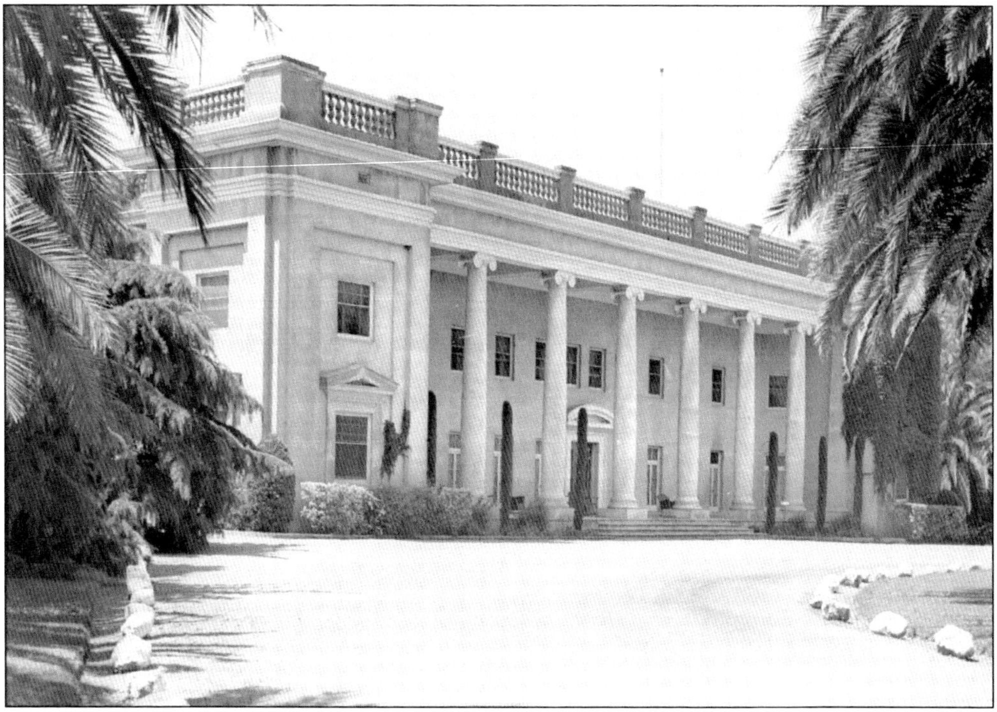

Dr. John Robertson was a leader in the treatment of mental disorders and addictions. He first opened his Livermore Sanitarium in 1894 on the former William Mendenhall estate at College and L Streets, using as his first building the old Livermore College. In 1904, Dr. Robertson had constructed a hydro sanitarium that relied on water (cabinet baths, showers, etc.) for the treatment of various disorders. The first building, the old college, burned in June 1909, and the new building pictured above was its replacement.

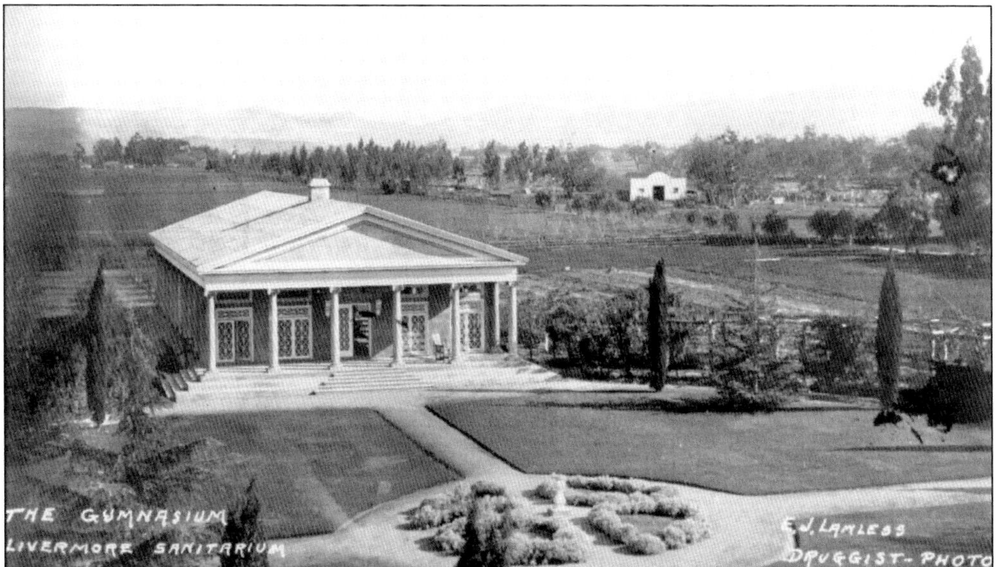

The year 1912 saw the construction of a gymnasium on the campus. This facility included a swimming pool, a two-lane bowling alley, and exercise equipment.

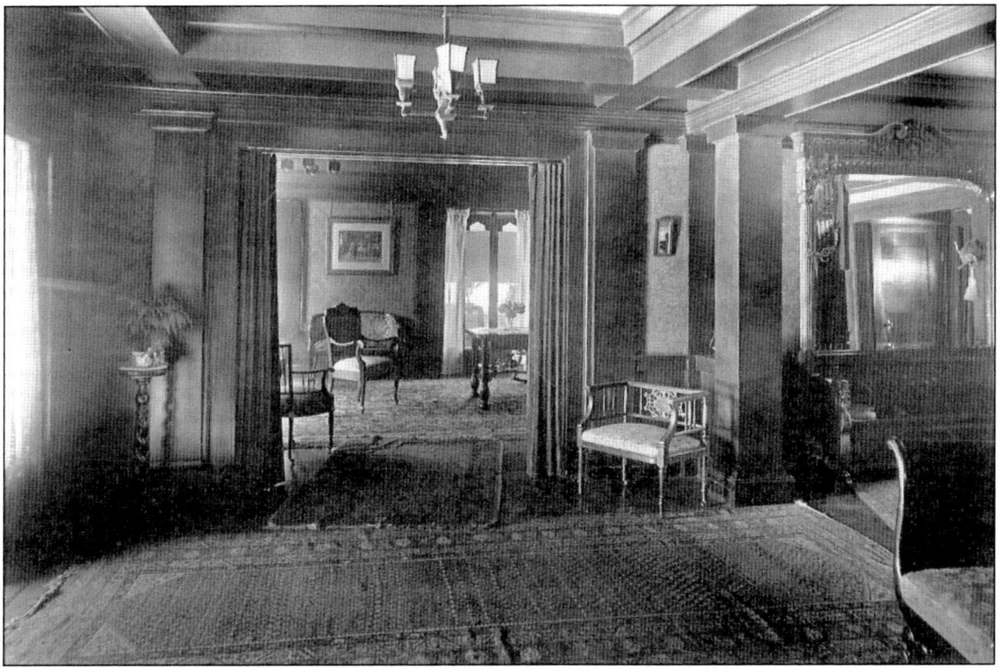

The sanitarium management did not skimp on creating a restful atmosphere as part of treatment. In 1920, there were over 120 patients at the sanitarium. By the 1960s, however, as new methods of psychiatric care were devised, the number of patients declined, and the facility closed. The property is now an upscale housing development.

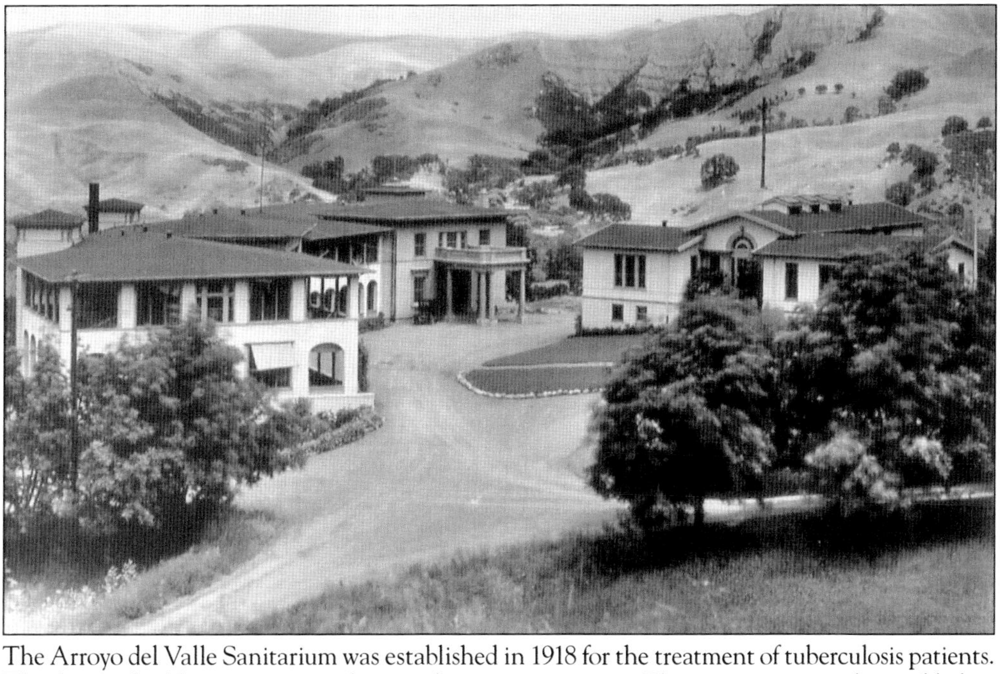

The Arroyo del Valle Sanitarium was established in 1918 for the treatment of tuberculosis patients. The disease had been most prevalent in the inner city areas. The sanitarium was located below the Cresta Blanca winery on Arroyo Road. It closed around 1960 after the discovery of penicillin rapidly decreased the incidence of the disease.

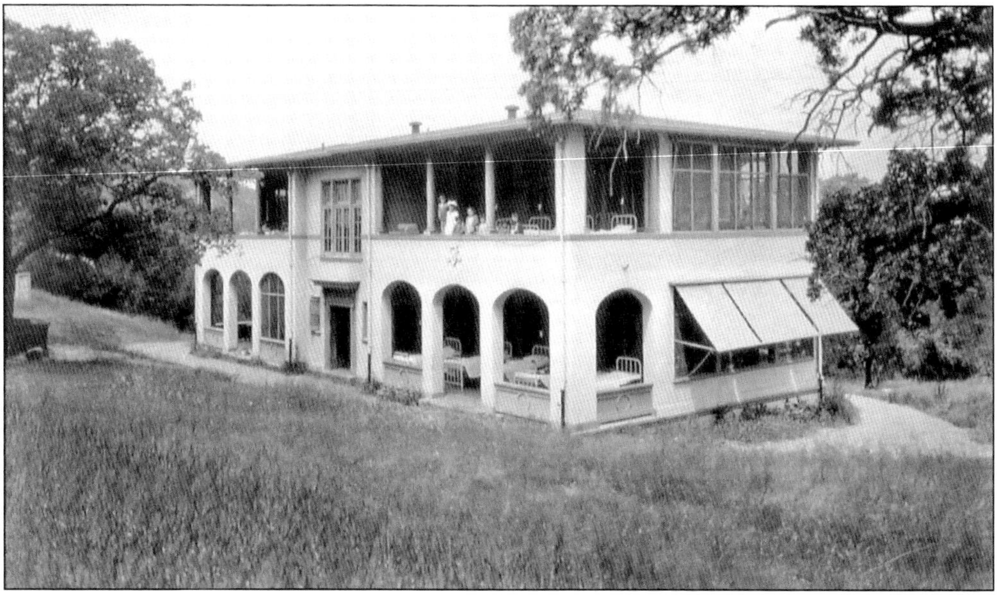

Several of the treatment buildings were constructed to take advantage of the warm, dry climate in the area. Sleeping in fresh air was one of the treatment methods for tuberculosis.

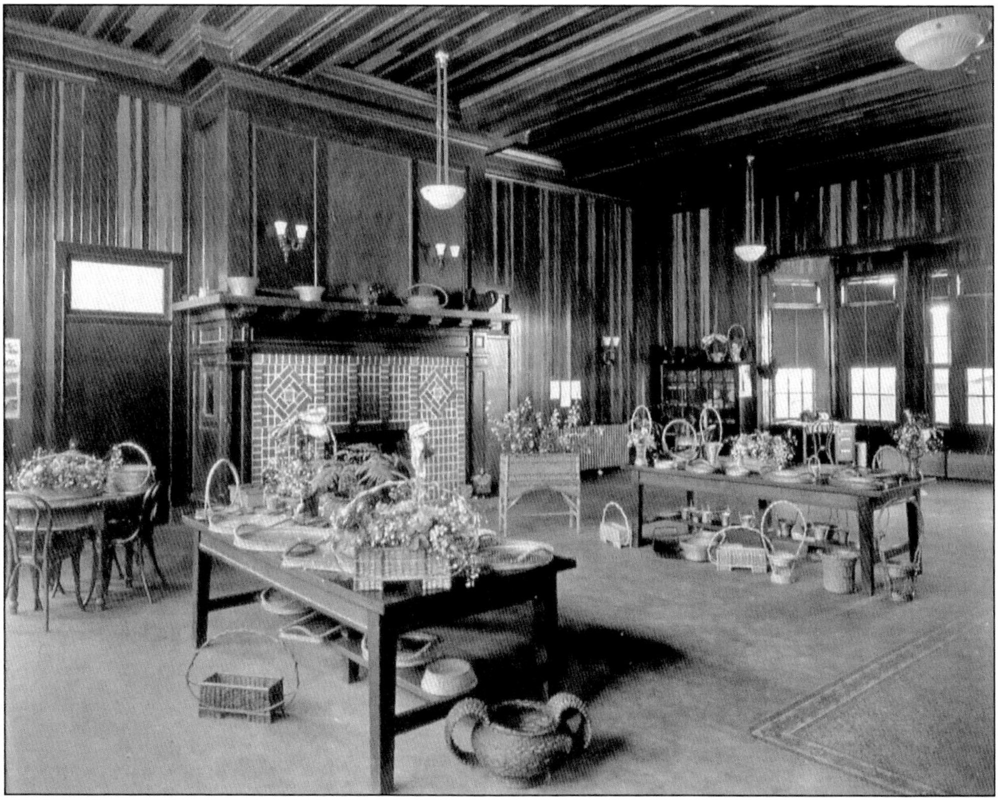

Activities of many kinds kept the patients busy. In early 1919, patients issued their first newsletter, "The Stethoscope." By 1923, Del Valle Farms had been established to help children continue their education while undergoing treatment.

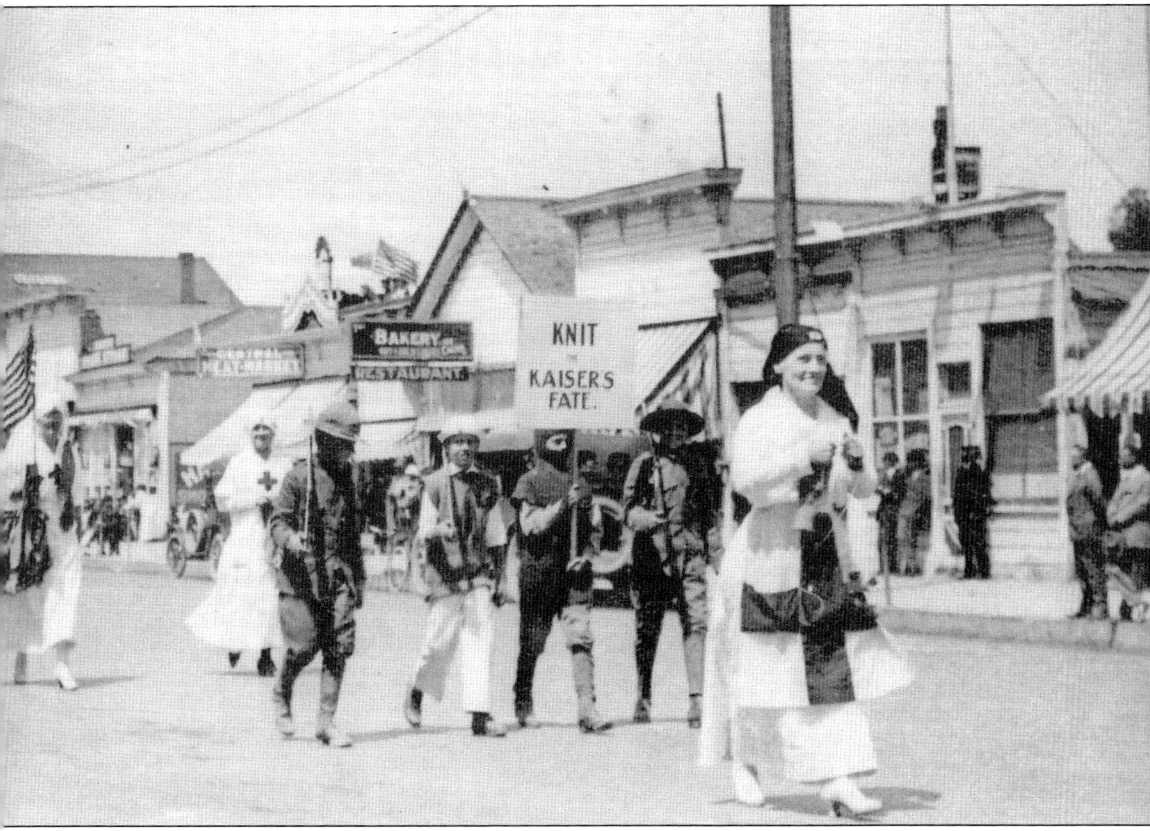

During World War I, many cities across the nation conducted donation drives for the American Red Cross. In the spring of 1918, the town of Livermore conducted its second donation drive. On May 20, 1918, local women active in Red Cross affairs paraded up First Street. Led by Gertrude Wilson, three of the young men behind her are identified as Wesley Madison, Wallace Meyers, and the McVicar boy. Carrying the American flag is Mrs. Ernie Uttendorfer, and to her left is Mrs. Madison. The townspeople met, even exceeded, its goal in three days.

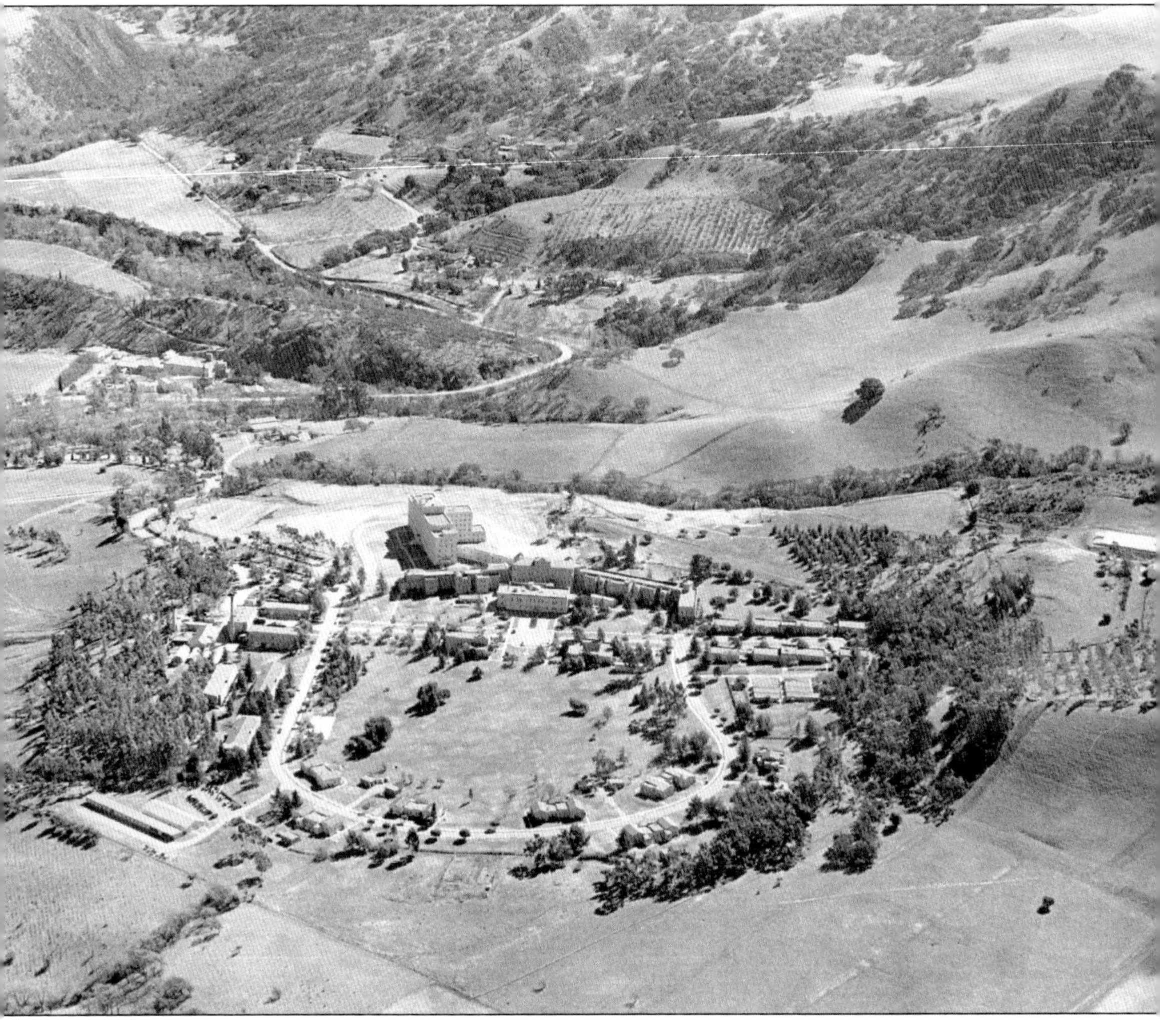

The U.S. Veterans Department chose the old Dos Mesa/Cresta Blanca vineyard of 200 acres in 1922 for the site of a hospital that specialized in care for tubercular-disabled veterans. Even before it was finished, plans were in process to enlarge the facility. Located about three miles south of town, the hospital complex became a small community of its own. The buildings in the center of this photograph comprise the hospital complex. On the left side of the picture are warehouses and other support facilities. At the bottom, along the circle drive, are residents of the medical staff.

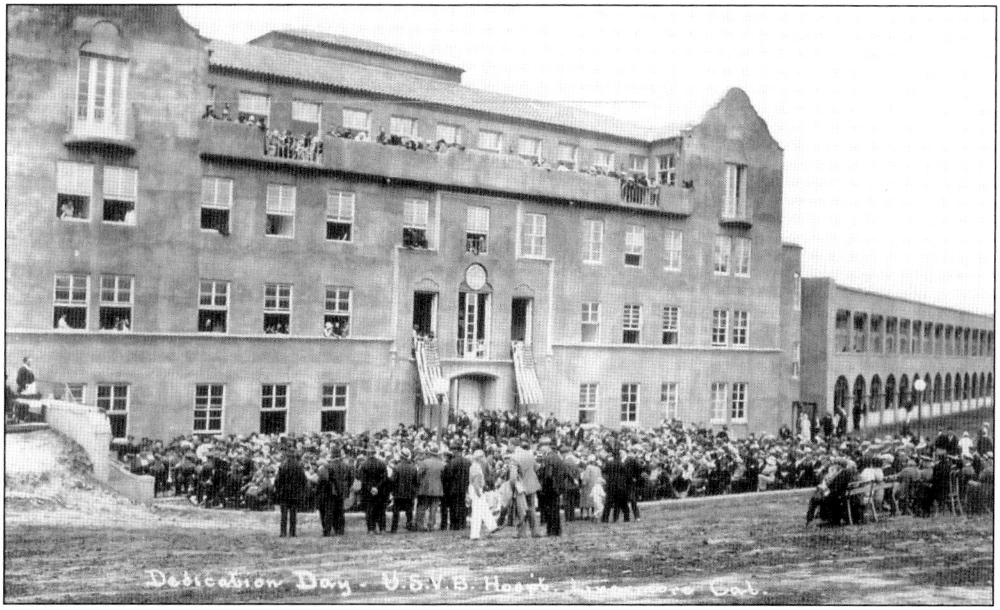

Dedication day at the new veterans hospital in 1925 was a gala occasion. Some 2,000 people attended the dedication ceremony. The contingent of dignitaries included the local Congressional representative, the chairman of the Alameda County Board of Supervisors, and representatives of various fraternal and veterans' organizations. The announcement that the road from Livermore to the hospital would be paved brought applause from the audience.

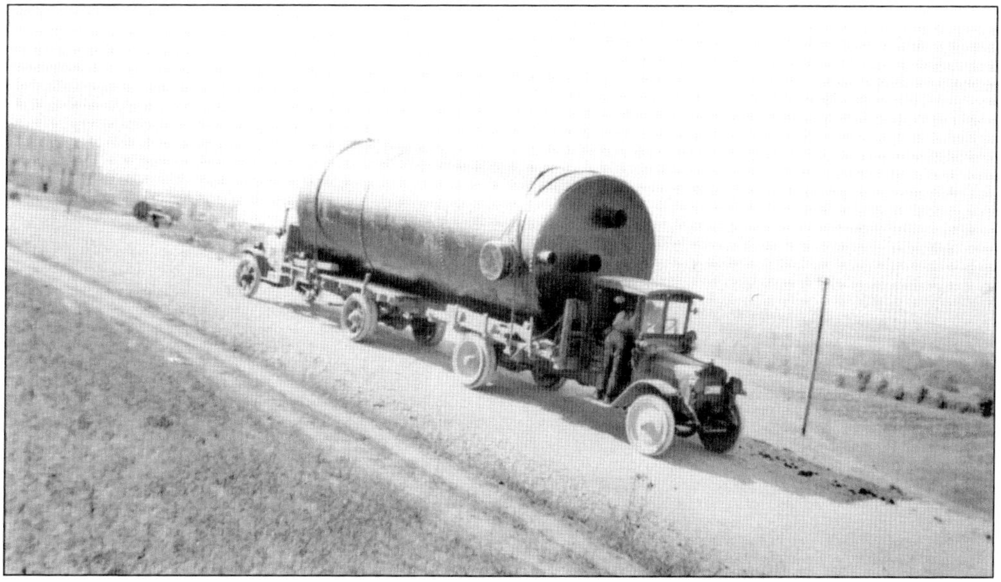

In 1924, Billy Wilson met the challenge when his California Transfer Company was chosen to move a fuel tank from a downtown rail siding out to the veterans hospital.

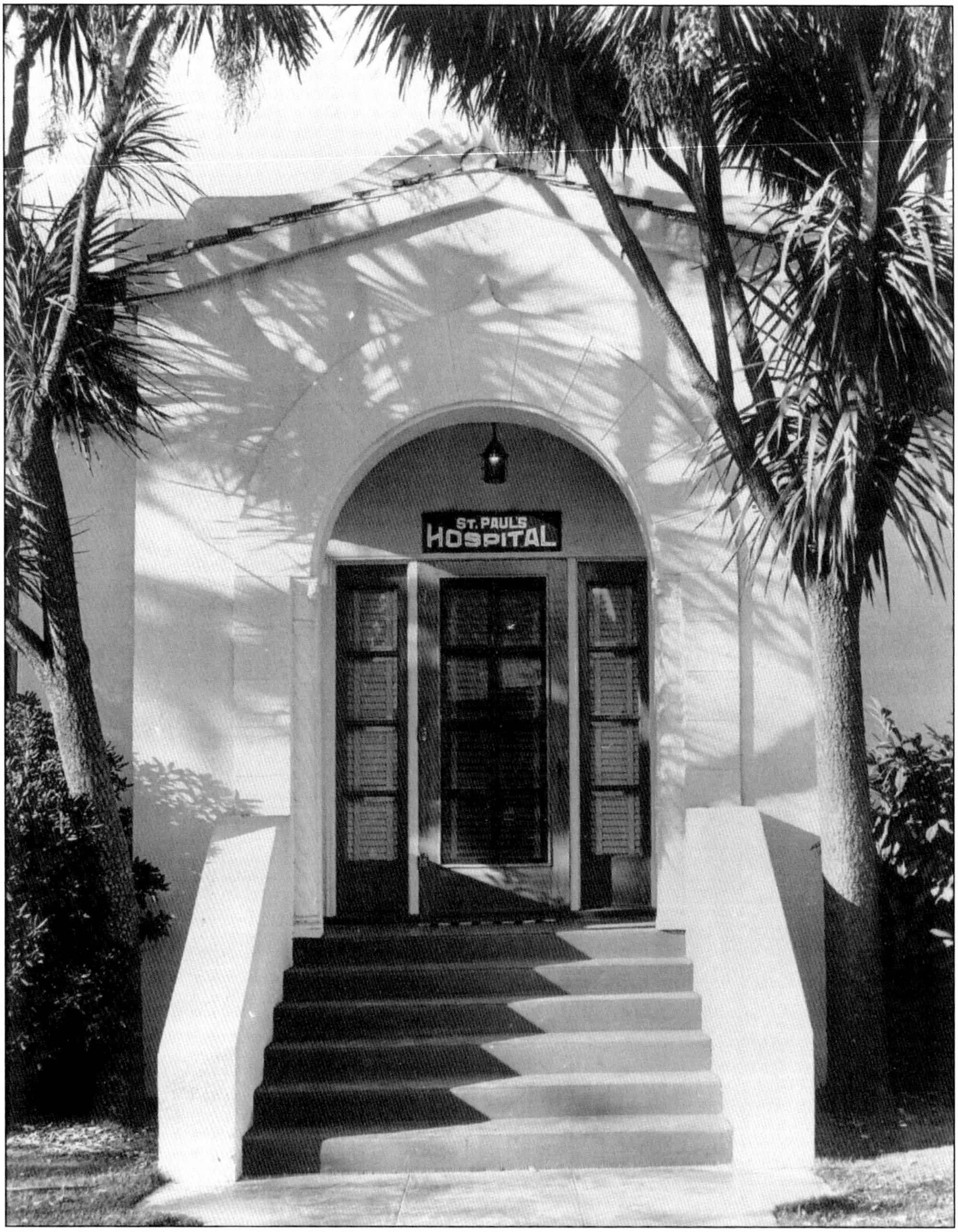

St. Paul's Hospital was established in 1927 by Dr. Paul Dolan. It was located at Eighth and J Streets. Until 1961, when Valley Memorial Hospital opened its doors, most births in Livermore took place at St. Paul's. The building now houses an elder care facility.

Seven

INDUSTRY

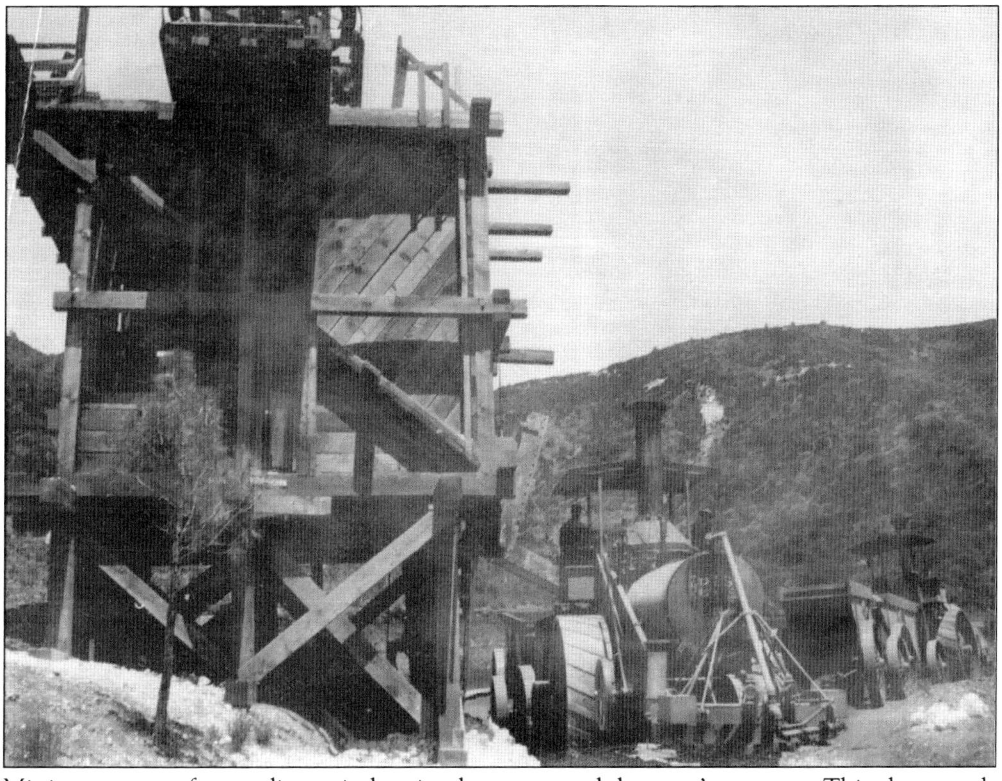

Mining was one of many diverse industries that supported the town's economy. This photograph was taken at the magnesite mines outside of town.

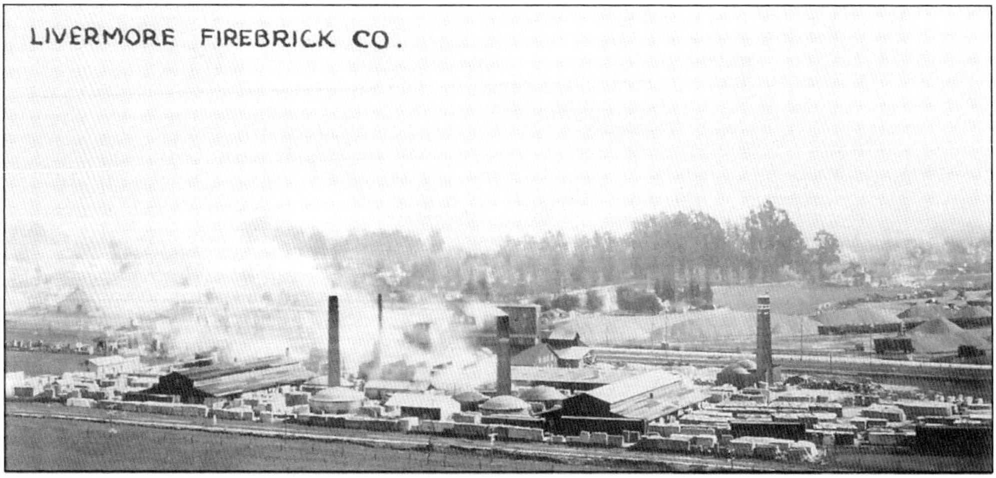

Livermore Fire Brick Company was established in 1911; in the later years, it was worked intermittently until 1949 when it closed. Located on Stanley Boulevard west of town, the company had ready access to the railroad to ship their product to market.

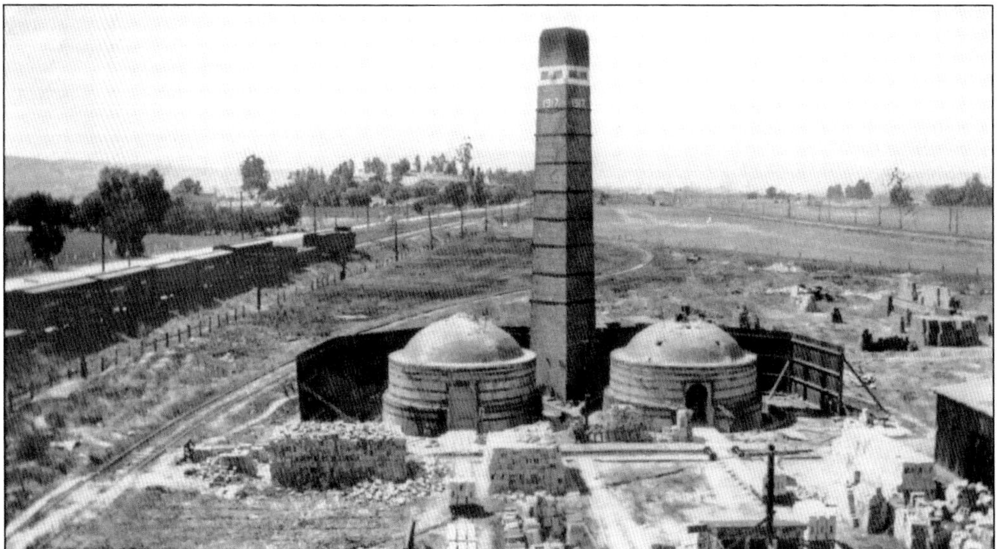

This bird's-eye view shows the retorts for firing the bricks. On the left side in the background is a view of Stanley Boulevard and Oak Knoll Cemetery. Livermore bricks were shipped to Washington State and Hawaii. Many of Livermore's buildings were constructed of local brick. One reason for the closure of the plant was because a source of local clay was never found.

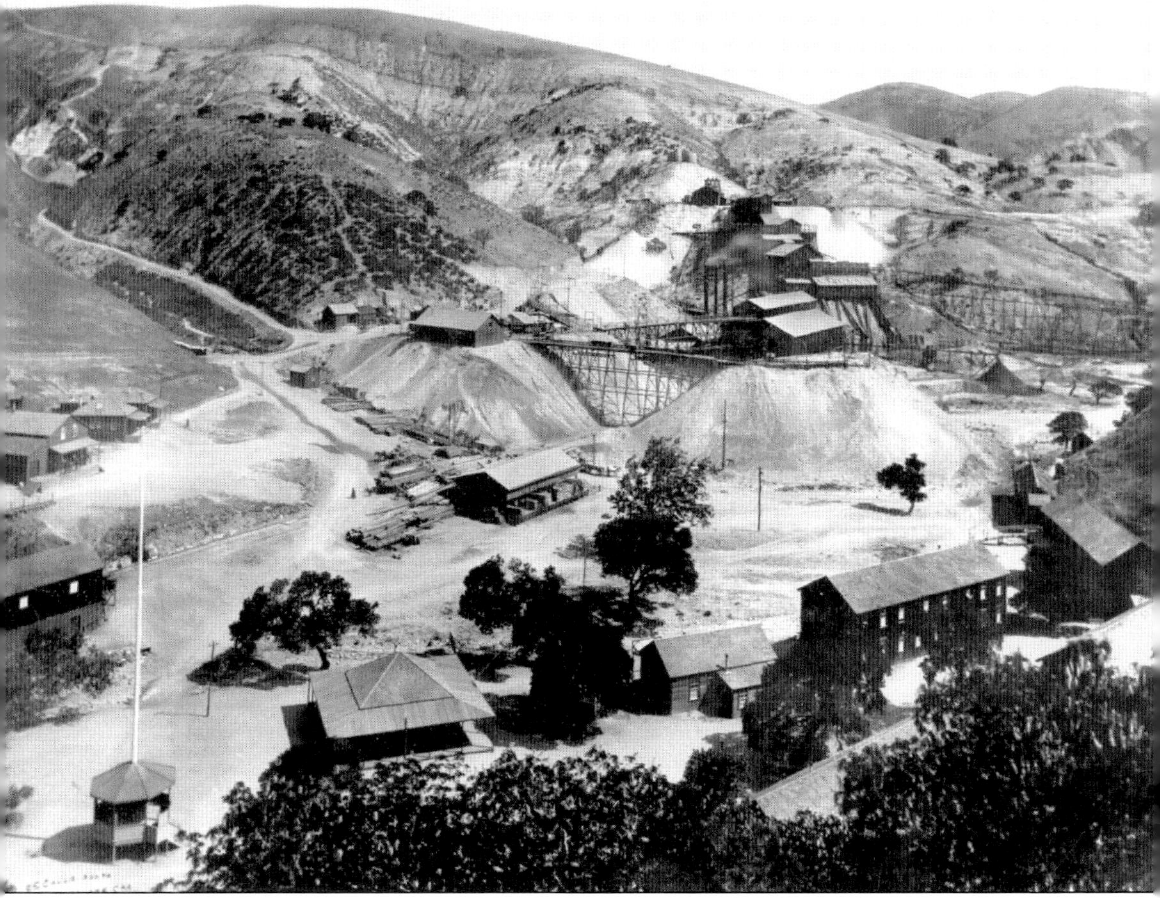

Coal was first discovered in Corral Hollow in 1855. It was a soft coal and the coal seams tilted down at a 60-degree angle. This photograph of Tesla dates from 1898. The company store is pictured at the lower right and illustrates typical company housing for miners and their families.

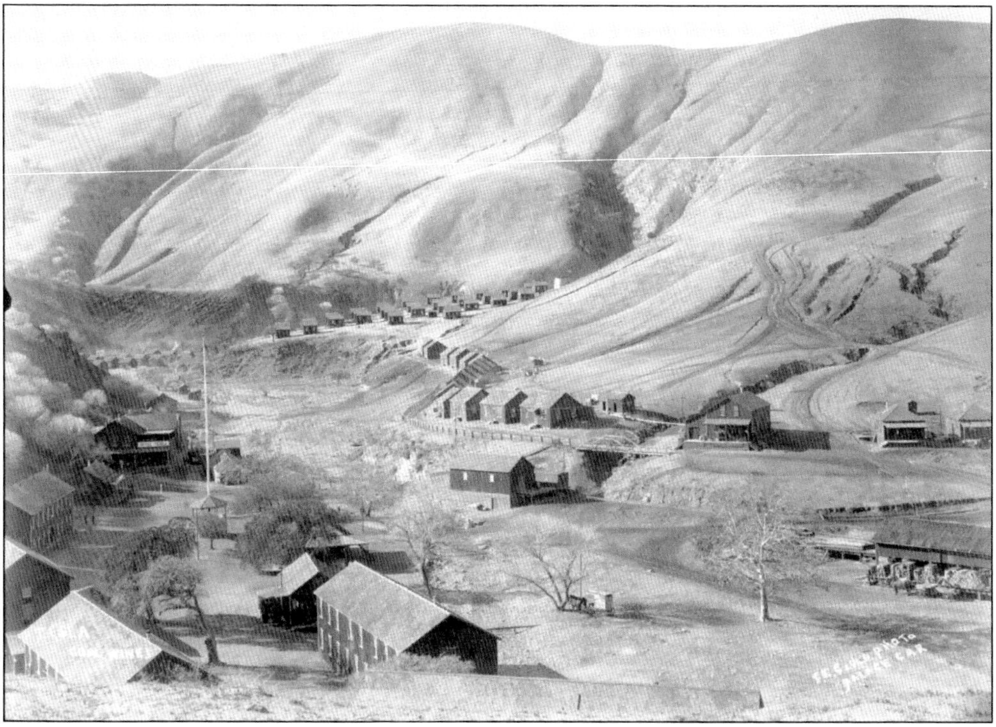

In the far distance is typical housing for Tesla miners and their families. A house usually rented for $6 to $8 a month.

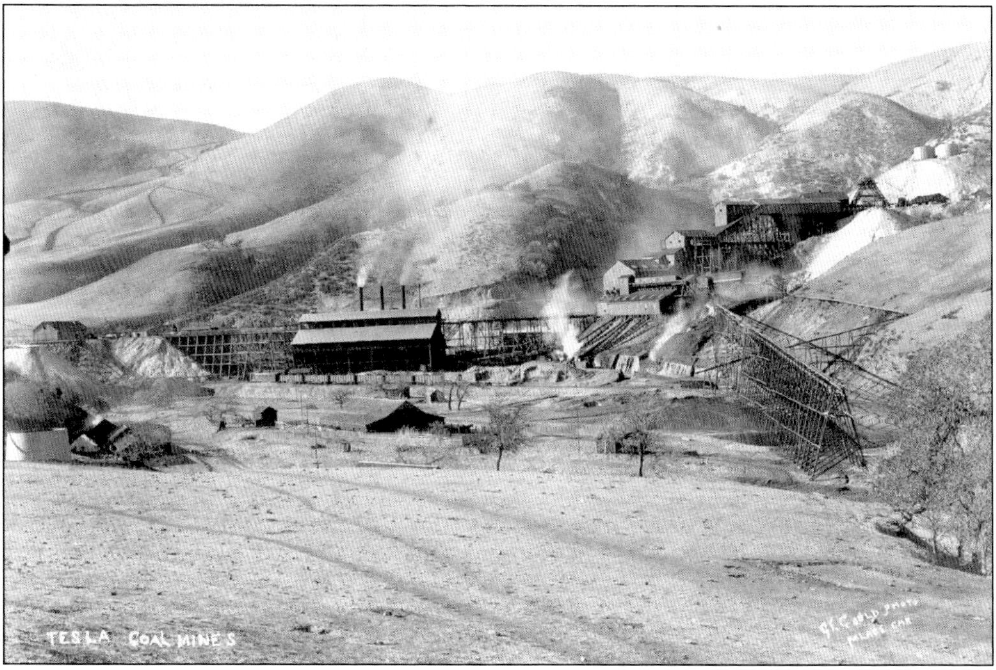

By 1900, James Treadwell had taken control of the mines and invested a large amount of money in the infrastructure. There appeared some financial chicanery going on, and the mines were intermittently closed. In 1907, they shut down completely.

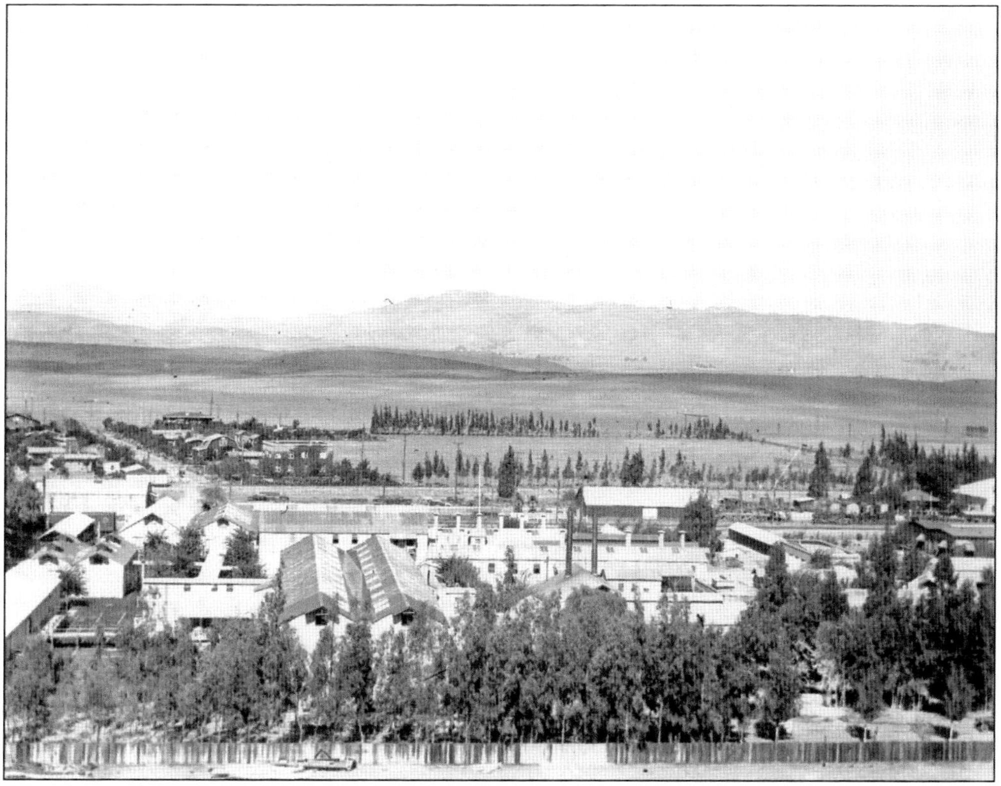

Coast Manufacturing and Supply Company (CM&S) arrived in Livermore in 1913. The company product was black powder fuse for dynamite.

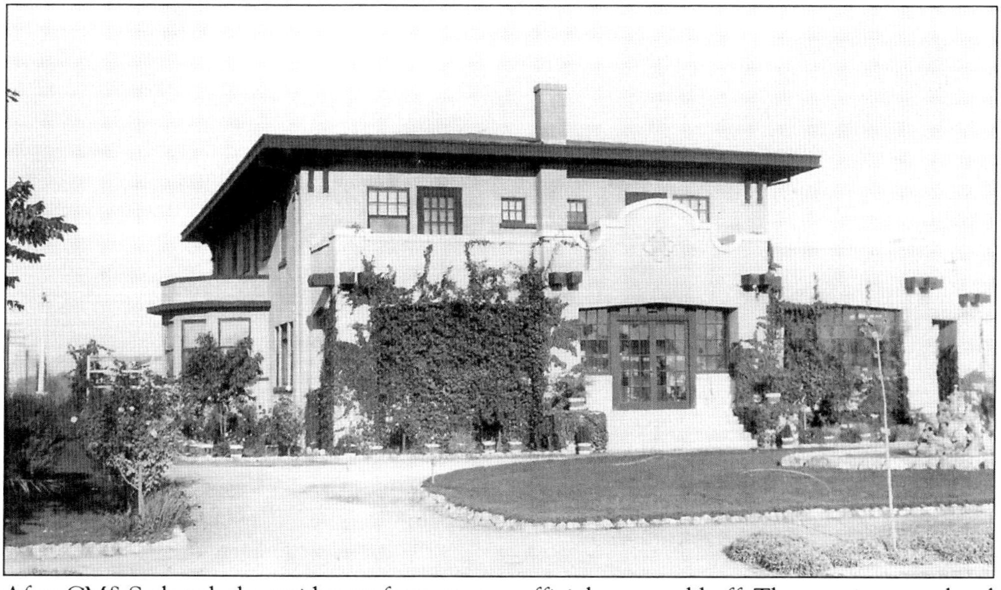

After CM&S closed, the residences for company officials were sold off. The area is now a local historic district that includes the president's home, pictured here.

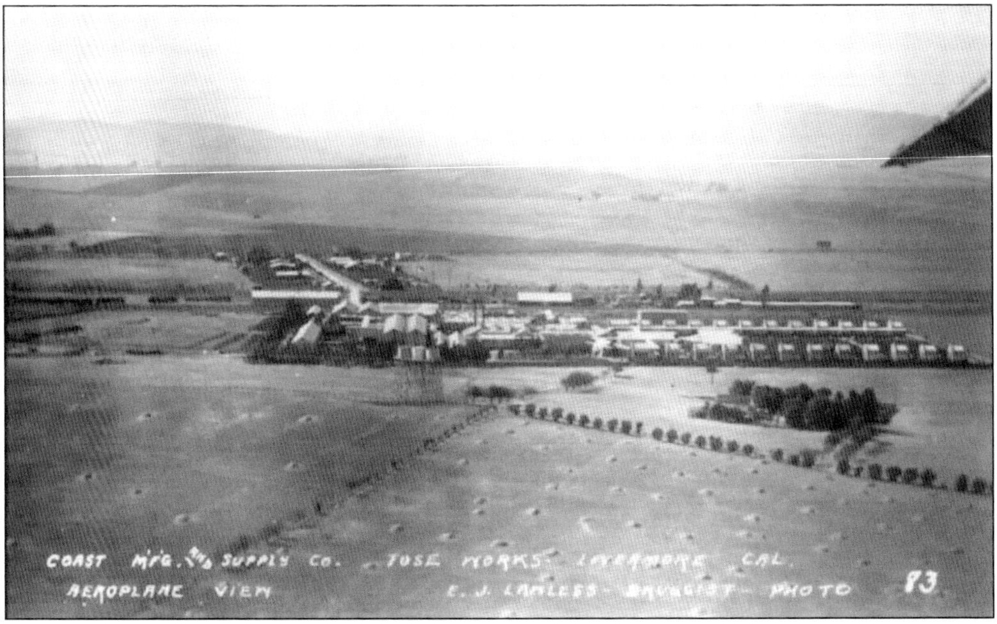

Coast Manufacturing employed up to 20 Chinese workers from 1913 until around 1924. Their dexterous hands were particularly adept at handling the "fuse line." Their quarters were located in the grove of trees, pictured here below the plant.

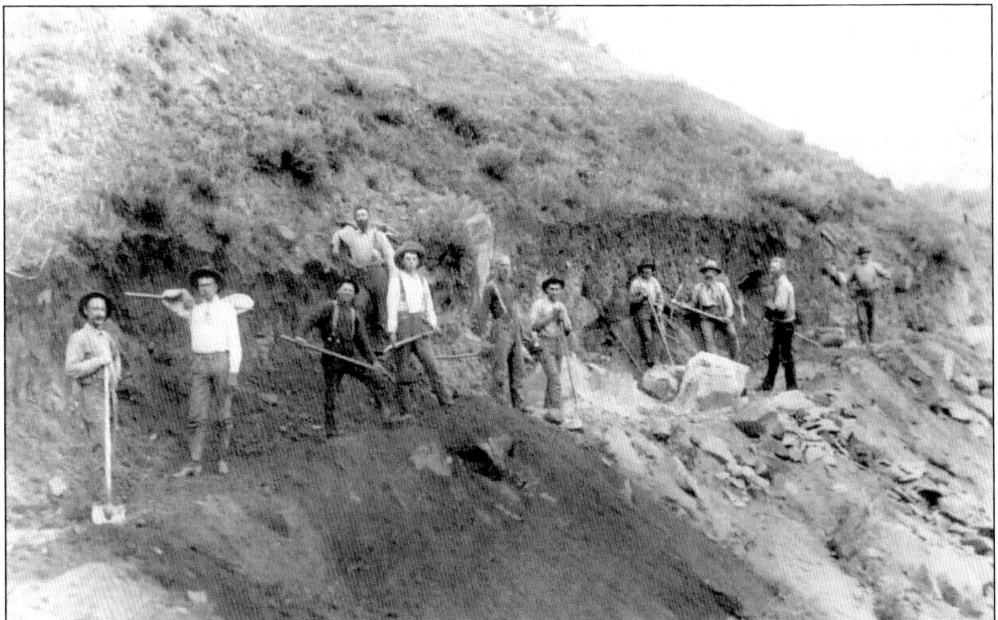

Before 1890, any product from the mines had to be transported into Livermore by horse or mule. Cutting down a slope was hard labor for this crew creating a roadway.

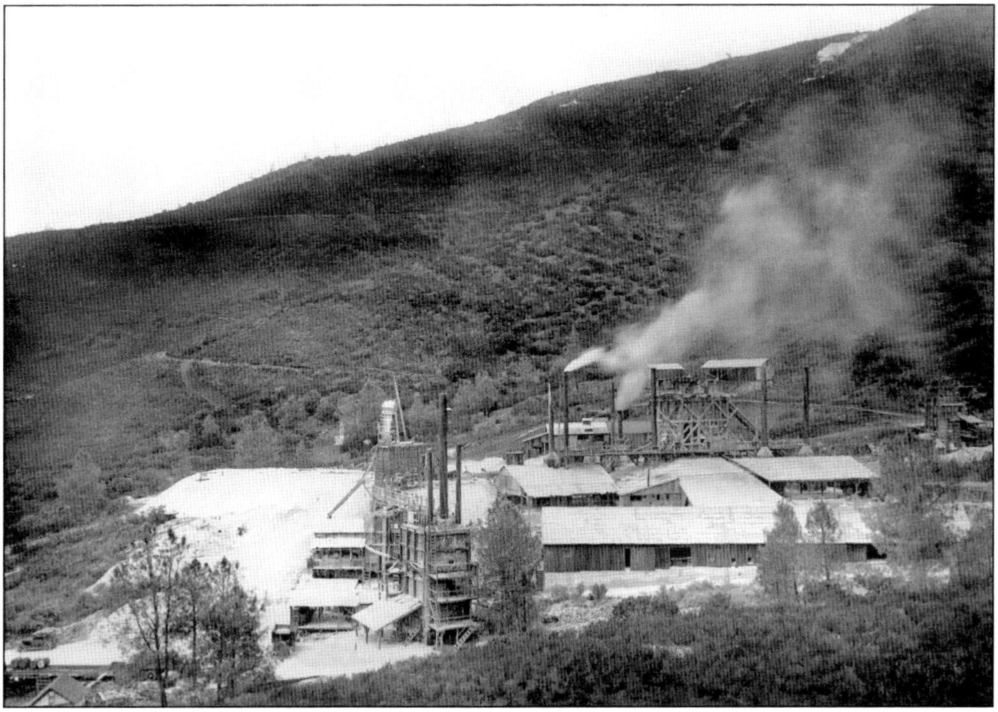

Magnesite is "calcined" (pulverized) to prepare the ore for commercial purposes.

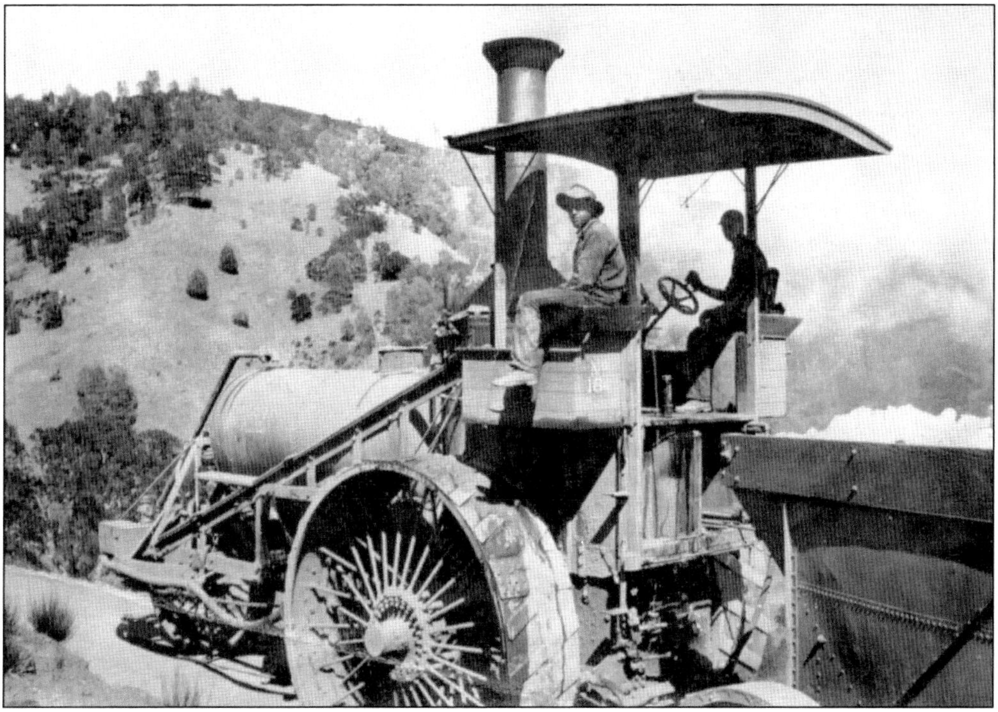

In the 19th century, magnesite was packed out on mules and horses; later a three-wheeled tractor pulling mine cars brought the product down to the shipping point in Livermore. By 1920, trucks were hauling the magnesite into town. On the return trip, trucks brought up fuel for the furnaces.

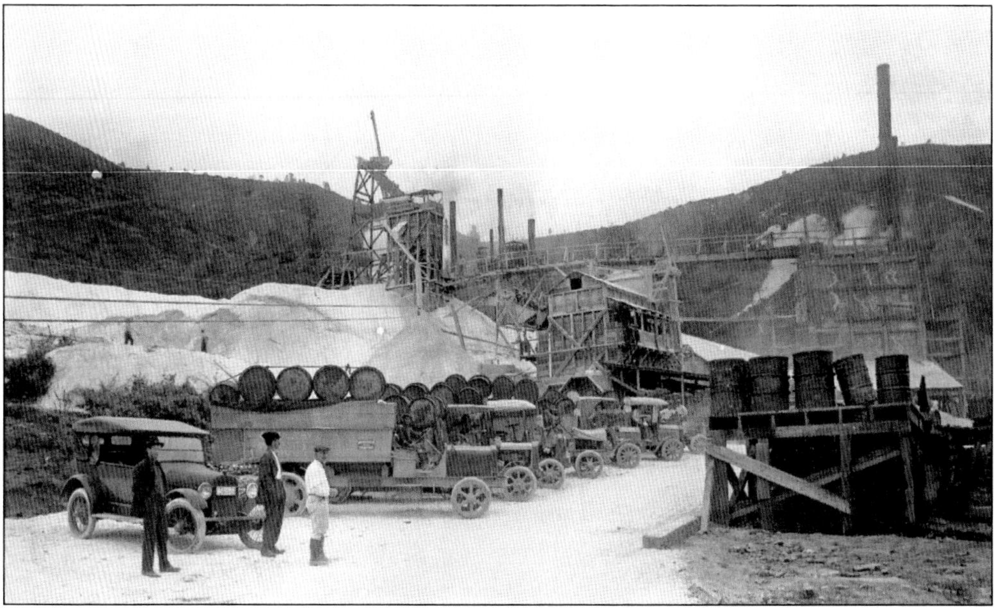

In the 1880s, magnesite mines in the hills south of Livermore were being exploited. Mining this mineral was big business about the time of World War I. This product is an ingredient in today's Milk of Magnesia.

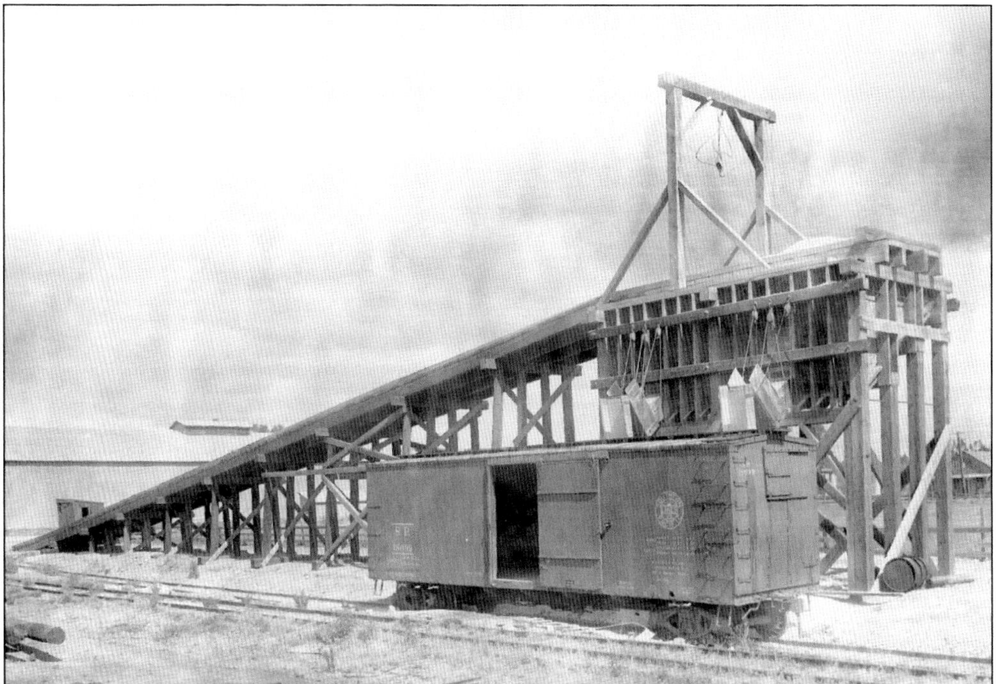

A truck loaded with magnesite backed up the ramp and the product was dumped into a boxcar. There were two ramps in Livermore, one on each rail line.

Eight

BUSINESS

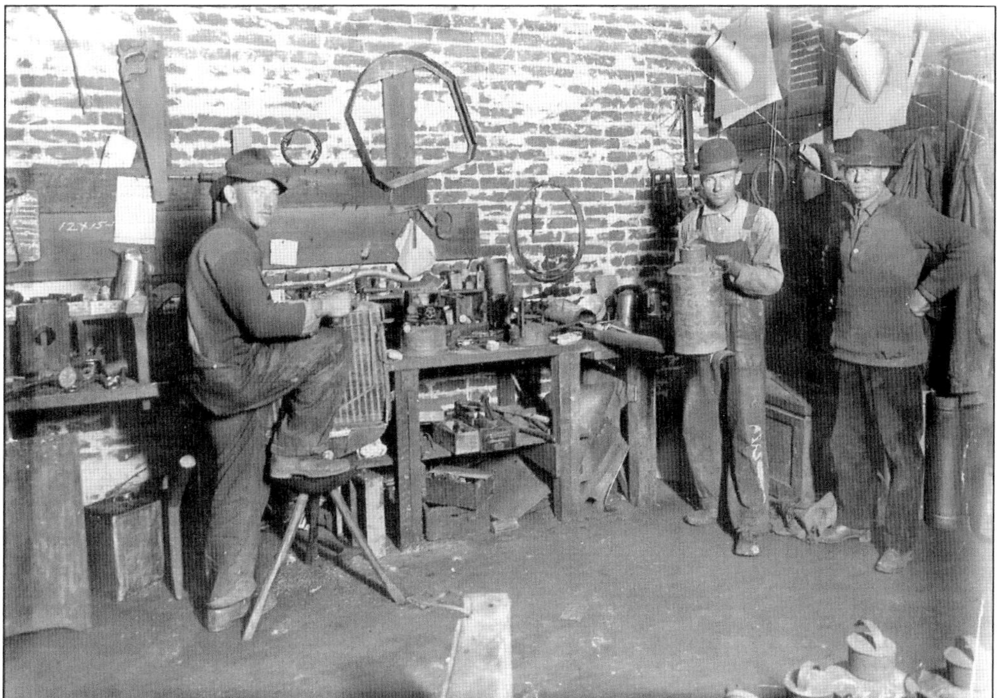

The Valley Hardware Company was located next to the Odd Fellows building on First Street. Pictured here *c.* 1920, the business would be bought out by the Livermore Commercial Company in 1929.

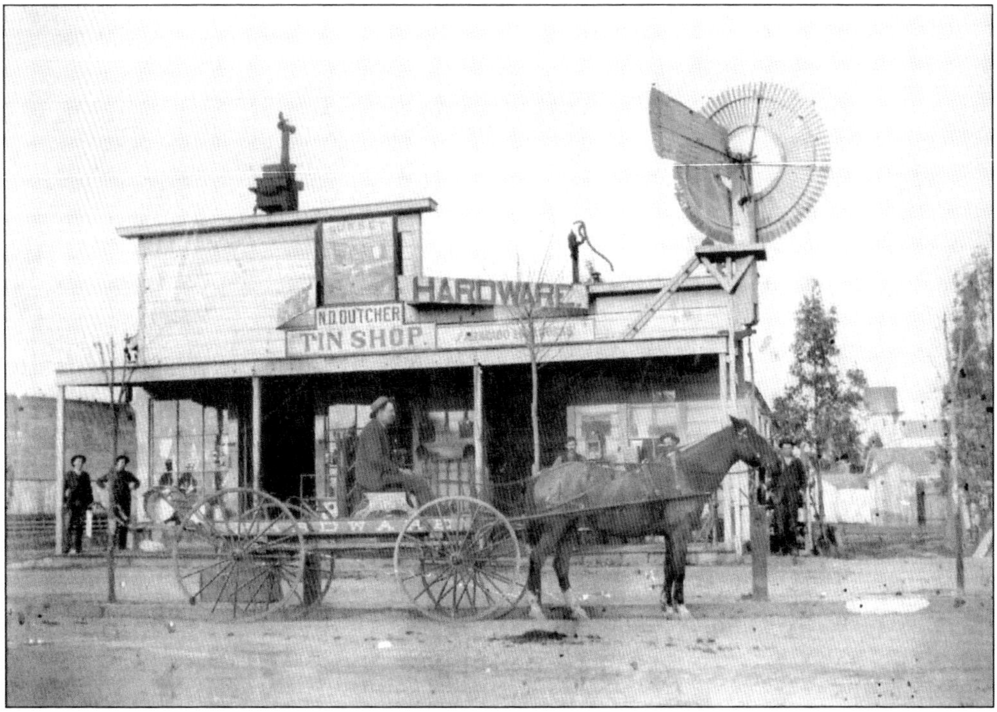

In 1876, Norris Dutcher's tin shop could be found on the east side of Livermore Avenue midway between First Street and the CPRR railroad tracks.

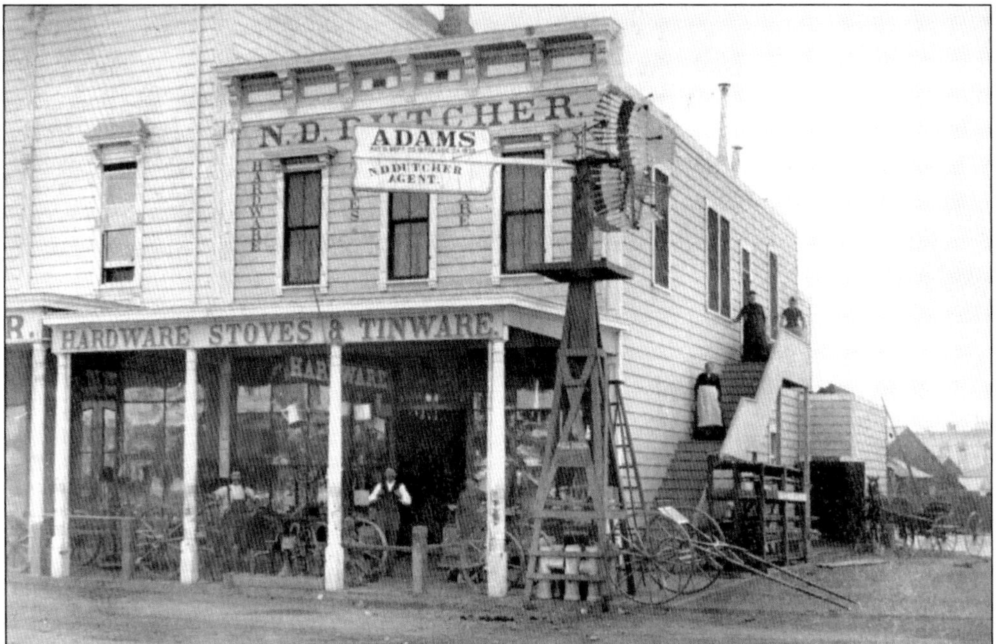

By 1884, Dutcher had moved his business to First Street, east of Livermore Avenue. Within 15 years, N. D. Dutcher Hardware was the largest hardware and tinware business outside of Oakland in Alameda County.

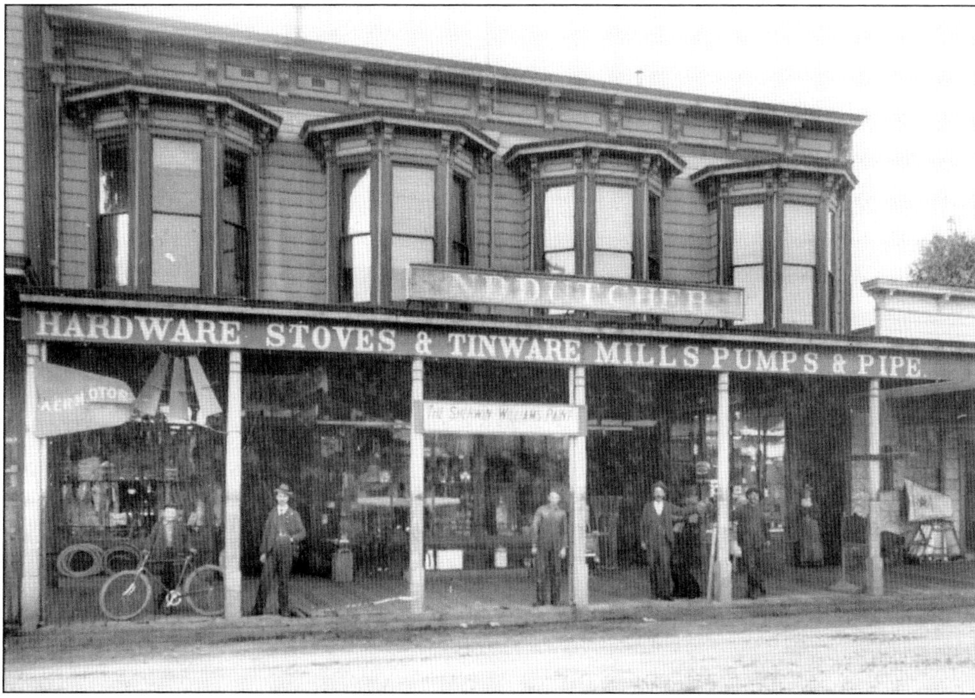

Around 1896, Dutcher had enlarged his building again.

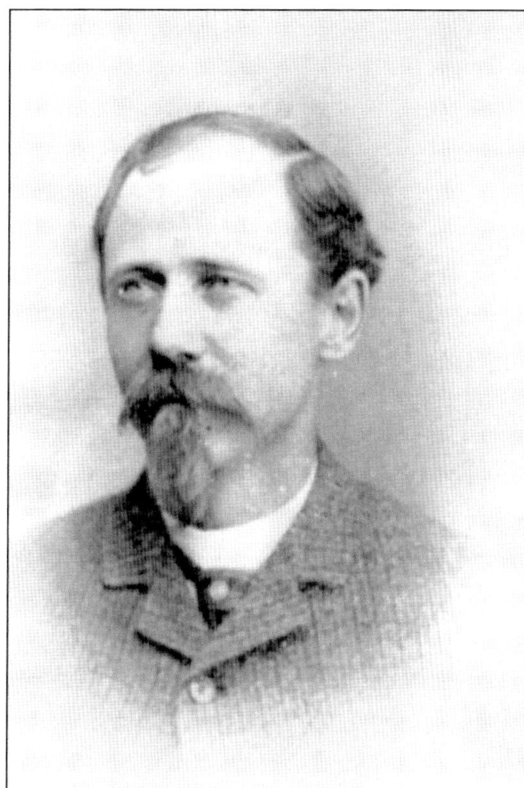

Norris Dutcher came to Laddsville in 1868 and began work as an apprentice blacksmith with James Beazell and later with R. N. Caughell. He worked as a store clerk for Charles Whitmore at his store at First and K Streets, and in 1876, he and his brother opened a tin shop under the name Dutcher Brothers. The partnership was dissolved in 1877.

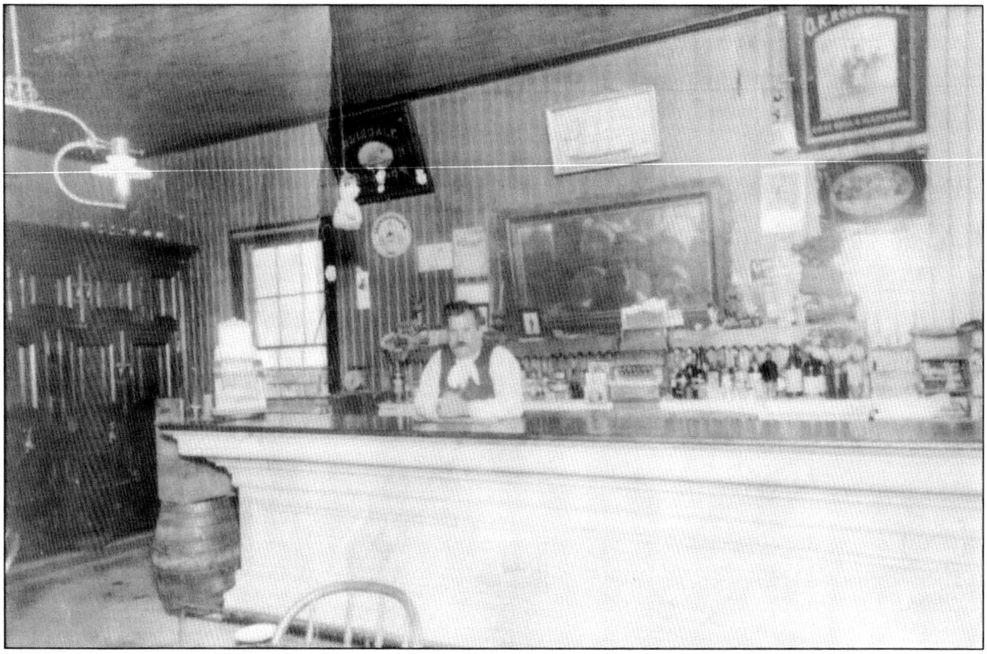

John Azevedo tended his Bismarck Saloon at the southeast corner of Chestnut and Livermore Avenue in 1912. By 1916, he had converted his place into a grocery store.

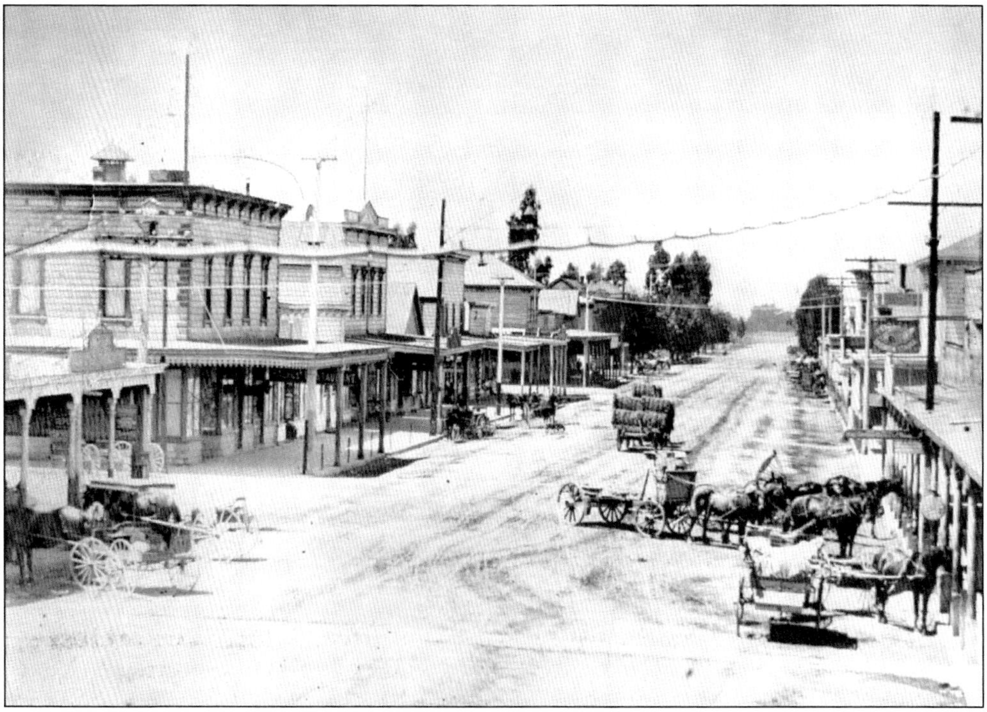

It was a lazy day in Livermore when this photograph was taken from the Livermore Hotel balcony around 1890. Buggies are clustered around the post office, right, while townsfolk pick up their mail. The wires running across the upper third of this photograph are the telephone lines. Livermore was the 29th town in California to have telephone service.

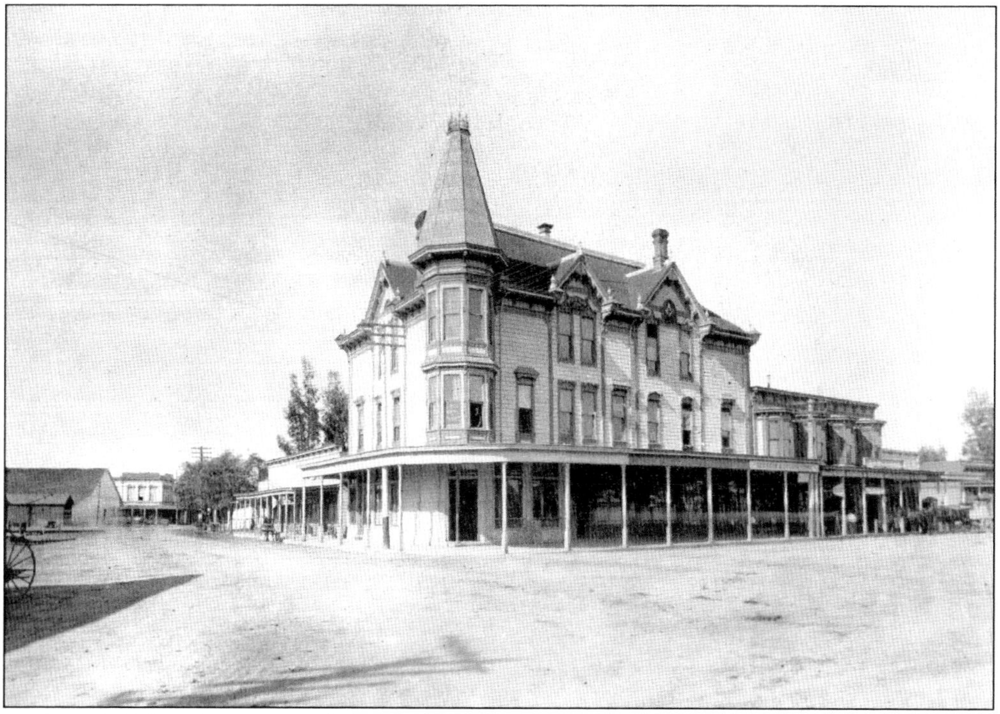

Andrew J. McLeod constructed this building in 1886 as a replacement for his Bank Exchange building that burned in 1882. It was the only three-story building in Livermore until modern times. The third floor was home to the local Masonic lodge until 1907.

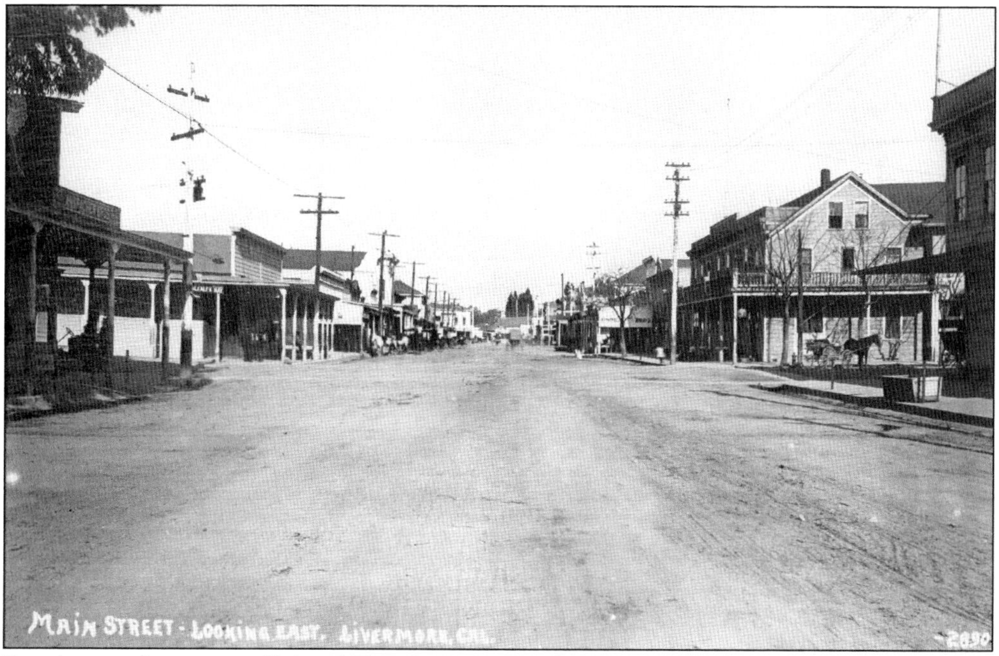

Standing at the corner of M and First Streets around 1890, a visitor might have seen this vista to the east. On the right is the Washington Hotel, on the left is Anspacher Brothers Mercantile, and in the distance is the Livermore Hotel.

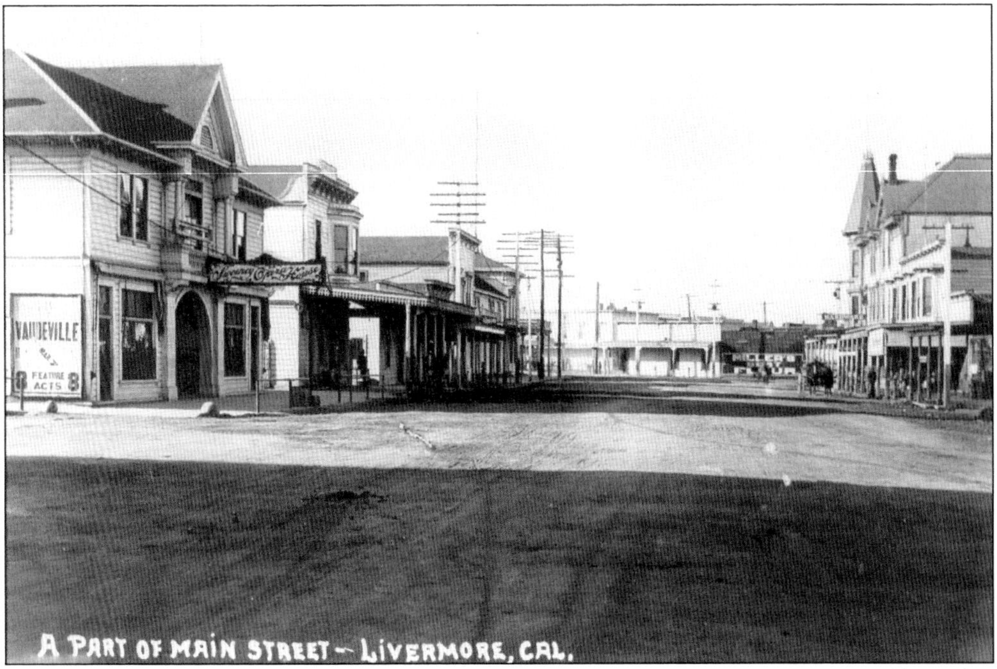

Standing at the intersection of First and McLeod Streets, looking west, a visitor would see this view around 1910. Sweeney's Opera House is on the left. N. D. Dutcher's hardware store and the McLeod Building are on the right.

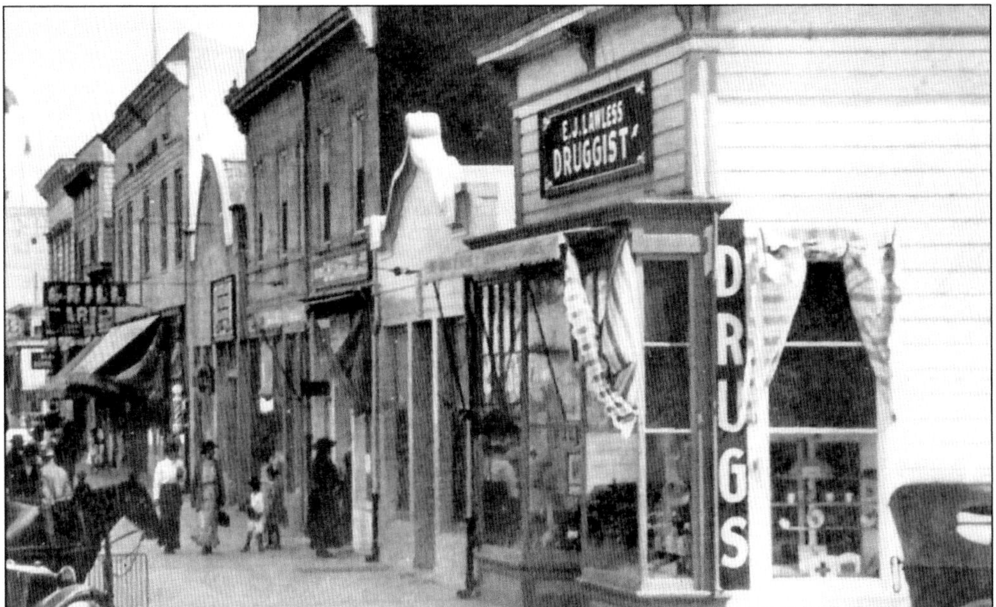

E. J. Lawless's drugstore was located on the southeast corner of First and K Streets. This photograph is dated after 1912 because the previous building was destroyed by fire in 1911.

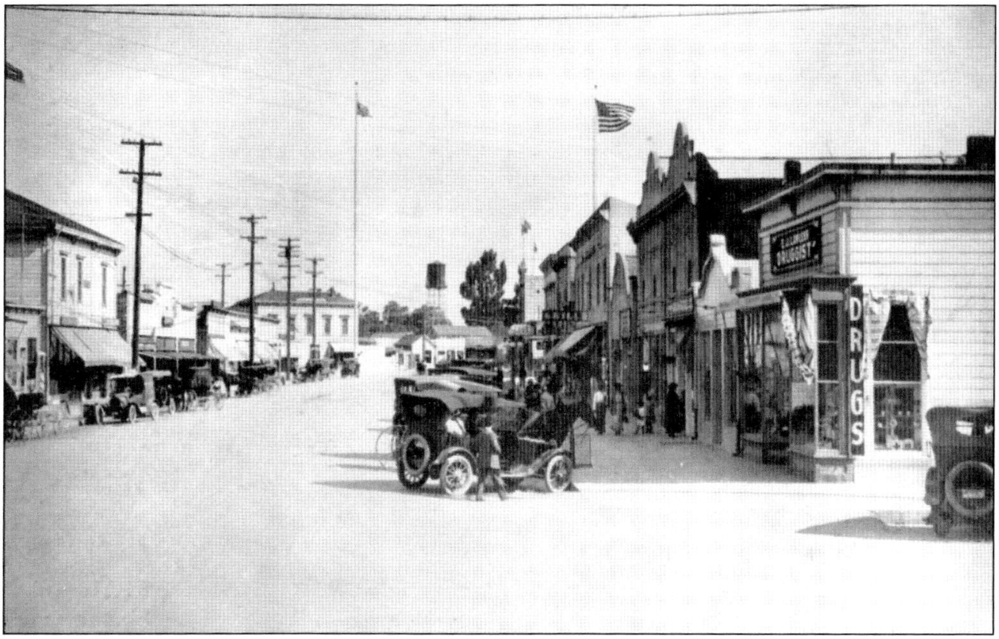

First Street, the commercial center of the community, was always a busy thoroughfare. By 1915, when this photograph was taken near the corner of K and First, the automobile had generally replaced the horse and buggy. Canvas awnings on the storefronts were replacing the old wooden sunshades.

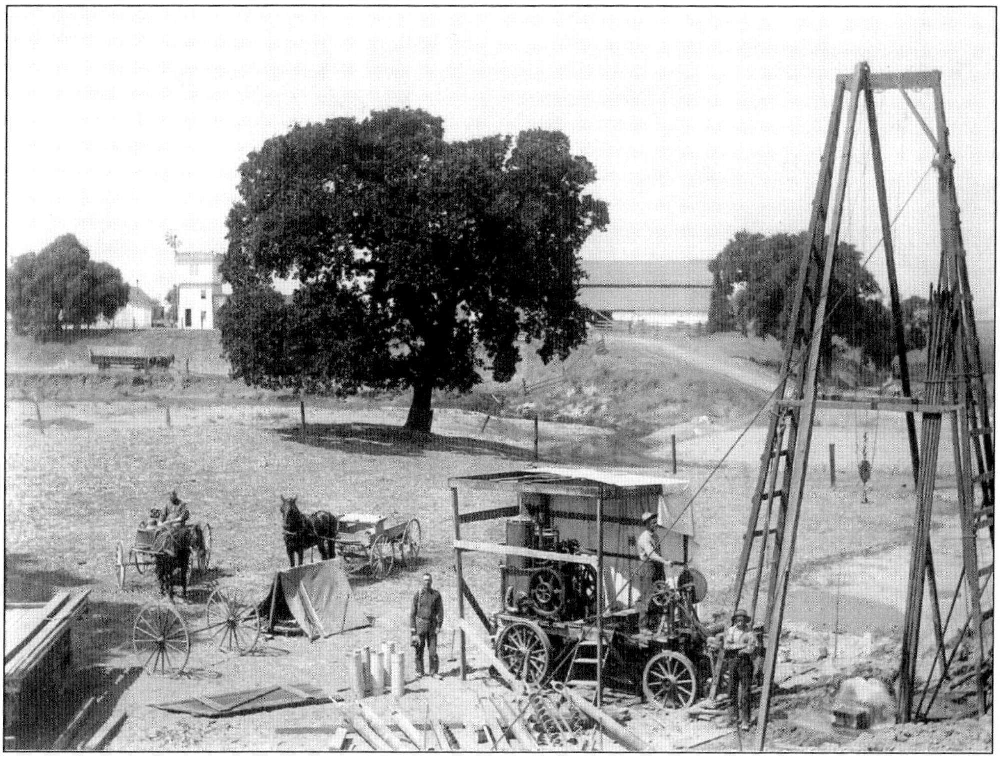

Fred Brenzel was one of the local well drillers. Here he is practicing his trade about 1900.

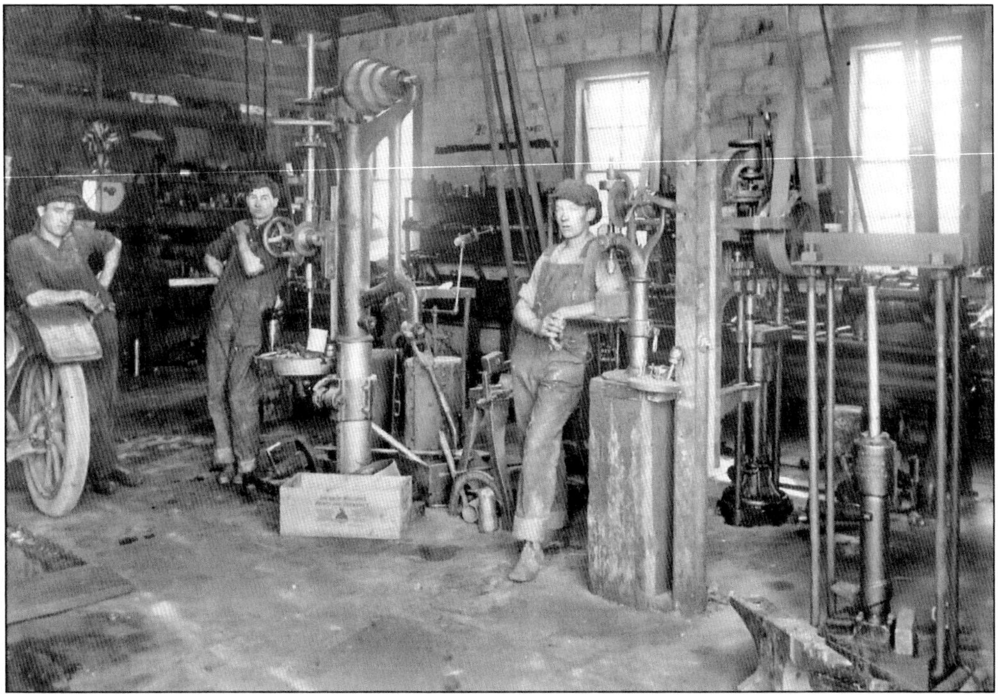

Opposite McLeod Street on the north side of First Street was the Valley Garage. Working in the machine shop are George Johnson, John Neinberg, and Harry (Skinny) Johnson.

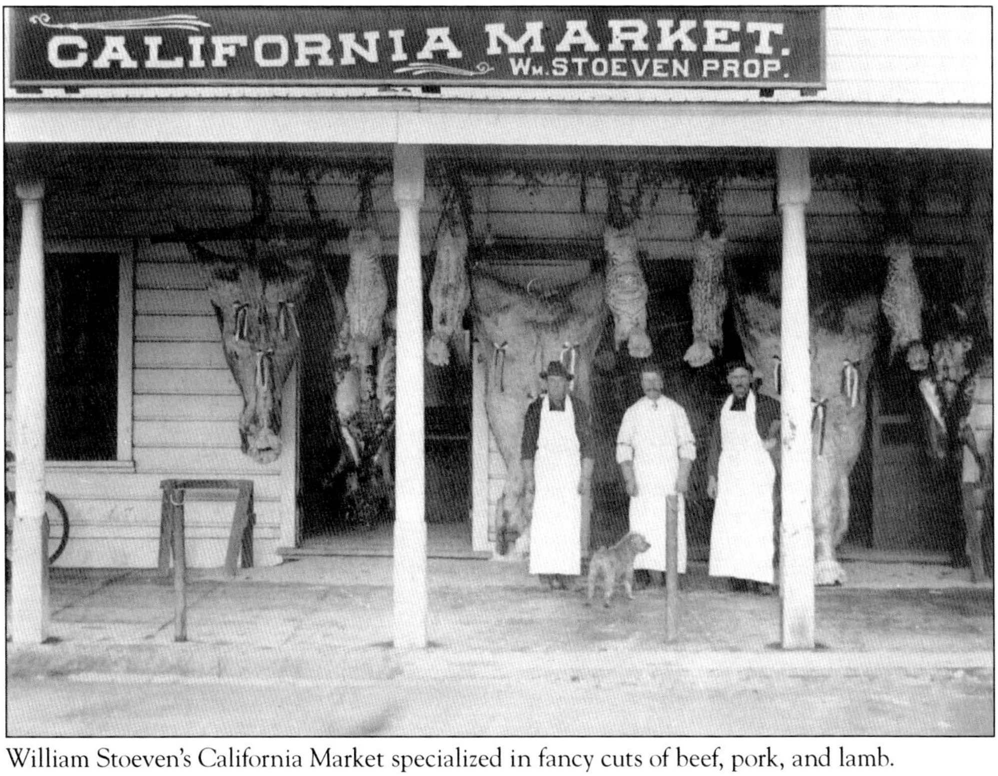

William Stoeven's California Market specialized in fancy cuts of beef, pork, and lamb.

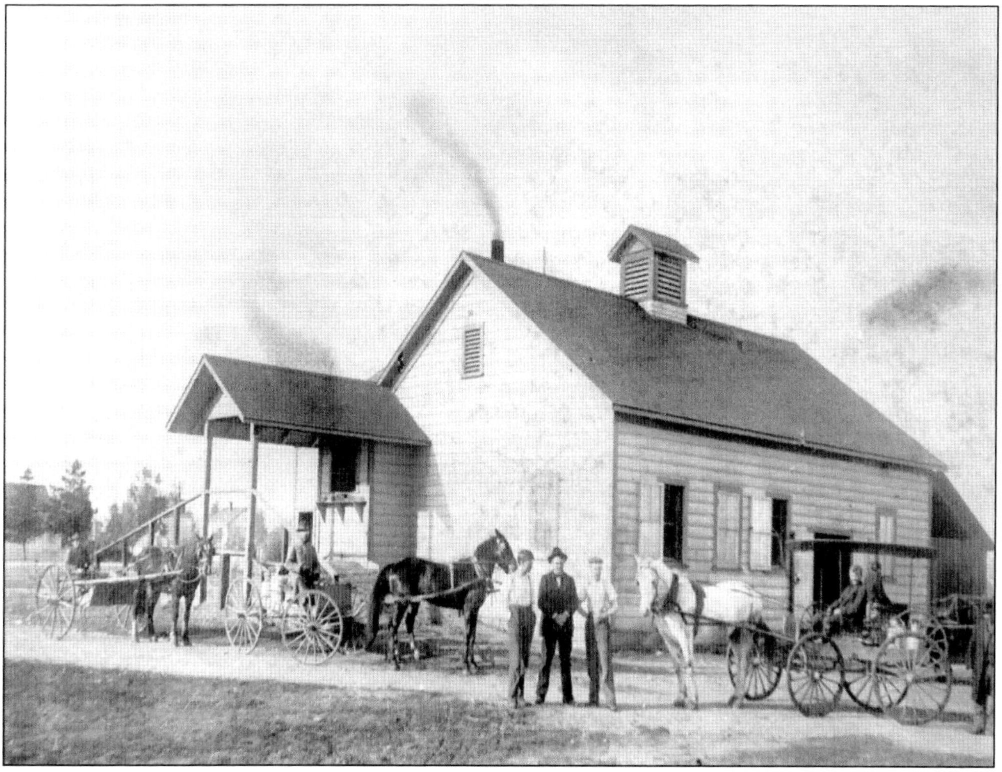

The Livermore Creamery at Sixth and Maple Streets, pictured here about 1900, was under the management of Archie Young. His younger brother, Fred, took over the business in 1912.

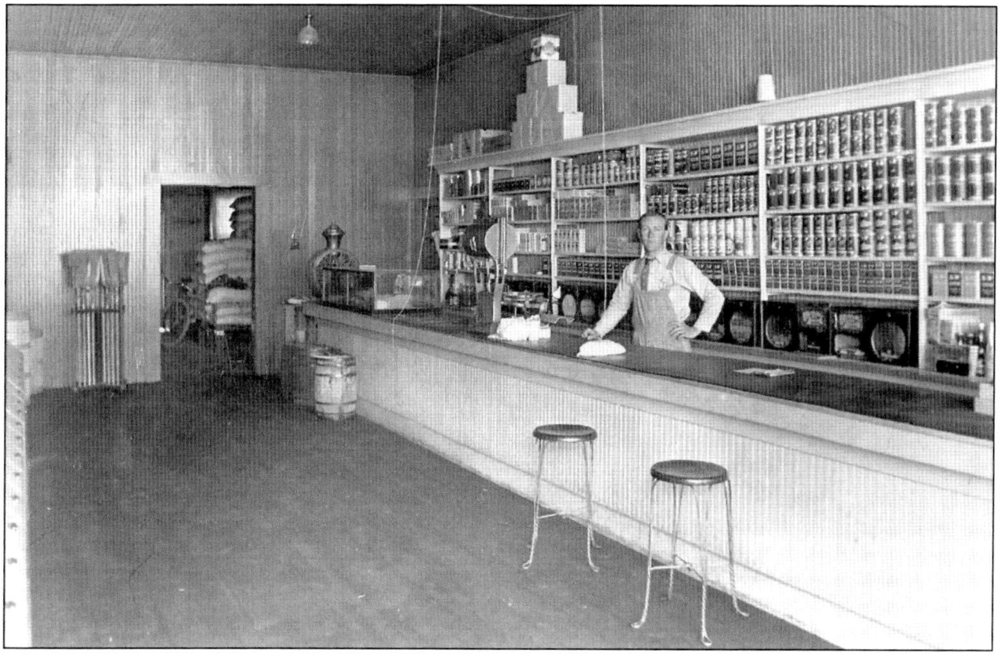

The Livermore Commercial Company was located on Livermore Avenue with an entrance on First Street. The store clerk was Joe Callaghan.

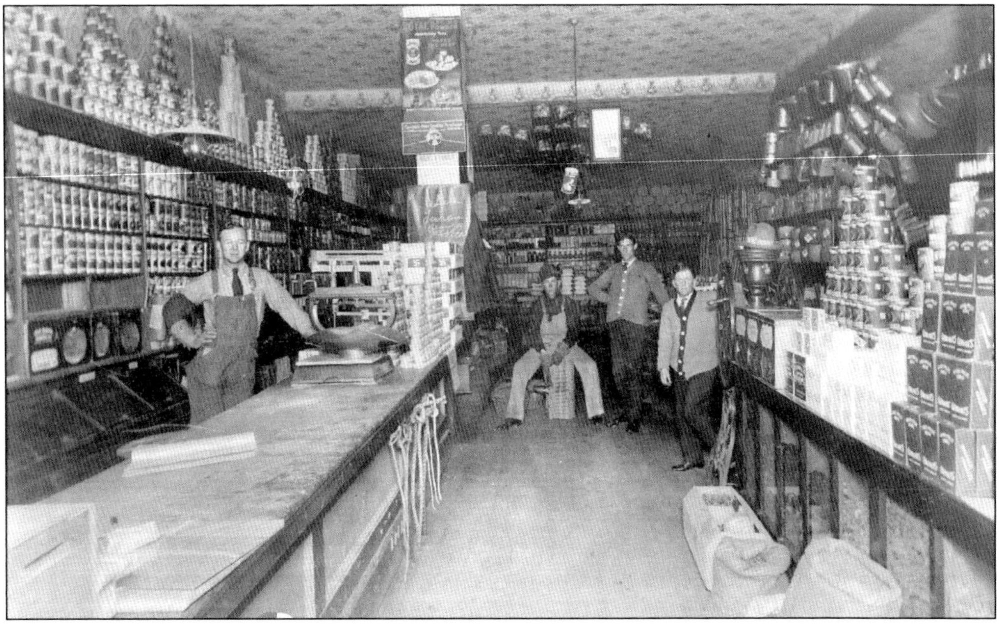

George Beck's grocery was located on First Street until he moved to the newly built Foresters Hall in 1915. His staff included Archie Bowles (behind the counter), Jessie Bowles, Marshall Pratt, and Roy Beck.

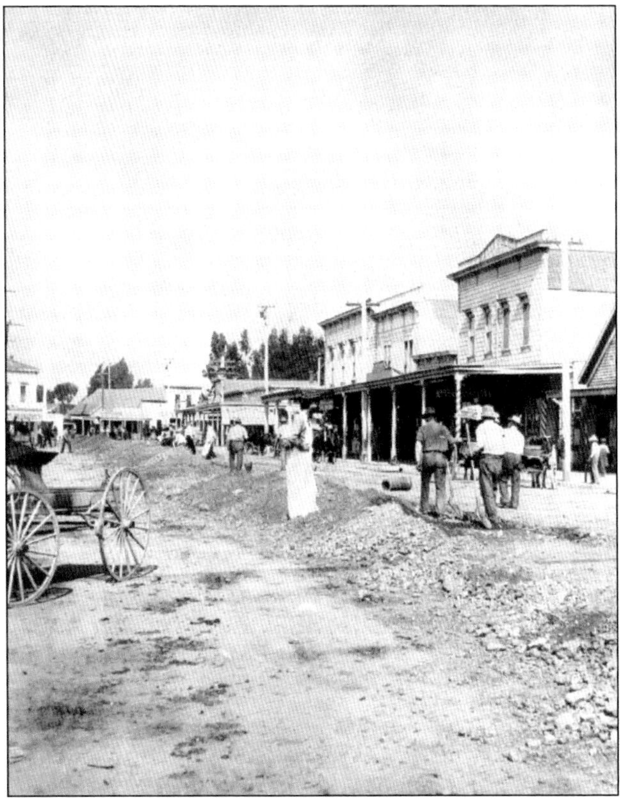

To help alleviate the problem of muddy streets, the town trustees authorized the installation of a storm drain down the middle of First Street in 1909. Mally's Hotel between J and K Streets is in the background on the right side.

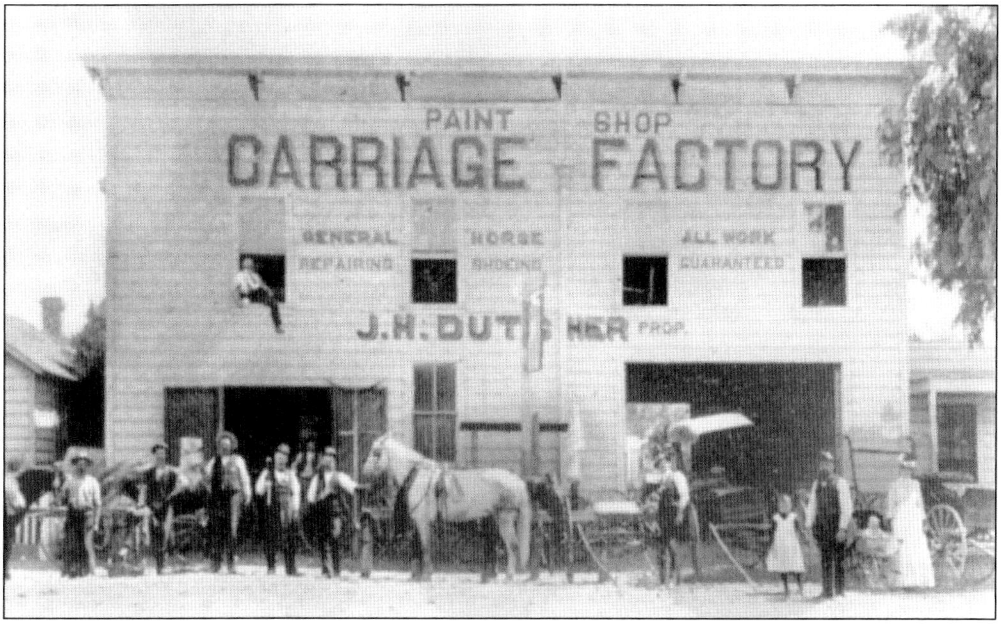

A necessary business in Livermore in 1896 was Jay Dutcher's Carriage Factory. His service included carriage and buggy repair, horse shoeing, and carriage repainting.

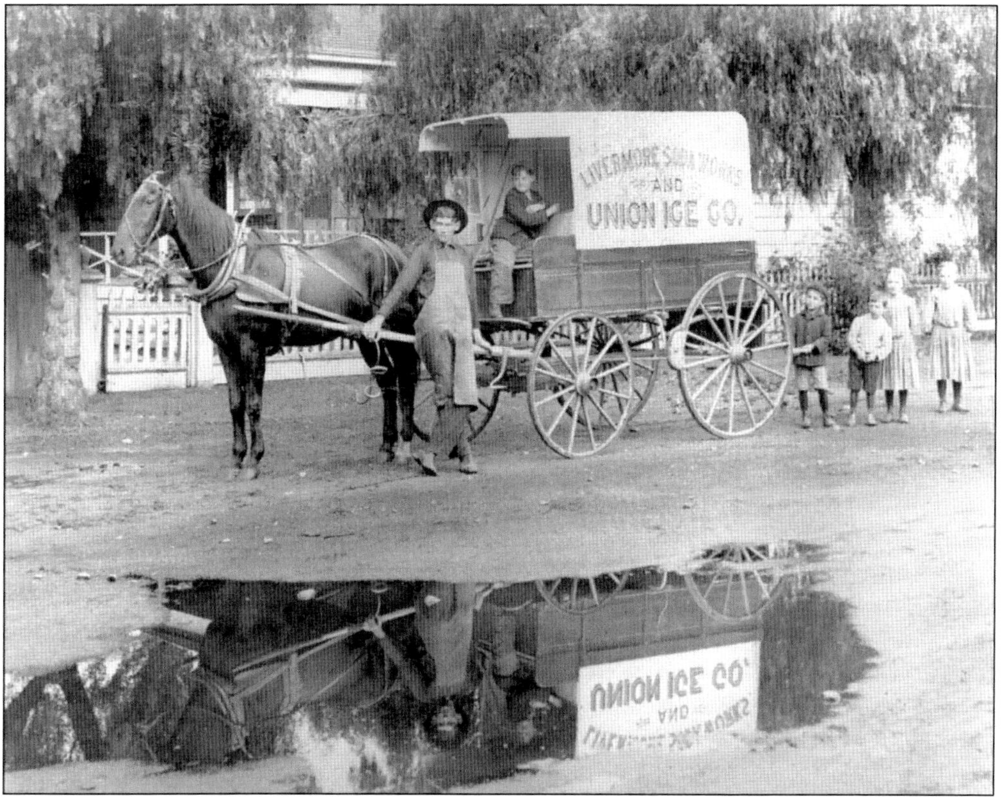

Ernest Uttendorfer delivered soft drinks and ice for the Livermore Soda Works and Union Ice Company. The soda works was located at Sixth and K Streets.

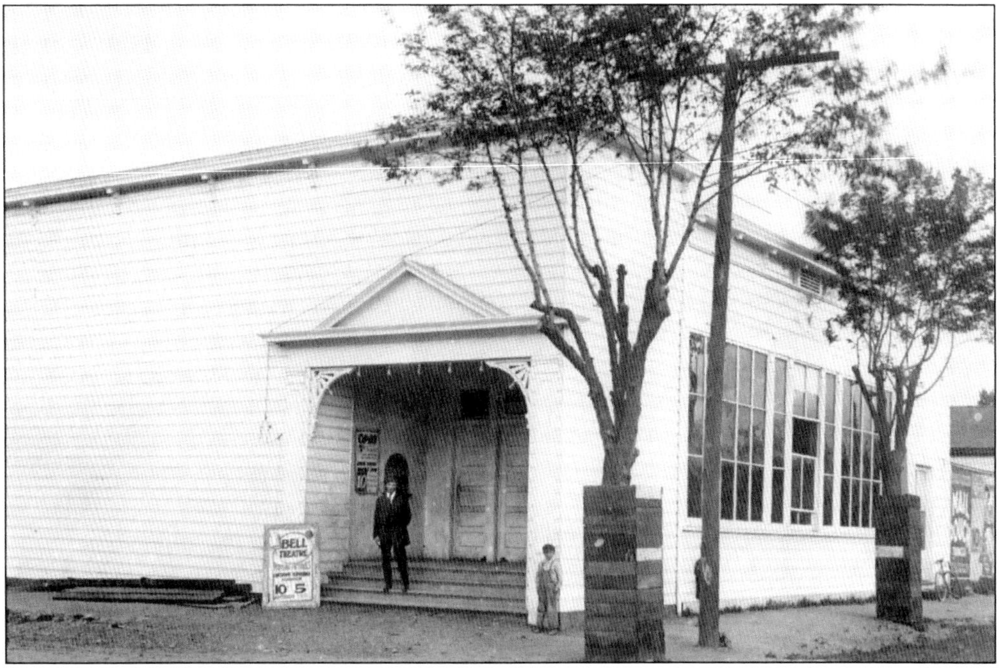

McVicar Hall at the southeast corner of Second and J Streets was a roller-skating rink by day and the Bell Theater by night. The movie theater moved to the Schenone Building around 1914. Five years later, the McVicar building was a victim of arson.

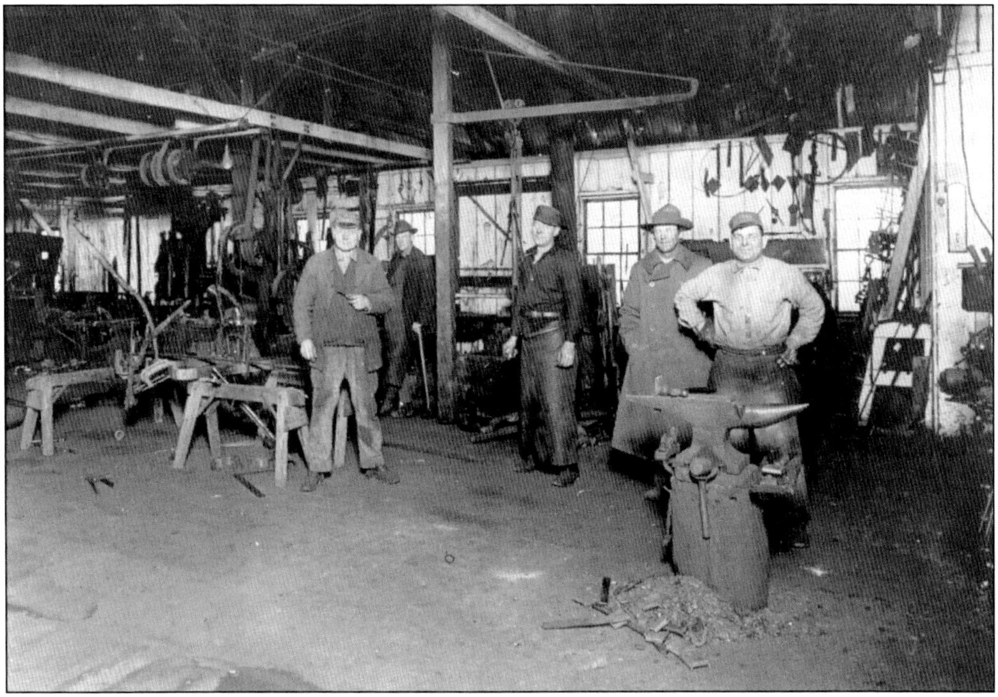

Bernhardt and Collldeweih's Blacksmith Shop had a lively business at the southwest corner of Second and L Streets. Here are Henry Collldeweih, unidentified, Roy Bernhardt, Tony Silva, and unidentified in the shop.

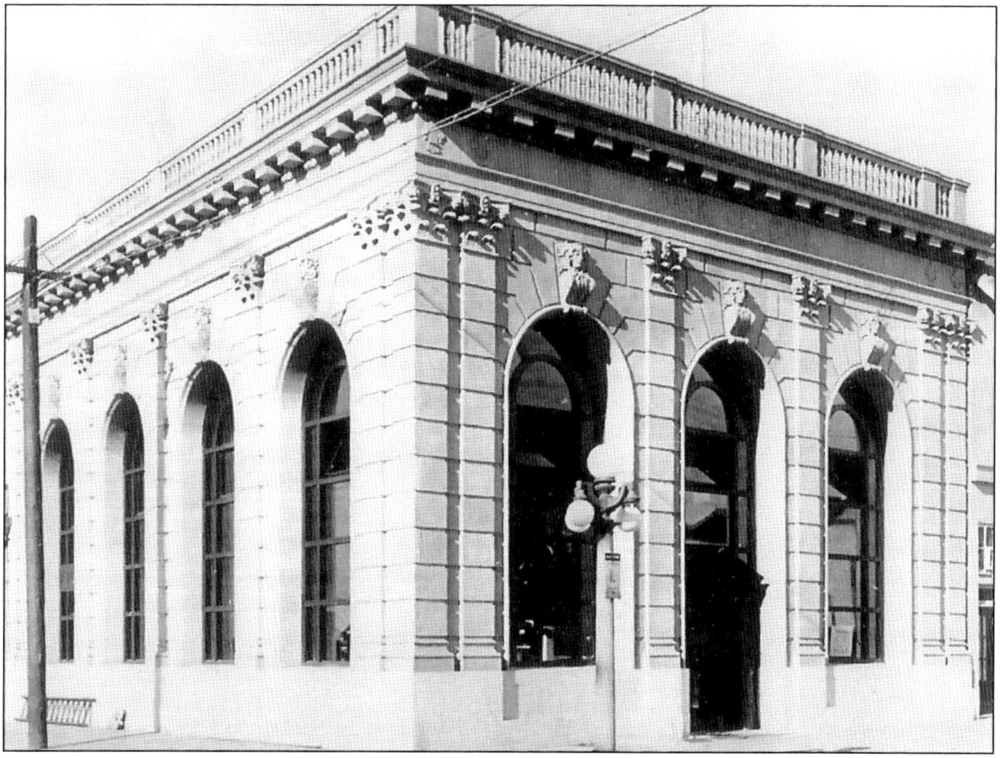

The Bank of Italy, which purchased the McLeod building, first opened a bank branch in a storefront on Livermore Avenue, just north of First Street, while the old building was being demolished. The bank constructed a new facility on the corner, opening for business on January 3, 1922, which still stands today.

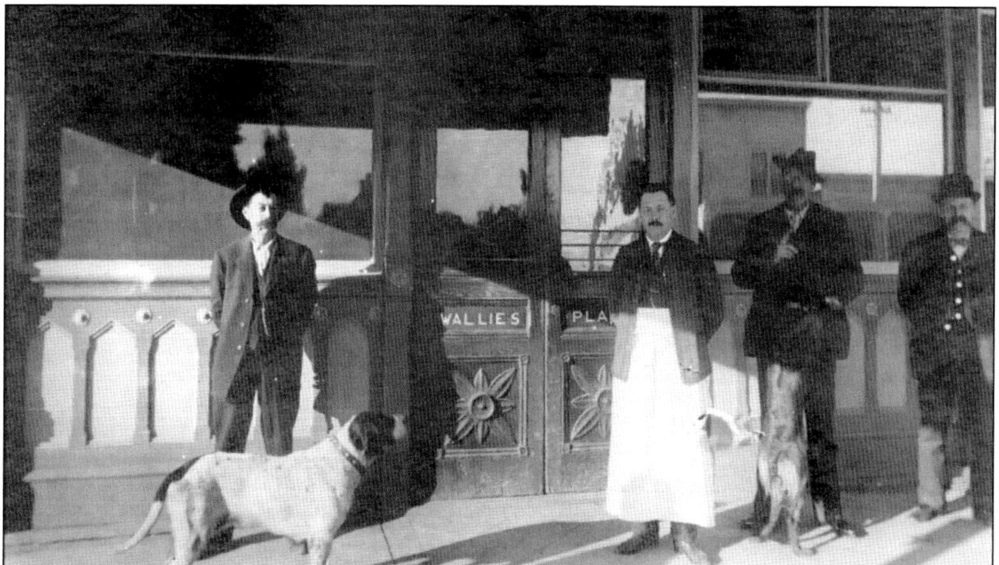

Wallie's Place on First Street near the flagpole was one of 22 saloons in Livermore at the turn of the 20th century. Farm hands who came in on Saturday night for a bath, a shave, and a beer kept Wallie Thomas busy dispensing beer brewed by the Livermore Brewery.

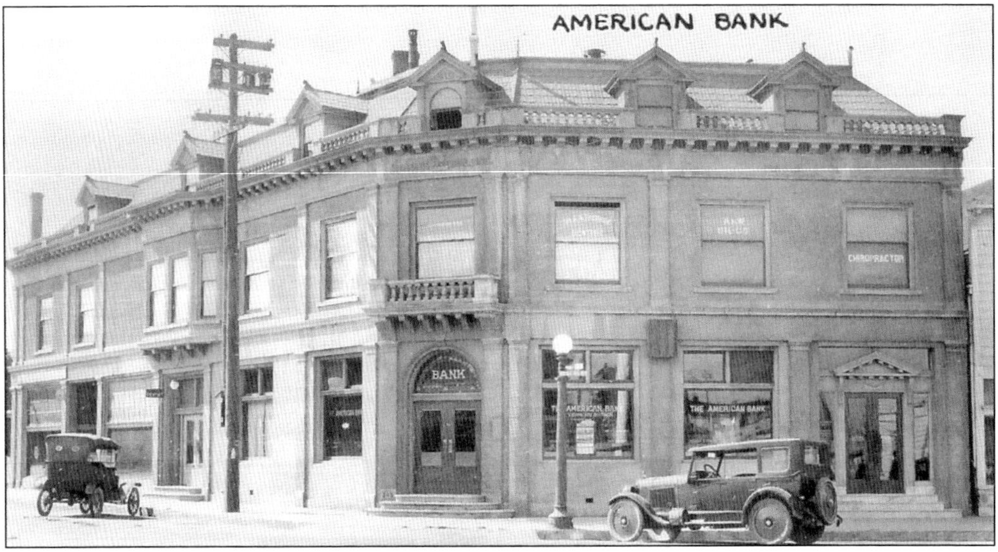

The Masonic Temple was constructed on the corner of First Street and Livermore Avenue in 1907. The upper floors were the lodge hall and professional offices. For many years, the ground floor housed banks—Livermore Savings Bank and American Trust Company that were later absorbed by Wells Fargo Bank.

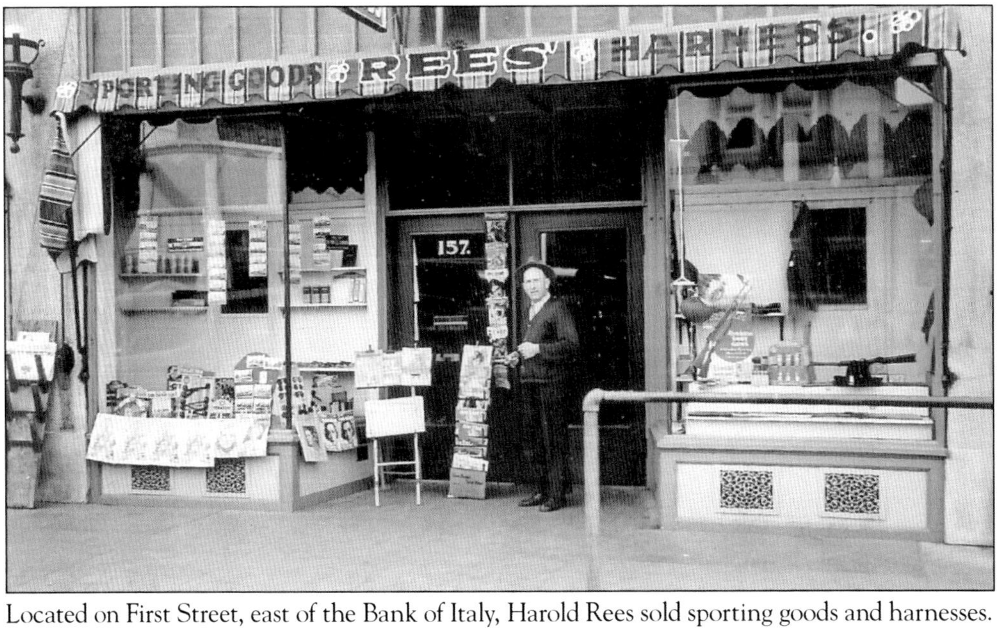

Located on First Street, east of the Bank of Italy, Harold Rees sold sporting goods and harnesses.

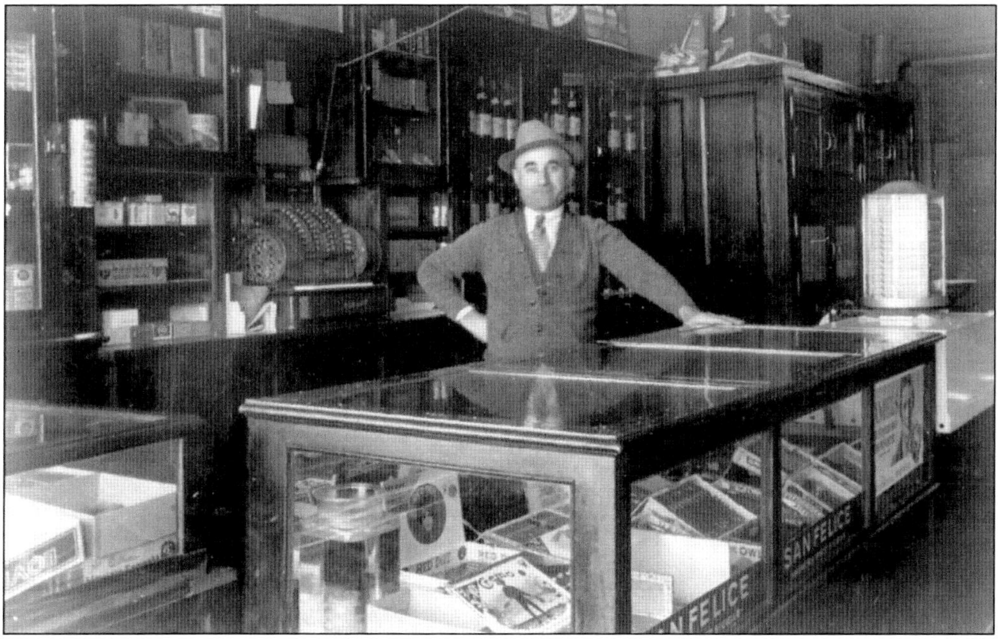

The location of the Hub, aptly named because it was located at a major intersection in the community, had been continuously occupied as a saloon since the town's beginning, although it was rebuilt in 1931. Joe Duarte was known for his fine selection of cigars.

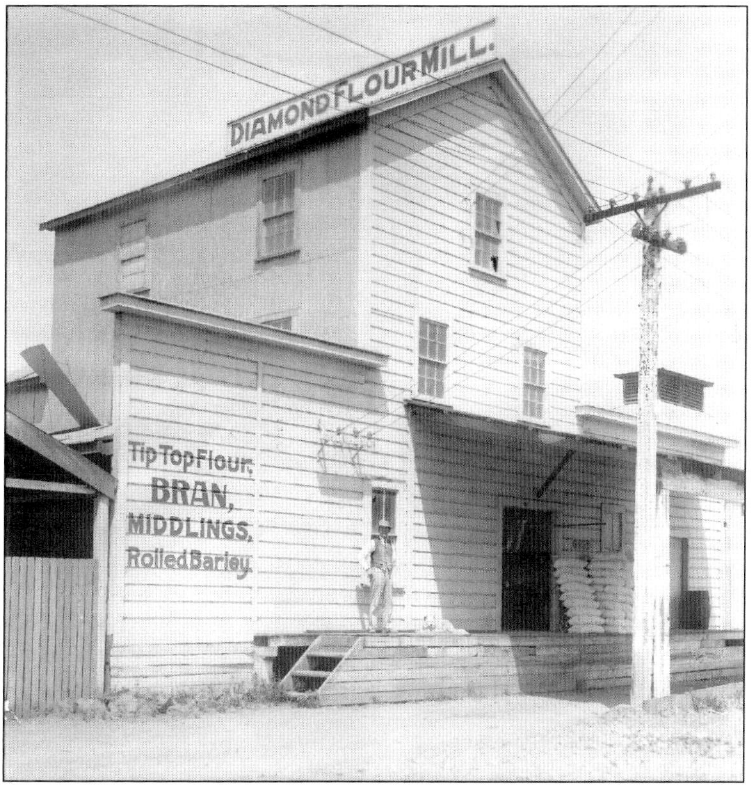

After Calvin Stevens's Livermore Valley Mills was destroyed by fire in 1882, a new mill, the Diamond Flour Mill, was built in 1884 at the corner of First and Maple Streets by W. F. and Antone Laumeister.

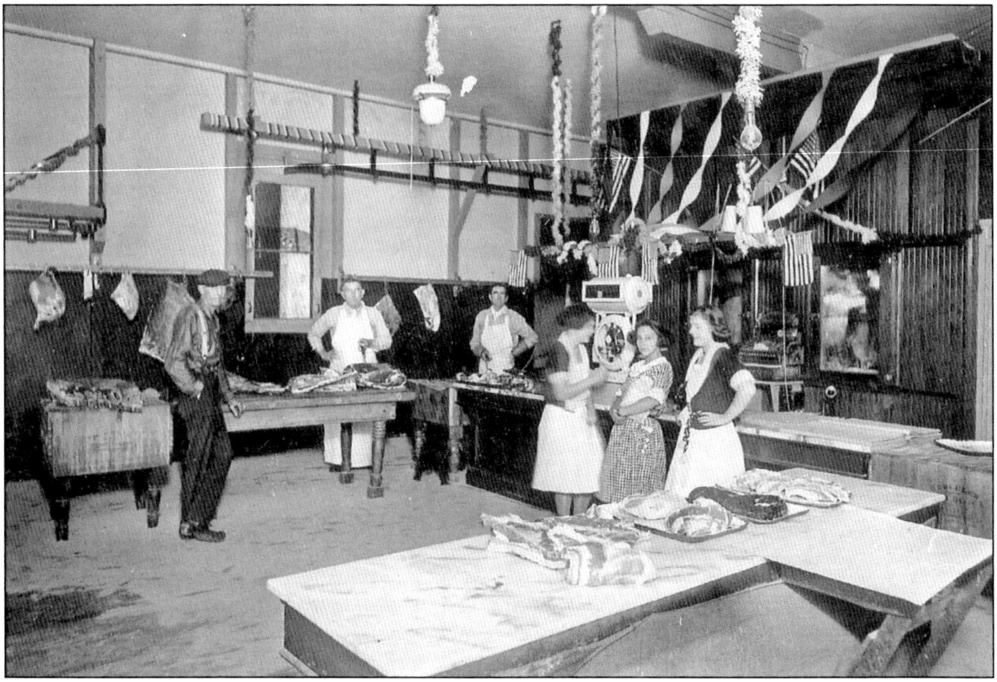

Dan Murray and George Collier were the proprietors of a butcher shop. Beginning in 1885, it was then located near Second and J Streets, a site later to become the location of the Foresters Hall.

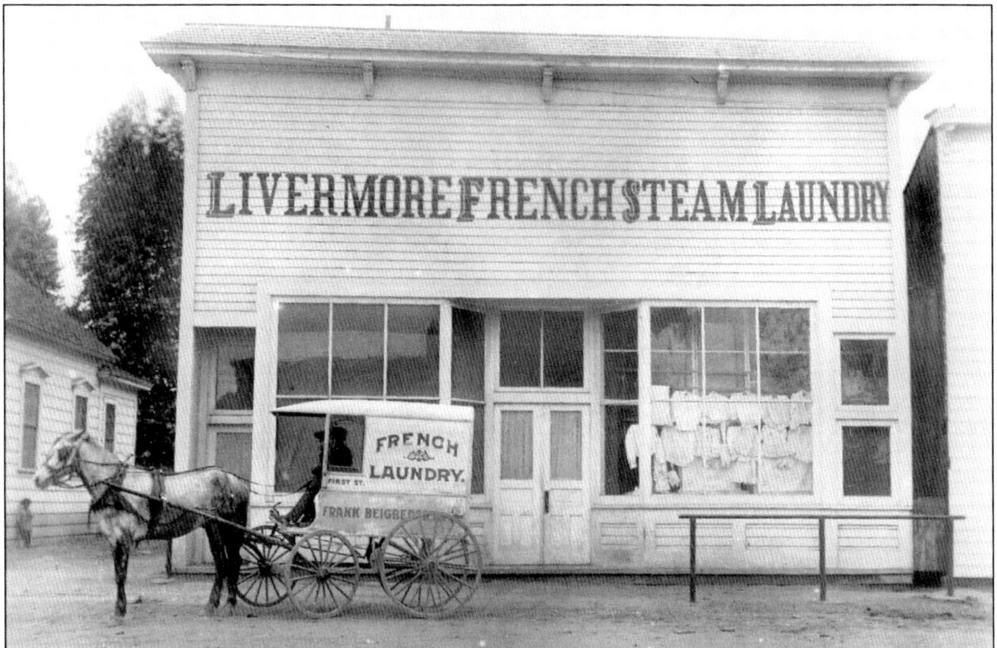

Frank Beigbeder's Livermore French Steam Laundry could be found on Second Street between Livermore Avenue and J Street. An arson fire in 1919 started in the old Bell Theater and spread east to consume Beigbeder's laundry, his home, and another residence at the Livermore corner.

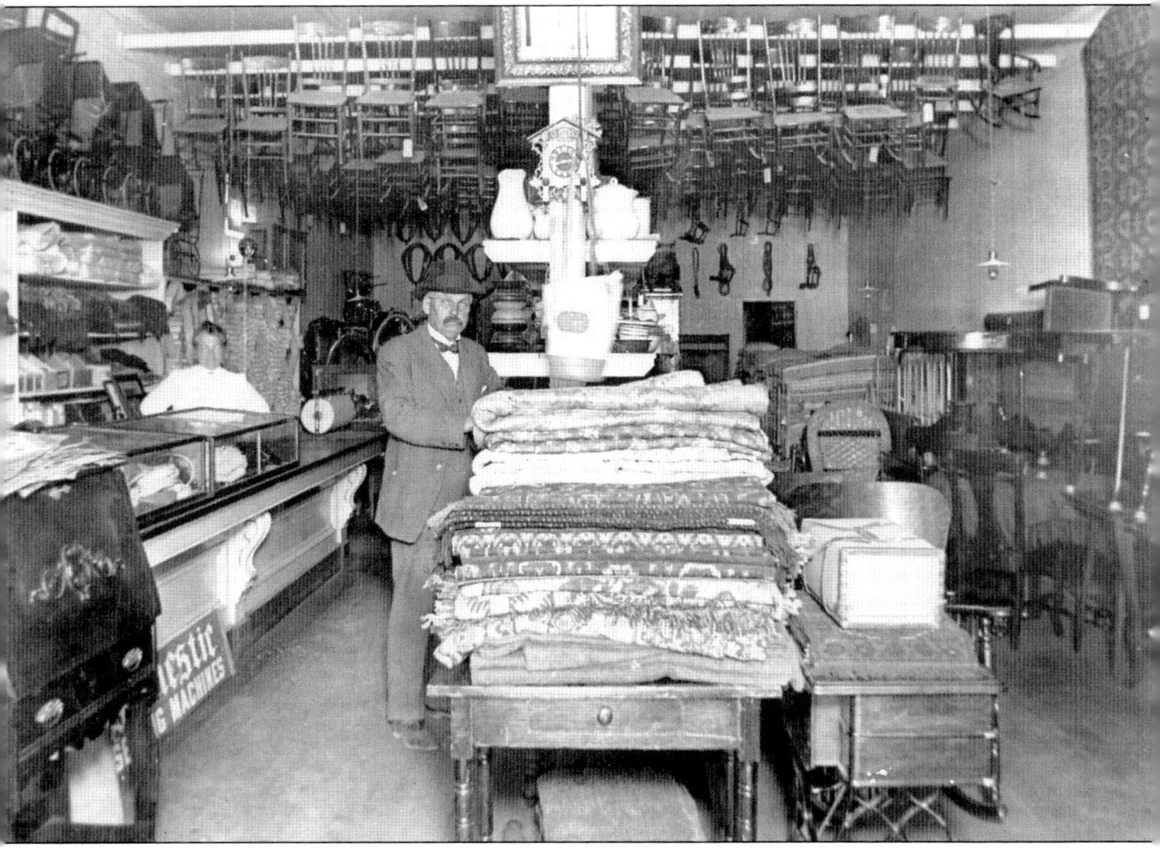

Theo Gorner came to Livermore in 1873 and purchased a harness business from George Beebe. He expanded his business by carrying a line of buggies and wagons. In 1884, he opened a furniture and upholstering business in the IOOF building. His stock in trade included tables and chairs, sewing machines, carpets and throw rugs, and even baby carriages. Gorner was also politically active as town treasurer and later town clerk in the 1870s. Although he passed away in 1911, his daughter Dora Gorner Meyers continued the business for another 40 years. Dora was the first woman member of the San Francisco Harness Dealers Association in 1915.

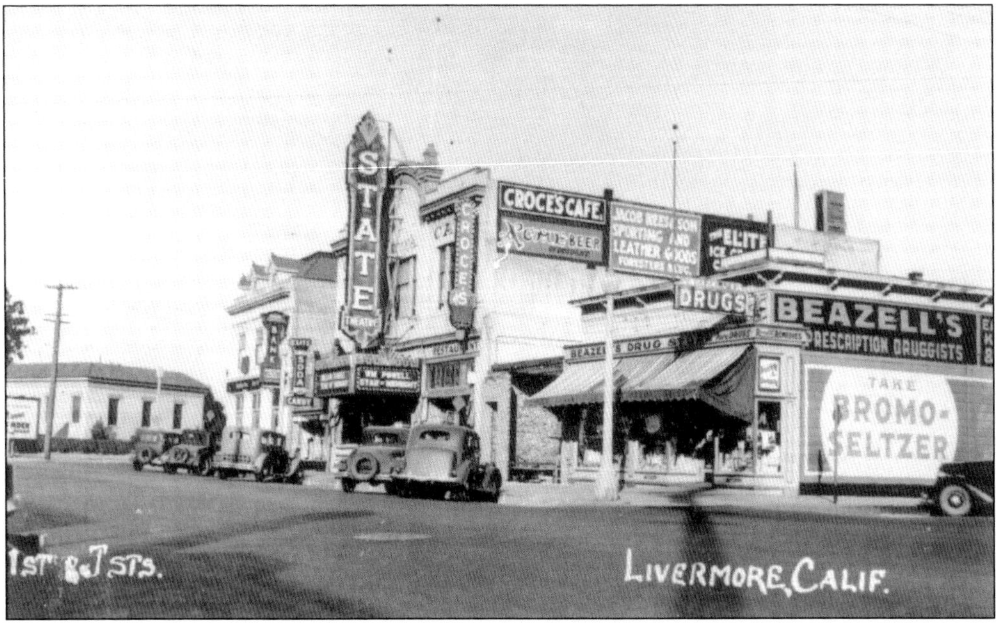

Standing on the north side of First Street, just west of J Street, one might have seen this vista after 1930. To the left of Beazell's Drug Store are the American Bakery, the Schenone Building with Croce's Café on the second floor, the Elite Ice Cream parlor, and the American Trust Company in the Masonic building. The structure on the left is the newly constructed telephone cross-bar station.

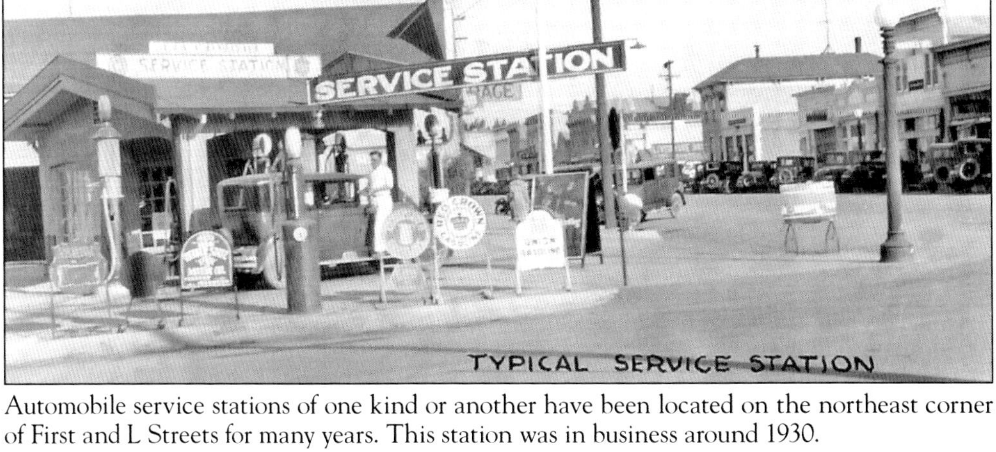

Automobile service stations of one kind or another have been located on the northeast corner of First and L Streets for many years. This station was in business around 1930.

Nine

SPORTS

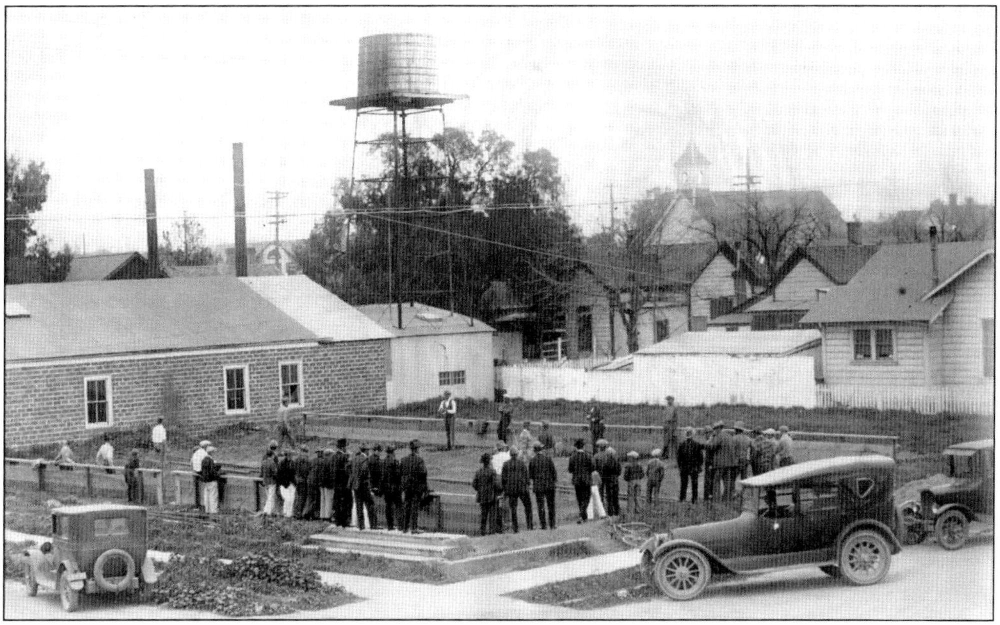

In 1927, an eight-lane horseshoe court was opened at the corner of Second and J Streets. A horseshoe club was organized with E. J. Lawless acting as president. Before this court, the public was encouraged to use the horseshoe courts on the American Legion Club House property at Third and McLeod.

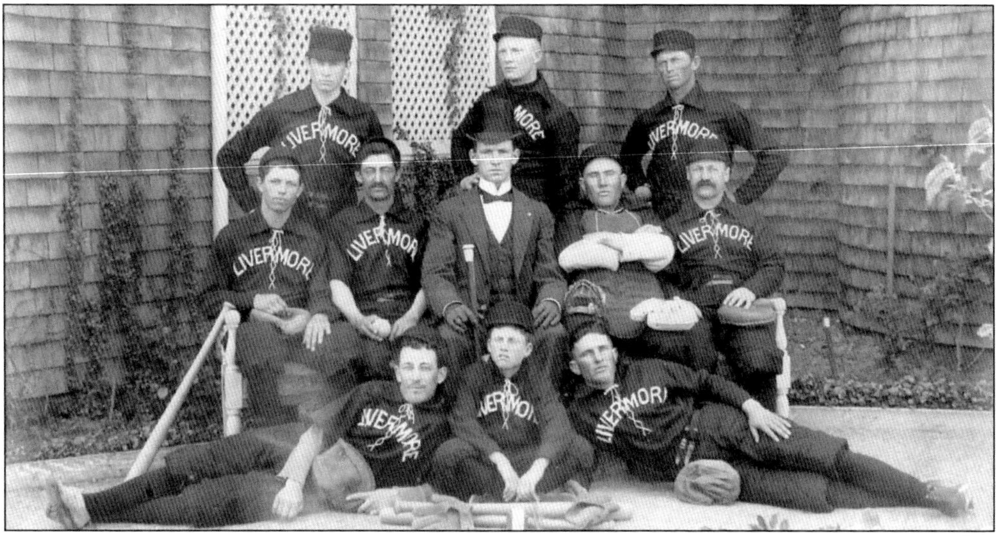

As early as 1875, the *Livermore Echo* mentions the formation of a club devoted to the pursuit of baseball. Many businesses and even the town newspapers (the *Livermore Herald* and the *Livermore Echo*) sponsored baseball teams. Games were played between teams from as far away as Oakland, Stockton, and San Jose. There were at least four baseball fields in existence by the beginning of the 20th century—McLeod's Field, the Second and M Street field, Foscalini's field in Laddsville, and Anspacher Brothers Warehouse field on First Street. From left to right, some of the son's of the town founders are identified among the members of this c. 1890 Livermore Baseball Club photograph: (first row) Mark Sanderson, Roy Beck, and Charles Reynolds; (second row) Charles Rathbone, Elsa McCaren, Andy Huper, Tom Rooney, and Wallie Mendenhall; (third row) Jack Hunter, Henry Huper, and Bill Johns.

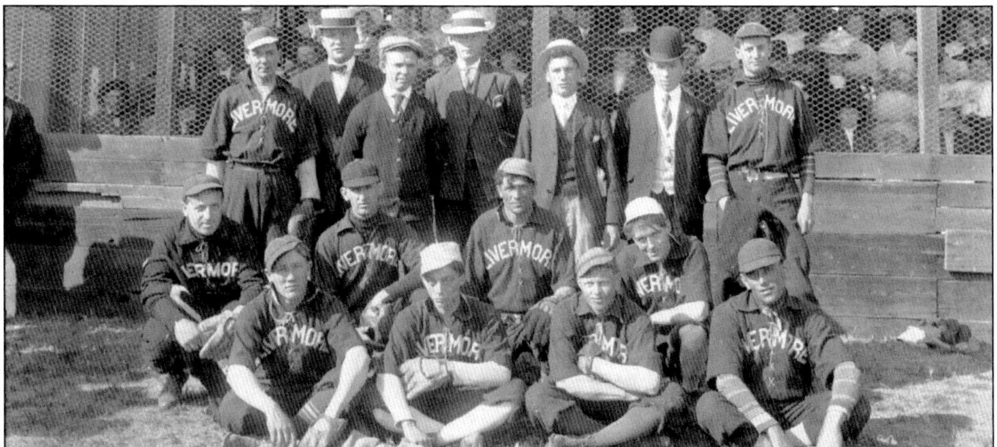

An article in the *Livermore Herald*, dated April 11, 1908, covering the Livermore Baseball Club, declares, "No Kicking in Sunday's Game, 'Battling Nelson' Acts as Umpire." Battling Nelson, also known as Durable Dane, was the world lightweight boxing champion between 1908 and 1910. The famous pugilist bought a 65-acre vineyard in Livermore and had a small hog ranch there as well. The 1908 Livermore Baseball Club pictured here, from left to right, are (first row) Joe Callaghan, William Barber, Art Holm, and Joe Cavanero; (second row) William Loenthal, Charles Taylor, Mark Draghe, and Ervin Wagoner; (third row) Charles Oswell, Henry Hupers, Battling Nelson, Ernest Utendoffer, two friends of Battling Nelson, and Charles Cullom.

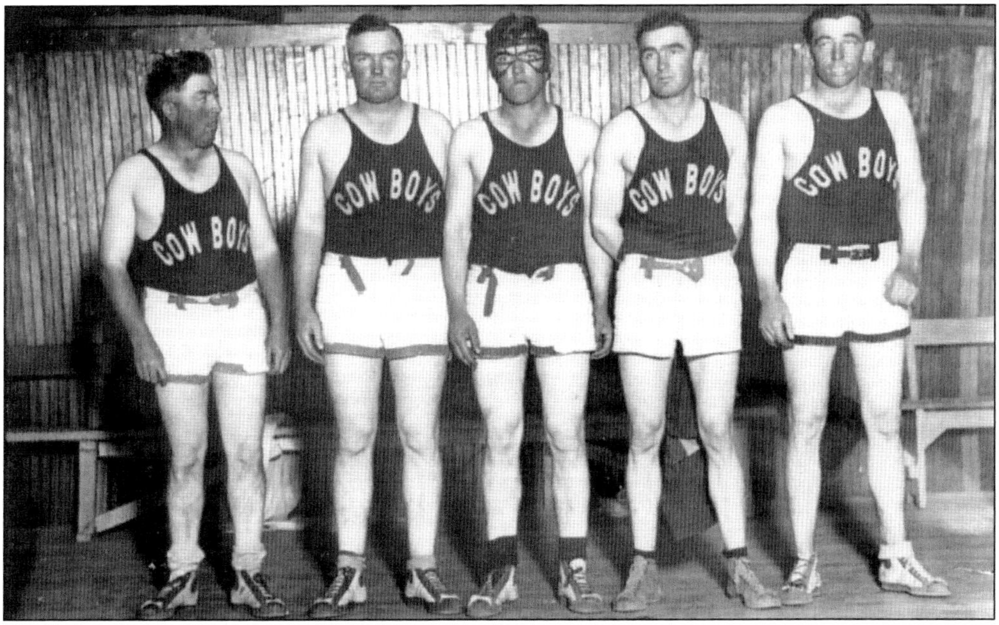

The McGlichey brothers are Livermore's best-known family of athletes. They were members of the 1920–1921 Livermore High School Basketball championship team. The 1920–1921 basketball season was a successful one for the Livermore High School team—they brought home the Oakland Tribune League championship. They traveled to the national championships, but were ultimately eliminated by the Kansas City Athletic Club, who consequently went on to win the nationals. Amazingly their mother attended her first game in 1926, content to wait at home and hear of their victories and personal glory after the games were over. Their father, John, however, never missed a game. He often was the official timekeeper and volunteer ticket taker at the games. Pictured, from left to right, are John, Joseph, Francis, William, and James McGlinchey.

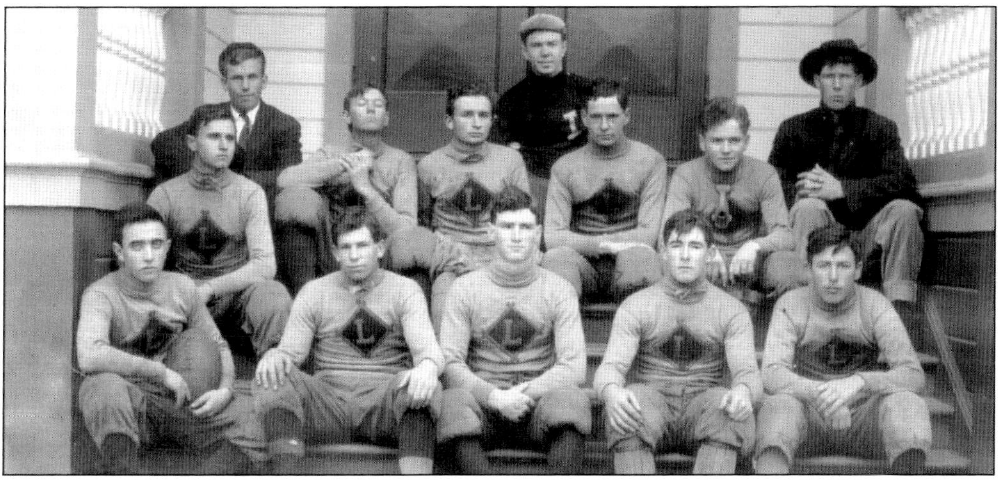

The early Livermore High School football teams were never known for successful seasons. Often sited as lacking weight and experience, the average team member weight in 1909 was 135 pounds. Members of the 1909 Livermore High School football team, from left to right, are identified as follows: (first row) unidentified, Arthur "Doc" O'Donnel, Charlie Sweet, Ellsworth Horton, and Dick Martin; (second row) Clinton Keller, Herbert Freericksen, Walter "Guy" Stickler, Maitland R Henry, and Desmond Teeter; (third row) Ted Mess, Ed Kennedy (coach), and Bill Crosby (coach).

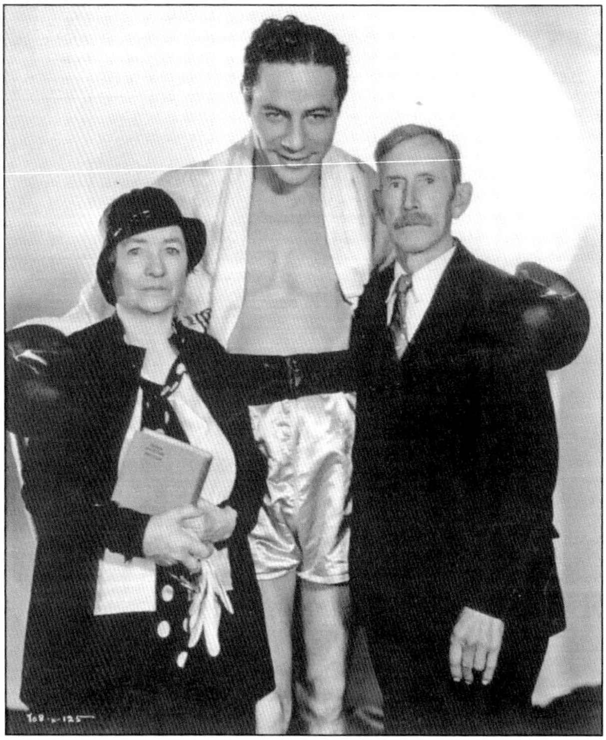

For many people in Livermore, Max Baer is the ultimate symbol of Livermore's sports professionals. Pictured in 1933 on the set of his MGM movie, *Prizefighter and the Lady*, Max Baer (center) visits with Mr. and Mrs. George K. Taylor from Livermore. Those that knew Max speak of his good nature and love of a good time.

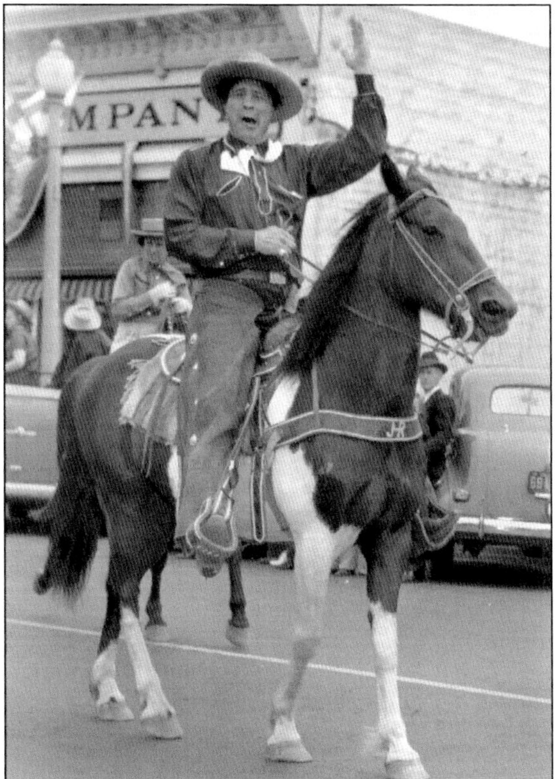

Max Baer, also known as the Livermore Larruper, was the city's most famous son through the 1930s. His professional boxing career spanned from 1929 to 1941. He was the Heavyweight Boxing Champion of the World in 1934. The *Livermore Herald* ran a continuing column from 1934 through 1941, called "Baer Facts." Here he rides in the 1941 rodeo parade greeting the crowds that he enjoyed so much. Max Baer's younger brother Buddy also took up boxing. In 1935, the brothers opened a gym in Livermore.

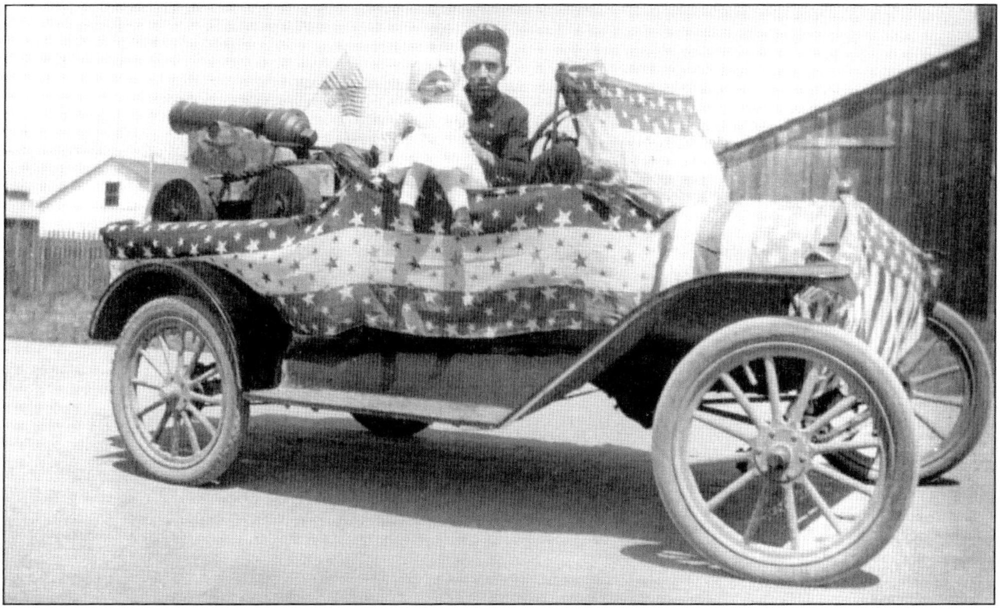

The first Livermore Rodeo took place in 1918 and was a fund-raiser for the Red Cross. One of the attractions of the 1918 rodeo parade was this bunting-decked horseless carriage, with the city's old cannon mounted on the back. The cannon was purchased in 1881 for $50 from the Fourth of July committee. Pictured here are Bill Henry and Margaret Clarke, daughter of Mr. and Mrs. Carl Clarke of Livermore. (Courtesy of Madeline Henry.)

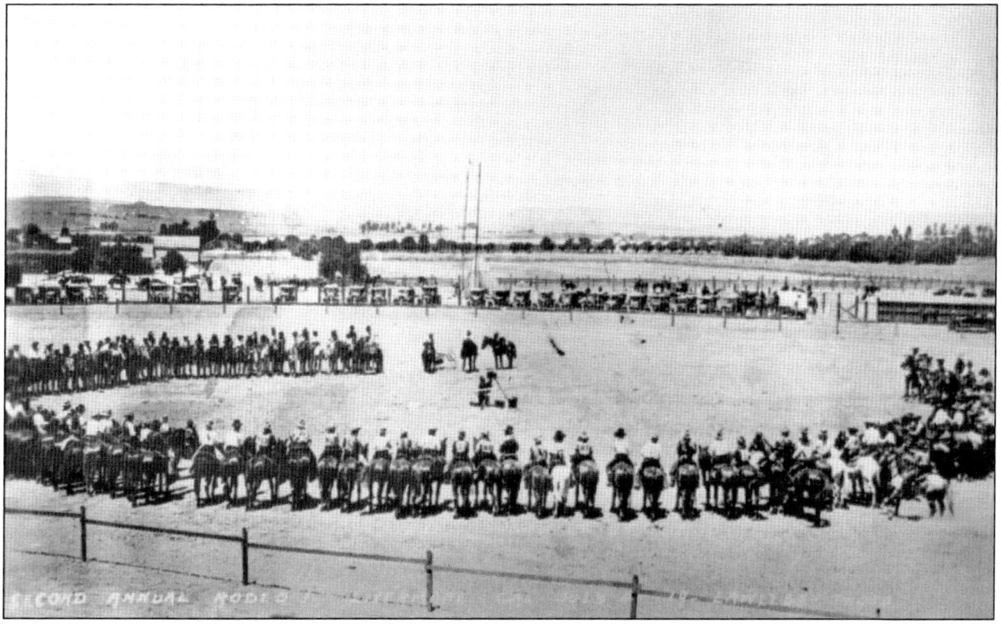

The grand entry signifies the beginning of the show at the 1919 second annual Livermore Rodeo. Angora "chaps" were popular at that time. The first annual Livermore Rodeo in 1918 included arena director Tom Holley and president John McGlinchey. There was a significant Spanish vaquero influence in their tack. (Courtesy of Madeline Henry.)

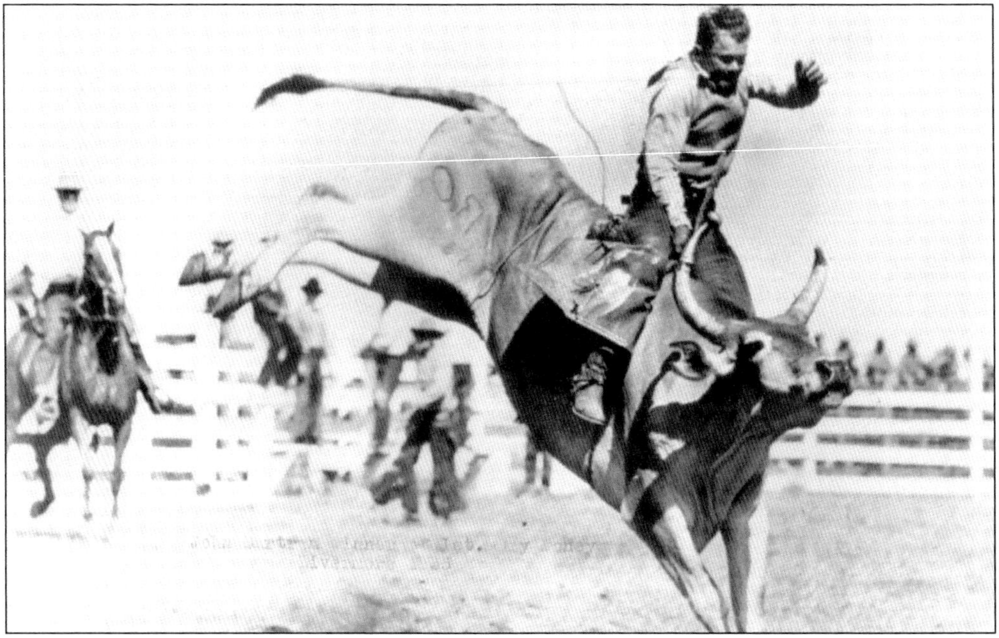

This 1935 photograph pictures John Bartram winning the first "Day Money" ever awarded at the Livermore Rodeo. John and his brother Dutch rode all three rough stock events and traveled extensively with the rodeo, performing at Madison Square Garden and at special performances in Australia. The rider behind John (at left) is former arena director Hugh S. Walker. (Courtesy of Lois Walker.)

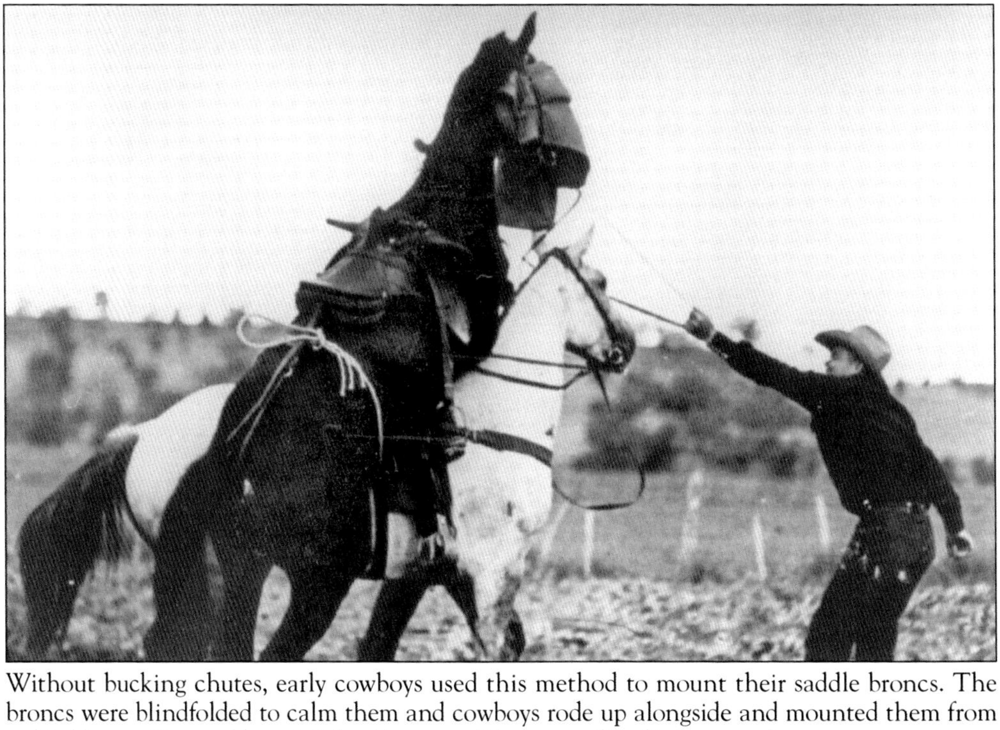

Without bucking chutes, early cowboys used this method to mount their saddle broncs. The broncs were blindfolded to calm them and cowboys rode up alongside and mounted them from a third horse. Pictured here is John Bartram. (Courtesy of Leslie Bartram.)

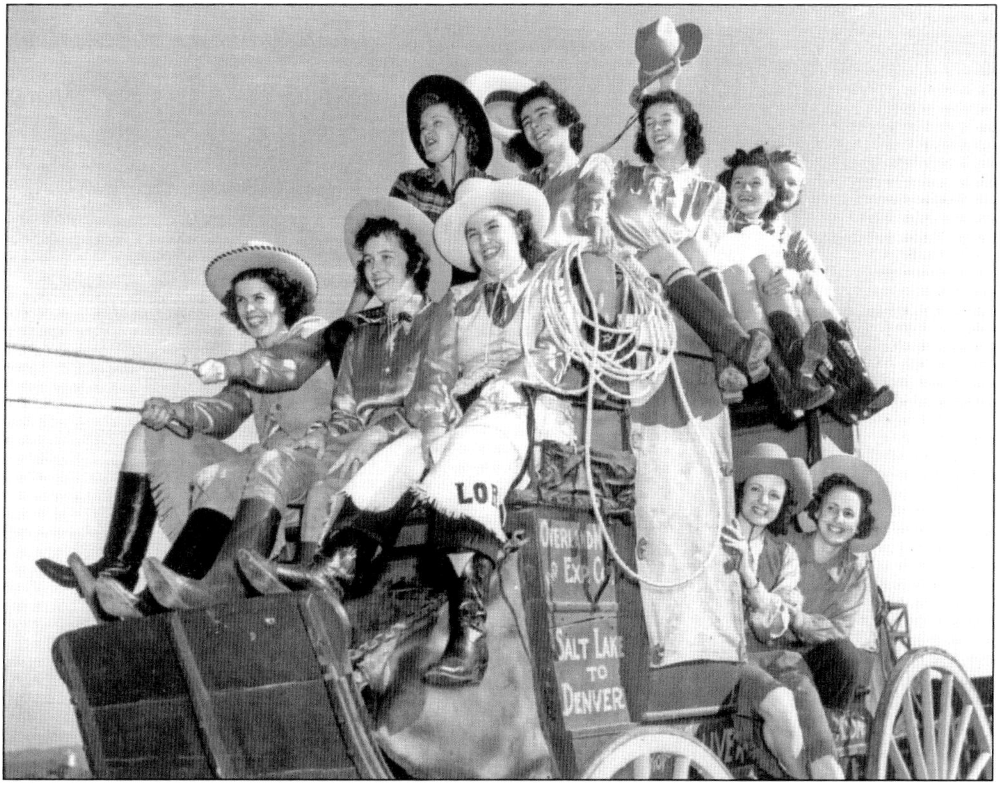

This 1939 Livermore Rodeo promotion photograph featured beauties Frances Temple, Mary Lee Beckmam, Loree Mulqueeny, Betty Kelly, Margery Temple, Isabelle Bonne, Betty Irwin, Carol Jean Huddleston, and LaVerne Jorgensen. (Courtesy of Carol Jean Famariss.)

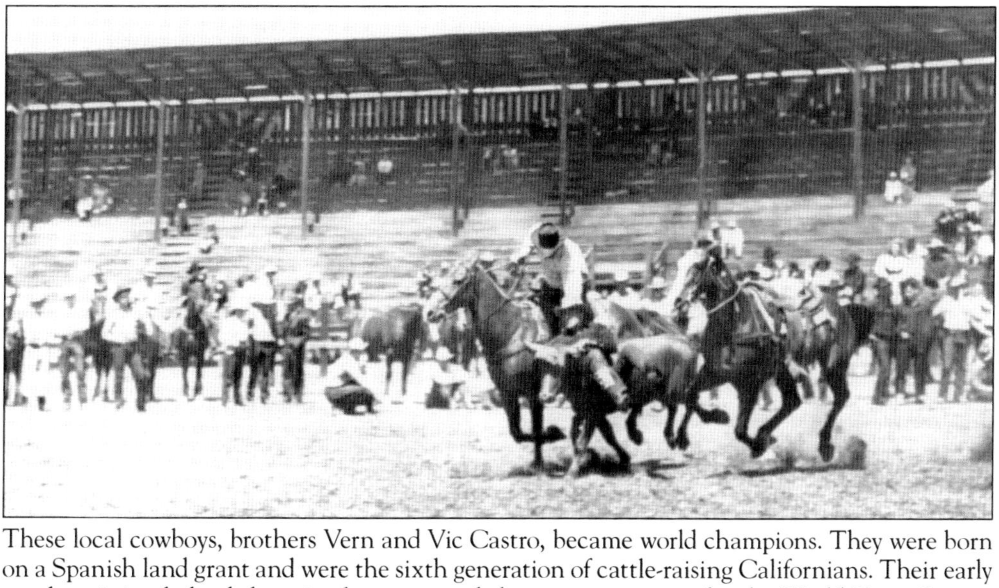

These local cowboys, brothers Vern and Vic Castro, became world champions. They were born on a Spanish land grant and were the sixth generation of cattle-raising Californians. Their early ranch training helped them in the arena and they went on to tie for the World Team Roping Championship in 1942. Pictured "bulldogging" are Vern Castro with Hazer and Vic Castro. (Courtesy of Loree Cornwell.)

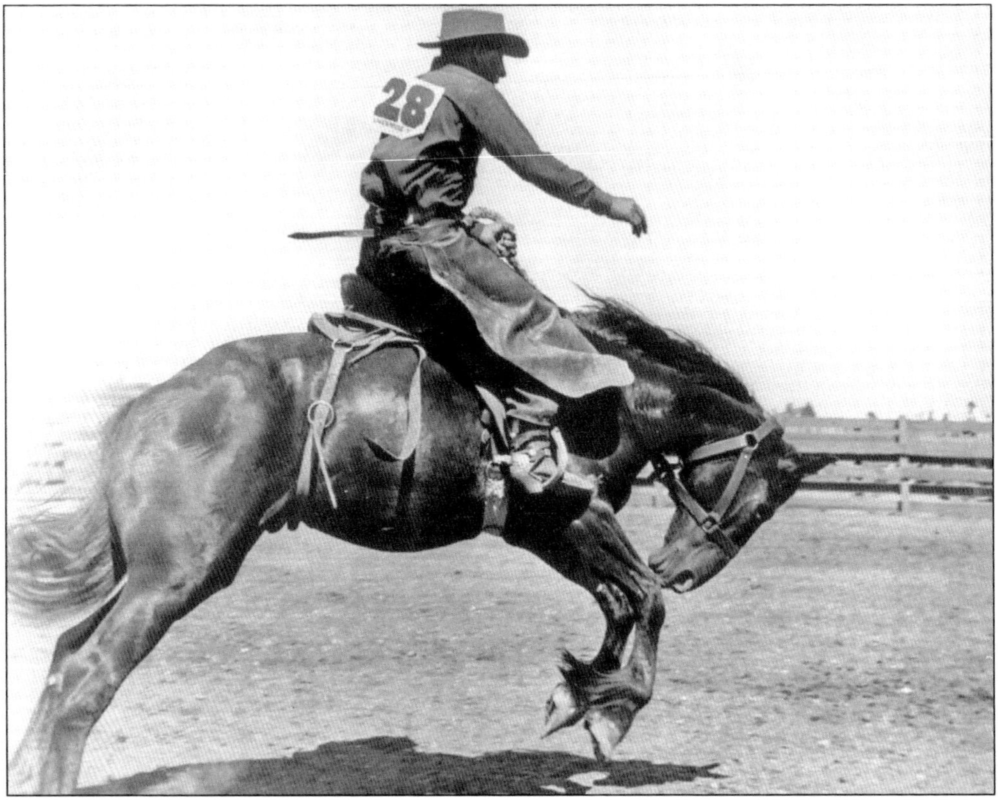

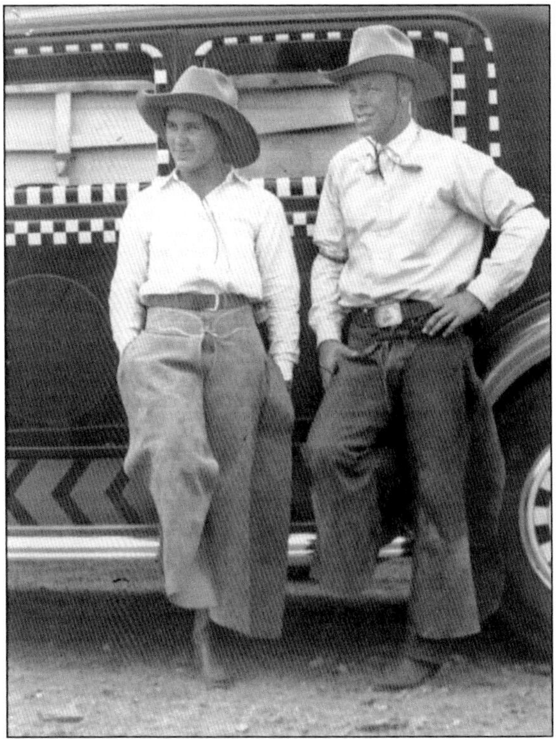

A local cowboy is riding a saddle bronc at the Livermore Rodeo in the 1940s. John Dobble was a cattleman in the Palomares Canyon area and rode rough stock until he was lassoed by his bride, Edna. (Courtesy Nick Dobble.)

On Sunday, June 10, 1935, 14,784 people attended the Livermore Rodeo. With contestants and families, there were probably over 16,000 people present. Pictured is Johnnie Schneider, Cowboy Champion of the World in 1935, with his first wife, Julia Freitas. They were married in 1931 in a brief ceremony as Johnnie was on his way to compete in the Salinas Rodeo. They went on tour throughout California during the remainder of the rodeo season and returned to Livermore to make their home in the fall. Several of Johnnie trophies and memorabilia are on display in the Rodeo Hall of Fame.